Hamas

Hamas

A Beginner's Guide

THIRD EDITION

Khaled Hroub

First published 2006 by Pluto Press. Third edition published 2025 by
Pluto Press
New Wing, Somerset House, Strand, London WC2R 1LA
and Pluto Press, Inc.
1930 Village Center Circle, 3-834, Las Vegas, NV 89134

www.plutobooks.com

British Library Cataloguing in Publication Data
A catalogue record for this book is available from the British Library

ISBN 978 0 7453 5087 5   Paperback
ISBN 978 0 7453 5089 9   PDF
ISBN 978 0 7453 5088 2   EPUB

This book is printed on paper suitable for recycling and made from
fully managed and sustained forest sources. Logging, pulping and manufacturing processes are expected to conform to the environmental
standards of the country of origin.

Typeset by Stanford DTP Services, Northampton, England

Simultaneously printed in the United Kingdom and United States of
America

Contents

Preface to the Third Edition

This book was originally written and published shortly after Hamas's victory of the Palestinian Legislative Council elections in 2006 in the West Bank, the Gaza Strip and East Jerusalem. The win shocked not only the movement itself but also the Palestinians, Israel, the USA and the broader region. That victory marked a turning point in both Hamas's political trajectory and Palestinian politics as a whole. This pivotal event has served as a recurring reference point throughout the chapters of the First Edition.

In 2007, Hamas took military control of the Gaza Strip, and its fragile post-election government was subsequently dismissed by Palestinian President Mahmoud Abbas – a move that divided the Palestinians between the West Bank and Gaza Strip, marking a new chapter for both the movement and the Palestinian people. By the end of the following year, Israel launched its first war on the Hamas-controlled and Israeli-blockaded Gaza Strip. In the years that followed, several competing dynamics emerged: the rise of Hamas's military and political power; the intensification of Israel's wars and attacks on Gaza; the worsening conditions for the 2 million Palestinians living in the Strip; and the deepening of Israeli occupation and settlements in the West Bank. These early changes and their impacts inspired the publication of an updated Second Edition of the book in 2010, shaped by a central new development: Hamas's control over Gaza.

The attacks of 7 October 2023 and the subsequent genocidal war on Gaza have prompted the release of this Third Edition. Even before this pivotal moment, the centrality of the original event that inspired this book – Hamas's 2006 electoral victory – had gradually faded. More pressing and brutal realities had come to define the lives and politics of both Gazans and Hamas, including the series of wars on Gaza (2008–2009, 2012, 2014, 2018, 2021 and 2022), Hamas's performance as the ruling party in the Strip, and the consequences of 16 years of Israeli and international blockade on both Gaza and Hamas. External pressures imposed by Israel, combined with internal deterioration in nearly every aspect of life, set the stage for the explosion in October 2023. These attacks can only be understood as the inevitable outcome of a context that had been steadily boiling for years. October 7 is not just an event, but a consequence.

Producing an updated edition of this book, centred around the events of October 7, posed a challenge: how to account for the 13 years that have passed since the last edition. One option was to update all the chapters by incorporating major events and their consequences since 2006. However, this approach would have diluted the focus on Hamas's 2006 victory, which shaped the First Edition, and resulted in a nearly new and considerably bulkier book. Instead, I opted for a more practical approach: adding new chapters that both bring the discussions up to date and address October 7 and the ensuing war. At the same time, significant updates have been made to the chapters introduced in the Second Edition (2010), which now serve as a bridge between the first two editions (2006, 2010) and the new chapters added in this edition. In doing so, I have preserved the original chapters (1–9) almost in their entirety, maintaining their focus and tone, with only minor updates and revisions where necessary. The new chapters rely heavily on original material, including Hamas's documents issued recently, speeches by its leaders and media interviews given by its spokespersons – all in Arabic. The translation to English is mine and any mistakes, if any, in this regard are also mine.

A final note is necessary. In the previous two editions, I made several judgements and predictions regarding Hamas's politics, ideology and actions. The passage of time has put these assessments to the test, and most have been validated. The most haunting prediction, one I wish had been proven wrong, was the inevitable explosion in Gaza if the brutal Israeli blockade and the inhumane conditions imposed on the Strip and its people continued without change.

Introduction to the First Edition

In January 2006, Hamas stunned the world by winning the democratic elections for the Palestinian Legislative Council of the limited Palestinian Authority in the West Bank and the Gaza Strip. Bringing Hamas into the unprecedented glare of the limelight, this victory shocked many Palestinians, as well as Israel, the United States, Europe and Arab countries. It also left the defeated Palestinian Fatah movement, Hamas's main rival which had led the Palestinian national movement for more than 40 years, completely shattered.

Despite the shock and surprise, Hamas's victory in those elections was in fact almost unavoidable. The cumulative failure over the past years to end a continuing brutal Israeli occupation of Palestinian land and people had only deepened the frustration and radicalism within the Palestinian people. Palestinian frustration and suffering has never ended since the creation of Israel by war in 1948. With British collusion and American support and against the will and interest of the native population, the piece of land that had been known for many hundreds of years as Palestine became Israel. In this war to create Israel the Palestinians lost more than 78 per cent of the land of Palestine, including the western part of their capital Jerusalem. What remained to the Palestinians were two separate pieces of land known as the West Bank (of the Jordan River) adjacent to the country of Jordan, which included a fragment of their old capital city, East Jerusalem, and the Gaza Strip on the Mediterranean bordering the Egyptian Sinai Peninsula. As a result of the 1948 war, hundreds of thousands of Palestinians were driven out from their cities and villages to neighbouring countries by Zionist forces. These 'refugees' have become one of the most intractable problems of the conflict, growing in number with their descendants to more than 6 million by the year 2006.

In 1967, Israel launched another successful war, this time not just against the Palestinians but also against all the bordering Arab countries. Palestinian losses were nearly complete. With this war Israel occupied the West Bank and the eastern part of Jerusalem, which had been under Jordanian rule, and the Gaza Strip, which had been administered by Egypt since the 1948 war. Israel also invaded Syria's Golan Heights in the north, and Egypt's Sinai desert in the south, and staunchly occupied them all in the name of Israeli security. Yet, for the Palestinians, the losses were multiple. The Israeli army forced another mass transfer of Palestinian refugees, this time from the West Bank cities and villages to neighbouring countries. Many of the refugees who had been uprooted to the West Bank during the 1948 war were moved on yet again, and with even more new refugees because of the 1967 war. The problem of Palestinian refugees had worsened.

Weakened Arab countries, along with the nascent Palestinian national liberation movement, failed in their military efforts to regain the land they had lost to Israel in 1967. Two years prior to that war, Yasser Arafat and other Palestinian activists in the West Bank and Gaza Strip and neighbouring Arab countries established Fatah, the Palestinian national liberation movement. Fatah declared a no-ideology affiliation and a secular outlook. Around the same time, and with other smaller leftist factions, the Palestine Liberation Organization (PLO) was established as a national umbrella front for the Palestinian struggle, with the clear leadership of Fatah. The goal of the PLO was to 'liberate Palestine': that was to say, the land that had been occupied in the war of 1948 and which had become known as Israel. Yet, after the devastating loss of the West Bank and Gaza Strip in 1967, the goal of the PLO had to be reduced. Instead of liberating Palestine, it focused on the liberation of only the two more recently lost parts of the land, the West Bank and the Gaza Strip. This goal was seen at this time merely as an intermediate phase which would not affect the long-term goal of liberating the entire land of Palestine.

From the mid-1960s to almost the mid-1980s, the PLO-led Palestinian national movement embraced armed struggle as the principal strategy to liberate Palestine. Arab weakness coupled with continuous international and Western support of Israel made the Palestinians' mission of liberating their land almost impossible. Achieving no success over decades of struggle, the PLO made two historic concessions by the end of the 1980s. It relinquished its long-term goal – the liberation of Palestine – by recognizing Israel and its right to exist. It also dropped the armed struggle as a strategy, for the sake of a negotiated settlement that hoped to regain the West Bank and the Gaza Strip and establish an independent Palestinian state.

In 1991, the United States convened the Madrid Peace Conference in the aftermath of the first Gulf War (1990–1991) and the expulsion of Saddam Hussein's troops from Kuwait. With Arabs everywhere fragmented because of the Iraqi invasion of Kuwait, the ensuing war, and a weakened Palestinian position because the PLO had sided (verbally and politically) with Iraq against the American-led coalition troops, the PLO's negotiating position in Madrid was fragile. Not unexpectedly, the Conference failed to produce a Palestinian–Israeli peace treaty but succeeded in confirming the historic shift on the side of the PLO towards negotiation instead of armed struggle as its preferred strategy to end the conflict.

In 1993, an initial agreement was reached between the PLO and Israel, the Oslo Accords, after months of secret talks in Norway. Endorsed in Washington by the Clinton administration, the agreement was, in theory, divided into two phases: a five-year interim phase (essentially meant to explore and test the competence of the Palestinians to peacefully rule themselves and control 'illegal' armed resistance factions) starting in 1994, which, if it proved successful, would be followed by a second phase of negotiations on a 'final settlement'. The Palestinians were almost evenly divided in response to the Oslo Accords. Those who supported Oslo argued that it was the best deal that the Palestinians could hope to achieve given the unfavourable conditions they faced and the tilted balance of power that remained unassailably propitious to Israel. Those who opposed it argued that it simply constituted surrender to Israel, by recognizing the Israeli state and officially dropping the armed struggle without any concrete gains. In the five-year interim period, there was to be no addressing any of the major Palestinian issues such as the right of refugees to return, the status of Jerusalem, the control over Palestinian borders, and the dismantling of the Israeli settlements build intensively in the occupied West Bank and the Gaza Strip. According to the Accords, these issues were all to be relegated to the final talks, which as it turned out, would never take place anyway.

Hamas has consistently opposed the Oslo Accords, believing that they were designed to serve Israeli interests and compromised basic Palestinian rights. After more than ten years of Oslo, the Palestinians had become completely frustrated and their initial shaky trust in the sincerity of peace talks with Israel had evaporated. During the interim period of years that would supposedly pave the way for permanent peace, Israel did everything possible to worsen the life of Palestinians and enhance its colonial occupation of the West Bank and Gaza Strip. During that period of time, for example, the size and number of Israeli colonial settlements in the West Bank – a major obstacle facing any final peace agreement – doubled. With the failure of Oslo, a second Intifada erupted in 2000 against Israel, giving more power and influence to Hamas and its 'resistance project'.

In March 2005, Hamas made three successive historic decisions, each of which represents a milestone in the movement's political life. The movement decided to run for the Palestinian Legislative Council elections in the West Bank and Gaza Strip. It decided that along with other Palestinian factions it would put on hold all military activities, for an unspecified amount of time and on its own terms. And it considered joining the PLO.

Hamas seemed to have decided to move firmly towards the top of the Palestinian leadership. The most important of these three milestones was Hamas's decision to participate in the legislative elections in January 2006. This decision was a complete reversal to its previous refusal to take part in 1996 elections because Hamas perceived them as an outcome of the Oslo Accords. By way of justification of the new move, it argued that the internal circumstances had totally changed after the 2000 Intifada, thus compelling Hamas to such a radical change. Hamas was also becoming confident of its own strength, after having won almost two-thirds of the seats in the January 2005 partial municipal elections.

Hamas's decision to take part in the elections had a profound impact on the nature of the movement, on the Palestinian political scene and on the 'peace process' at large. At the level of its internal make-up, it would help politicize the movement – at the expense of its well-known militarism.

HAMAS

Founded in the late 1980s, Hamas emerged as a doubly driven religious-nationalist liberation movement, which peacefully preaches the Islamic religious call while harmoniously embracing the strategy of armed struggle against an occupying Israel. Its critics thought it seemed as if Hamas started where the PLO had left off. Its supporters felt that Hamas came at just the right time to salvage the Palestinian national struggle from complete capitulation to Israel. On the ground, Hamas hacked its own path in almost the opposite direction to the peaceful route then being taken by the PLO and other Arab countries that had concluded peace treaties with Israel, namely, Egypt and Jordan. It refused to come under the PLO as the wider umbrella of the Palestinian nationalist struggle and adopted the 'old' call for the liberation of Palestine as had been originally enshrined by the PLO founders back in the mid-1960s. Hamas rejected the idea of concluding peace treaties with Israel that were conditional on full Palestinian recognition of the right of Israel to exist.

With the lack of any serious breakthrough towards achieving even a minimum level of Palestinian rights, Hamas has sustained a continuous rise since its inception. After years of persistent struggle, it has become a key player both within the parameters of the Arab and Palestinian–Israeli conflict and in the arena of political Islam in the region. At the Palestinian level, it has shown a continuing popular appeal. By using myriad and interconnected strategies spanning military attacks, educational, social and charitable work in addition to religious propagation, it has succeeded in popularizing itself across the Palestinian constituencies inside and outside Palestine. With the gradual erosion of both the legitimacy and popularity of the PLO, Hamas's power has manifested itself in landslide victories in municipal elections, student union elections, syndicational and other elections held in the West Bank and the Gaza Strip.

In the area of political Islam and its various approaches to politics, Hamas has offered a unique contemporary case of an Islamist movement that is engaged in a liberation struggle against a foreign occupation. Islamist movements have been driven by a host of various causes, the vast majority of which were focused on the corrupt regimes of their own countries. Another stream of movements, the 'globalized Jihadists', have expanded their holy campaigns across geopolitical lines, furthering pan-Islamic notions that reject ideas of individual Muslim nation-states. Contrary to both of these, Hamas has somehow remained nation-state based, limiting its struggle to one for and within Palestine, and fighting not a local regime but a foreign occupier. This differentiation is important as it exposes the shallowness of the widespread (mostly Western) trivializing conflation of all Islamist movements into one single 'terrorist' category.

Hamas has undergone various developments and experiences, and there are clear maturational differences between its early years and its later phases. Over the years of the struggle, at historic junctures and decisive and sensitive turning points, Hamas has offered not only a fascinating case for study but, more importantly, a case of an emerging key player capable of affecting the course and the outcome of the Palestinian–Israeli conflict.

Vacillating between its strong religious foundations and political nationalist agendas, Hamas strives to keep a balance between its ultimate vision and immediate pressing realties. Although it will remain an open question to what extent the 'religious' and the 'political' constitute the make-up of Hamas, it is significant to witness the interplay between these two drives within the movement. Although the movement suppresses any implicit or explicit tension between the two, it is perhaps only a question of time and space, and the nature of certain events, before one of them succeeds in overriding the other. At the highly politicized junctures of Hamas's life, it has been clearly evident that the 'political' vigorously occupies the driver's seat.

Militarily, Hamas adopted the controversial tactic of 'suicide bombing', to which its name has become attached in the West and the rest of the world. The first use of this tactic was in 1994, in retaliation for a massacre of Palestinians praying in a mosque in the Palestinian city of Hebron. A fanatical Jewish settler opened machine gun fire upon the worshippers, killing 29 and injuring many more. Hamas vowed to revenge these killings, and so it did. Since then, all and each of Hamas's vicious attacks against Israeli civilians have been directly linked to specific Israeli atrocities against Palestinian civilians.

Although no more brutal than what the Israelis have been doing to Palestinians for decades, the suicide attacks have damaged the reputation of both Hamas and the Palestinians worldwide. Hamas's justification for conducting these kinds of operation has many grounds. First, it says that these operations are the exception to the rule and are only driven by the need to retaliate. It is an 'eye-for-an-eye' policy in response to the continual killing of Palestinian civilians by the Israeli army. Second, Hamas says that it keeps extending an offer to Israel by which civilians on both sides would be spared from being targeted, but Israel has never accepted this offer. Third, Hamas leaders say that Israeli society as a whole should pay the price of the occupation of the West Bank and Gaza Strip, just as much as Palestinian society is paying the price for that occupation: fear and suffering should be felt on both sides.

At the socio-cultural level, Hamas has had mixed fortunes. Its grassroots social work in helping the poor and supporting hundreds of thousands of Palestinians has been admired and praised. This sustained work, which has been marked by competence and dedicated sincerity, has bestowed on the movement a high level of popularity. At election times, this has paid off considerably. Combined with its military and confrontational action against Israel, Hamas has been functioning on several fronts at the same time, and this has not failed to impress the Palestinians.

However, many secular Palestinians have feared that Hamas has been indirectly, if incrementally, transforming the cultural and social fabric of Palestinian society. Hamas has seemingly exploited its socio-political capital and popularity to advance its cultural and religious agenda. Although there have been only a few occasions when Hamas members have attempted to impose certain religious morals on society, and these cannot really be described as a phenomenon, they have been enough to create anxiety among more secular Palestinians. Many Palestinians support the nationalist liberationist and social work of Hamas, but not its religious ideal. Hamas purposefully overlooks this fact, and instead considers any vote for its political agenda as a vote for its religious one too.

HAMAS IN POWER

The reasons behind the Hamas victory in the 2006 Palestinian Legislative Council (PLC) elections, and the significance of this victory, merit a closer look. Hamas triumphed for a host of reasons. In the first place, the movement has indeed reaped the benefits of long years of devoted work and popularity among the Palestinians. At least half the voters supported Hamas for its programme and its declared objectives – and also for its warmth and the helping hands that it has kept close to the poor and needy. The other half of Hamas's voters were driven by other forces. The failure of the peace process, combined with the ever-increasing brutality of the Israeli occupation, left the Palestinians with no faith in the option of negotiating a peaceful settlement with Israel. The gap in the debate on 'peace talks versus resistance' was closing as the date of the election approached, with the notion of 'peace talks' losing ground, yet without clear and definite support for Hamas's 'resistance' concept either. The latter was vague, and many Palestinians were wary about its meaning and mechanisms. But the frustration of the peace talks had by then taken its toll and contributed largely to the defeat of the Fatah movement, the upholder and main force of the Oslo Accords and what had resulted from them.

Another major factor that helped Hamas to win those elections was the failure of the Fatah-led Palestinian Authority in almost all aspects. It failed not only externally, on the front of the peace talks with Israel, but also internally, with its management of day-to-day services to the Palestinian people. Mismanagement and corruption were the 'attributes' that came to mark Fatah's top leaders, ministers and high-ranking staff. As unemployment and poverty reached unprecedented levels, the extravagant lifestyle of senior Palestinian officials infuriated the public. The elections gave the people the chance to punish those officials. The chickens were coming home to roost, and Hamas was to be the beneficiary.

Thus, it can hardly be said that the Palestinian people voted for Hamas primarily on religious grounds. There was certainly no overnight popular conversion to Hamas's religious fervour or even its political ideology. Christians and secular people voted for Hamas side by side with Hamas members and exponents in all constituencies. Hamas's support of Christian candidates won them seats in the parliament. A Christian was appointed to the

Hamas cabinet as the minister of tourism. The vast spectrum of Hamas's voters in these elections supported the suggestion that the people were voting for new blood, and for a nationalist liberation movement that promised change and reform on all fronts, more than for Hamas the religious group.

The Hamas election victory itself represents something significant not only for Palestinians but also for other Arabs, Muslims and beyond. At the Palestinian level, it is a historic turning point, where a major shift has taken place in the leadership of the national liberation movement. For the first time in more than half a century Palestinian Islamists have moved into the driver's seat of the Palestinian national movement. It seems that almost overnight the Islamists have replaced the long-lived secular leadership that controlled the destiny of the Palestinians and their national decision-making for decades. This fundamental change, furthermore, was realized through peaceful means and without violence, giving Palestinians as a whole – including Hamas – a great sense of pride. Not only are the Palestinians theoretically competent and ready to practice democratic rule, but they have also done so by embracing democracy on the ground and accepting its outcome. Moreover, the campaigns for the elections with their contrasting platforms gave the Palestinians the chance to revisit their strategy over the conflict with Israel, as it had previously been designed and pursued by the Fatah movement.

For Hamas itself, this victory is the greatest challenge that the movement has faced since its emergence. Almost abruptly, all Hamas's ideals and slogans have been brought down to earth to face the harsh realities on the ground. It could be safely said that the post-election Hamas will be considerably different from the organization we used to know before the elections. At the Arab and Muslim level, Hamas's victory is almost unique: political Islam has reached power in a democratic process and will not be deprived of its victory. Islamist movements throughout the region were jubilant at Hamas's triumph and considered it to be their own victory. Existing Arab and Muslim regimes, on the other hand, have watched the rise of Hamas to power with obvious anxiety and suspicion, and fear that it will encourage their local Islamists to vigorously pursue power. Secular constituencies and individuals in the Arab countries remain divided. They support the nationalist liberation side of Hamas, but they continue to be agitated by its religious and social substance.

At the international level, a Palestinian government led by Hamas has been a most unwelcome phenomenon among the fruits of democracy. The West in particular is now caught in the dilemma of either accepting this disquieting result, to show the Arab and Muslim world that its call for democracy in the region is sincere, or joining Israeli efforts to bring down Hamas's government and risk losing credibility. The West decided early on to join the blockade on the new Hamas government, as part of a concerted effort by Israel, the United States, the European Union, some Arab states and the Fatah movement to oust it.

Strategically, many Palestinians have looked at Hamas's victory as benefiting the ultimate ends of the Palestinian nationalist movement in both the short and long term. Hamas's presence at the heart of the Palestinian decision-making mechanism furnishes further, and much needed, legitimacy to the Palestinian Authority (PA). It also brings more integrity and trust to the entire make-up of Palestinian politics. Hamas had never previously participated in the Palestinian Authority constructed by the Oslo Accords, on the basis that both the Accords and the Authority had capitulated to Israel and made unacceptable concessions. Capitalizing on a 'free-ride' type of discourse, Hamas has not only succeeded in amassing astonishing popularity, but it has also challenged the leading position of Fatah, the backbone of the PLO and the strongest party in mainstream Palestinian society. The inclusion of Hamas in the political process will now deprive Fatah of the erstwhile free-ride politics it came to abuse, and ensure it is held responsible for more 'real' politics along with other Palestinian parties.

More importantly, and at the level of the conflict with Israel, there cannot be a sustainable and final peace deal without a real Palestinian consensus, to which Hamas's contribution is central. Hamas's political position is pragmatic and hovers around accepting the concept of a two-state solution. If a decent final agreement can be reached, recognizing Palestinian rights according to Madrid Conference references and UN resolutions, Hamas will be unable to object. It seems that a moderate, co-opted and participating Hamas, even if it hardens the PA position, is far better than a radicalized and militarized Hamas.

Introduction to the Second Edition

WESTERN ENGAGEMENT WITH HAMAS

Two years after the blockade of the Gaza Strip, Mahmoud al-Zahar, a prominent Hamas leader in Gaza, wrote in the *Washington Post* (on 17 April 2008) the following: 'Sixty-five years ago, the courageous Jews of the Warsaw ghetto rose in defense of their people. We Gazans, living in the World's largest open-air prison, can do no less.'* It is not only this statement but also the developments on the ground over the four years since Hamas won the elections in 2006 which have confirmed one thing: the refusal to accept that is necessary to engage with Hamas has been devastating by all measures political and human, and almost exclusively for the Palestinians.

Here is an irony followed by an ironic question: the majority of Israelis support direct talks with Hamas, but the international community does not! According to a *Haaretz*-Dialogue poll conducted in March 2008, 64 per cent of Israelis say that their leaders 'must hold direct talks with the Hamas government in Gaza toward a cease-fire and the release of captive soldier Gilad Shalit [captured by Hamas in June 2006]'. Another poll in November 2009 showed that 57 per cent of Israelis supported a plan proposed by Shaul Mofaz, the second-ranking leader of the Israeli Kadima party, which includes talking to Hamas. The ironic question that follows has a British flavour, alas, and ponders the experience and lessons of the direct and indirect talks with the IRA, as revealed in a book by Tony Blair's Chief of Staff, Jonathan Powell.

---

* Mahmoud al-Zahar, 'No Peace Without Hamas', *Washington Post*, 17 April 2008, www.washingtonpost.com/wp-dyn/content/article/2008/04/16/AR2008041602899.html.

The two main lessons concluded in Powell's *Great Hatred, Little Room: Making Peace in Northern Ireland* (2008) were the need to 'talk to the enemies' and to 'create consensus on their front', which could lead to a consensual negotiated agreement. These two common-sense lessons are not hard to learn. Yet both have been discarded by the British and other Western governments, let alone Israel, in their dealing with Hamas. The consequences of their 'no-talking' policy have proved to be scandalous on the Western side and disastrous for the Palestinians.

Responding to Hamas's surprising victory in the January 2006 Palestinian elections, Europe joined an American-led effort to boycott Hamas and its subsequent government. The Western capitals, along with Tel Aviv, have thereafter imposed a set of conditions on Hamas that the movement had to meet if it wanted Hamas and its electoral victory to be acknowledged by the 'international community'. In fact, it would not have been possible for the movement to completely fulfil those conditions unless it were to agree to dispose of the very cards that made its democratic election victory possible: in other words, to voluntarily commit political suicide. Somehow, the movement went a long way towards risking doing just that, as 'Hamas in power' stretched itself and its positions half-way by agreeing to meet the three conditions of 'recognizing Israel', 'renouncing terrorism' and 'adhering to previous agreements between Israel and the Palestinian Authority'. Repeatedly, official Hamas statements have accepted the idea of a Palestinian state within 1967 borders, constituting a *de facto* (if not spoken) recognition of Israel. Hamas announced a unilateral truce by which it stopped all its military activities until Israel resumed its incursions and attacks against the Gaza Strip; and it declared in a statement of the national unity government in March 2007 its 'respect' for previous agreements between Israel and the Palestine Liberation Organization (PLO). For Washington and Brussels, those incremental moves by Hamas were not enough. Yet Hamas could stretch no further, otherwise it would have jeopardized its own unity and coherence. What the

West refuses to see is that this also brings jeopardy to themselves, as a first disunited, and then fragmented Hamas would unleash a complete Iraqization of the Gaza Strip and a wholesale catastrophic situation.

Hamas's failure, after its election victory, to bring about political achievements which would have offset the rising anger within its own ranks, especially from the idle military, was exacerbated by the enormous pressures and crippling interdictions coming from external players. To make things worse, some influential Fatah leaders and groups in the Gaza Strip vowed to create further security chaos in an effort to bring Hamas's government down. All the conditions, internally and externally, were ripe, and they precipitated Hamas's pre-emptive, violent military take-over of Gaza in June 2007 – displacing the remaining Fatah leadership and controlling all security forces – which has led to an unprecedented political and geographical split between Palestinians.

The greatest opportunity to appear during the span of the four years following Hamas's electoral victory was the short-lived national unity government of 2007. Brokered by the Saudis after the intensification of Fatah–Hamas clashes in the Strip, this government offered, for the first time in over 20 years, a chance for the creation of a viable Palestinian consensus. However, Western positions towards the unity government did not change, despite the extra mile that Hamas had gone towards meeting the West. The stances of the United States and the European Union lacked not only insightfulness but also the required sense of pragmatism. This complete lack of support for the unity government by the West drove Hamas further to the edge, forcing them to seek more support from Iran and Syria. The national unity government represented the great missed chance to bring the movement back into the fold of internal Palestinian politics, where the focus would be driven by exclusive Palestinian interests. Had the Palestinians been encouraged by the United States and the European Union, if not pressured, to have a unified leadership – with Fatah and Hamas at the heart of it – the road forward to making peace would have been better paved. By way of comparison, creating a national consensus and broader platform of polity is precisely what the United States and the European Union have been trying to achieve in Iraq. But not so in Palestine.

Since the emergence of Hamas in 1987, the Palestinian polity has been divided into a 'peace camp' and a 'resistance camp'. These function in complete disharmony, and the resultant effort of these two camps has been more harmful to the Palestinians than to Israel. With the signing of the Oslo Accords in 1993–1994, the rift between the two approaches had become wider and deeper. The Northern Ireland common-sense lesson of creating consensus on the other side suggests that the inclusion of Hamas in the Palestinian political process would have been a vital condition for any potential peace and consensual agreement. Yet, this lesson was ignored, in favour of the premise of leaving the Palestinian leadership, dependent upon Arafat's charisma and power at the top of it, with the business of selling (or imposing) any reached deal on the Palestinians. No 'promised' deal was ever reached, and now Arafat is not around and gone with him is any potential of imposing a deal. Even if there ever was any validity in the logic of 'imposing' a consensus-lacking peace deal on the Palestinians, particularly one relying on an individual charismatic leadership, it now has no credibility whatsoever given the sheer weakness of the current Palestinian president Mahmoud Abbas and the unyielding power of Hamas and its political/electoral legitimacy. This is why the format of any Israeli–Palestinian negotiations that excludes Hamas is rendered obsolete. Even if a semi-miracle happened and an agreement was concluded by Israel and the Palestinian president, who would implement it, and how, in the Gaza Strip without Hamas's approval?

The hard-learned Northern Ireland lessons of dealing with the 'enemy' are not showing up in Western foreign policy, in Palestine at least. At one point during the conclusion of the Palestinian national unity government, according to a Hamas source, there were some signals coming from London that Ismail Haniya,

Hamas's prime minister, would have been invited to London along with the Palestinian president after the official declaration of government. Such a step, if it was really on the horizon, would have helped change the violent course of events that unfolded in the following weeks. It could have given a measure of international legitimacy to Hamas's leadership which it could have sold to its constituencies, and equally driven back those reckless Fatah leaders in the Gaza Strip who thought that Hamas's days in government were numbered. The same Hamas source went on to say that London eventually backtracked and refrained from inviting any Hamas minister, as did some other European Union countries. In Europe it is always said that the Palestinian president and some Arab governments, primarily Egypt and Jordan, pressured the Europeans to shut Hamas out even after the national unity government was formed. This pressure is not a surprise, though it is ironic that such weak governments, internally and regionally, could have the power to 'pressure' the European Union. Nevertheless, the real surprise is that the Western capitals yielded to the pressure.

Talking to Hamas also falls within a wider scheme of thinking about the rising power of Islamists in the Middle East. The key word here is engagement. And the argument is that Western governments should talk and engage with Hamas and other Islamist movements, especially when they are democratically elected and show readiness and eagerness for dialogue. The Turkish model has some wisdom to offer. The 'European agenda' of the government of the Turkish Justice and Development Party (AKP), with its Islamist background and constituency, has affected the total orientation and moderation of the party. Engagement, of course, may not change policies full scale and in short periods of time – that should be clearly acknowledged – but it certainly moderates people and blunts the edges of their radicalism.

Europe and in particular Britain have had a historically peculiar role to play in the Middle East, in the past and present. When it comes to Palestine, most Palestinians hold Britain responsible for originating their long-lived misery. It is the Balfour Declaration of 1917, by which the Jews were promised a homeland in Palestine by the British colonial power, that digs deep into the Palestinian psyche and is considered by many of them to be the 'mother of all these sins'. Britain shoulders a fair share of the historical responsibility for what happened to the Palestinians, and it should equally carry an equivalent share of the burden for relieving their current situation. Alas, what frustrates many Palestinians, and not only Hamas, is to see Britain and Europe merely reproducing American positions which are biased against their cause.

Despite all appearances, Hamas has not strayed too far from politics. It might be on the edge but there is still a good chance of bringing Hamas back into the fold before it is too late. Weakening Hamas provides space for more radical splinter groups attempting to emulate al-Qaeda tactics. Yet even the strategy of finishing off Hamas by excessive military means, and even the forms of war crimes as we have seen in the December 2008–January 2009 Israeli war, proved failures. The facts on the ground say that Hamas is there to stay, for it is not a marginal alienated group or on the fringes of the Palestinian society. It is a mainstream movement which won free and fair elections. The Gaza war aftermath has, if anything, proved Hamas's steadfastness that al-Zahar's statement to the *Washington Post* asserted.

Introduction to the Third Edition

THE ROAD TO OCTOBER 7

The goal of this book is to present a balanced account of the largely misrepresented and distorted case of Hamas. Drawing on decades of first-hand knowledge and original sources, this book moves beyond simplistic, black-and-white assessments, offering a nuanced perspective free from either glorification or vilification. Hamas is a complex socio-political and historical mainstream movement, embedded in the Palestinian people and their aspirations for freedom and independence.

In introducing this Third Edition of the book, there is an essential entry point to be made about Hamas, Palestine and the Palestinians. For most Palestinians, Hamas is deeply intertwined with Palestine's century-long national struggle for liberation and self-determination. As detailed in the introduction to the First Edition, the roots of Palestinian Islamism, which later evolved into Hamas, can be traced back to the 1940s in Jerusalem under British colonial rule. Consequently, Hamas emerged organically within the Palestinian context and has operated within the historical boundaries of Palestine, with the liberation of Palestine as its guiding principle. The Palestinian people's support and criticism of Hamas is largely based on its effectiveness in advancing the national cause of liberation. While many endorse its anti-Zionist and anti-colonial stance, others voice objections regarding its religious and social-religious agenda. Hamas garners wider support when its resistance efforts are prioritized over other aspects.

This updated edition is prompted by Hamas's 7 October 2023 attacks on Israel and the genocidal war that followed. The added chapters address these events and their consequences. This introduction places October 7 within the wider context of the Palestinian struggle and builds on what the first introduction offers, that is, the historical evolution of Hamas; and what the second introduction discusses: the disastrous consequence of the policy of isolating Hamas and disengaging with it. Isolation and aggressive blockade prompted Hamas to inwardly focus on building its own political and military capital and power in the Gaza Strip. This process of self-fortifying has guided Hamas's politics and resistance under siege that evolved during the long years of the Israeli blockade on the Gaza Strip since 2007. One line that connects Hamas's conduct and trajectory before and after the year 2007 is the cycle of unplanned and/or unexpected temporal successes that led to uncalculated losses and failures. October 7 and its aftermath are the most recent culmination of this cycle. What follows offers a closer look at this successive chain of costly success that eventually led Hamas and the Palestinians to where they are now.

That the Gaza explosion of 7 October 2023 'didn't happen in a vacuum' has been the view of most sensible people around the world. On the contrary, many observers, including this writer, had warned in preceding years of the impending explosion of Gaza, which ultimately manifested in the form of the October attacks. These have indeed stemmed from the volatile immediate and broader contexts whose collapse and spill-over were inevitable. The suffocating blockade on the Gaza Strip and its 2.3 million Palestinians which turned the Strip into a concentration camp, combined with the deepening of Israeli occupation and prolonged subjugation of the Palestinians in the West Bank and East Jerusalem, exacerbated tensions. The long-defunct peace process only paved the way for further expansion of Israeli settlement and annexation of land. The frustration and helplessness that have engulfed the Palestinians for years have intensified significantly over the past two decades.

Meanwhile, Israel grew more religiously extreme, converging to an almost collective denial of the notion of Palestinian nationhood. Leading Israeli parties, high ranking government officials, and the prime minister himself frequently dismissed the idea of a Palestinian state. Instead, officials and ministers (such as Bezalel Smotrich and Itamar Ben-Gvir) repeatedly and publicly called for the expulsion of the Palestinians, offering them one of three options: leave Palestine entirely; accept being unequal citizens under Israel's control; or face the wrath of the Israeli army. The Israeli occupation over the land that was supposed to become a Palestinian sovereign state, has only been consolidated: the settlements relentlessly expanded, a de facto annexation of Palestinian areas aggravated; and the daily humiliation, arrest and house demolitions have continued. All this has created an apartheid system between the Mediterranean Sea and the River Jordan that has racially elevated Jewish Israelis and downgraded the Palestinians. The Palestinian Authority (PA), established after the Oslo Accords in 1993 as a nucleus for a Palestinian state, has degenerated into a discredited body that functions at the service of Israel's security and its settlers in the West Bank.

Hamas, since having gained full control over Gaza in 2007, has faced massive pressures, externally from the harsh Israeli land, sea and air blockade, and internally from the rapid deterioration of the living and economic conditions of the Palestinians in the Strip. Hamas attempted various strategies to break the throttling conditions. Politically, it pursued reconciliation with the Fatah and the PA to end the Palestinian split; it improved its relations with Arab and regional countries showing moderation and diplomacy; and it offered long periods of 'calm' to Israel. None of these came to fruition; the Gaza cauldron kept boiling.

Facing multiple impasses, Hamas's survival strategy involved adopting soft internal and external politics and hard military build-up. Politically, Hamas espoused a more moderate approach in internal Palestinian politics towards the PA and Fatah by offering a series of reconciliation proposals. Externally and regarding Israel and 'peace' proposals, as well as regional and world powers, Hamas repeated its acceptance of a Palestinian state within the 1967 borders. In certain ways, the wider context of the impasse that besieged Gaza and Hamas as well as the Palestinians at large has been very much linked to Oslo's failure and its consequences – as discussed in the introduction to the First Edition.

Militarily, Hamas pursued a counter-(Israeli) containment approach. This is a mix of intensive build-up of military capabilities, and engagement in low-intensity military operations along the borders that was meant to keep alive the idea and image of resistance. With these forms of resistance, Hamas wanted to send a bold message to Israel that it is undeterrable, while avoiding large-scale military confrontations. All this has scored partial success during the years of the blockade, yet it remained far from breaking the impasse. The successive wars on Gaza in 2008–2009, 2012, 2014, 2018, 2021, 2022 and 2023 have exhausted the people and turned part of the anger against Hamas.

TEMPORAL VICTORIES, LASTING COST

Throughout its political life, and particularly since 2006, Hamas has endured a frustrating pattern of unexpected milestone successes that produced little long-term political gain – or these successes came along at a heavy cost. Efforts by the anti-Hamas camp, including Israel, the USA, the PA, and some Arab governments variably blocked the materialization of the movement's advances into concrete and lasting good fortunes on the ground. Within this pattern of unexpected but costly victories, three milestone successes stand out, the adverse consequences of each added to the growing desperation of Hamas that led to October 7. The first two are dramatic in nature, which are its 2006 victory in the elections of the Palestinian Legislative Council and its military takeover of Gaza Strip in 2007. The third one, which is less dramatic than the first two, is Hamas's continuation of its 16-year rule of the Strip against all odds. These events share the aspect of an unexpected and sudden achievement that comes with overwhelming responsibilities beyond the movement's capacity to handle them. October 7 also fits this pattern: a successful military move that brought about massive and devastating cost to the movement and the Gaza Strip at large. This pattern of unexpected victories and their adverse aftermath merit a closer look.

ELECTION VICTORY SURPRISING SUCCESS – 2006

In January 2006, Hamas surprised itself – and the world – by winning the Palestinian Legislative Council elections in the West Bank, East Jerusalem and the Gaza Strip. The movement ran for those elections, driven by survival instinct. It wanted to circumvent being targeted by the 'war on terror' campaign led by former US President George W. Bush, after the September 11 attacks of 2001. That campaign listed countries and organizations that the USA (and Israel) would pursue, including Hamas. Yielding to American pressure, the PA along with most governments in the region, became 'partners' in the American war on terror. The translation of this partnership in the case of the PA meant cracking down on Hamas directly.

In parallel, Bush launched 'The US–Middle East Partnership Initiative (MEPI)' that claimed to democratize the region.* It intended to mitigate the belligerent image of the war on terror, claiming that all efforts, 'war on terror' and democratisation, complemented a bigger project that aimed to bring democracy to Arab countries. Within this context, a major objective of Hamas's participation in the Palestinian elections was to protect the movement from the looming suppression and crackdown, and present itself as a democratic political entity integrated within the Palestinian system. Hamas, thus, used one American campaign, the promotion of democracy in the region, to dodge the other campaign against terror.

Hamas wanted to secure a strong position in the Palestinian legislature, even if the powers of the Council were restricted by

---

* For more details on The US–Middle East Partnership Initiative (MEPI), see https://mepi.state.gov/.

Israel. In this case, Hamas would greatly influence the Palestinian decision-making, while staying away from the burden and messiness of the executive authority that functions in accordance with the Oslo Accords. However, against its initial plans, Hamas won the elections and found itself in an undesirable position: a resistance force rose to become the ruling party of the PA that operates within the framework of the Oslo Accords which Hamas opposes.

Lacking real experience in running ministries and leading a nation-wide authority, Hamas was desperate to convince other Palestinian groups or independents to join forces with them and form a coalition government. That effort was in vain. Fatah had outrightly refused to join such a government and encouraged others to do the same. Trying to gain regional and international acceptance, the Hamas government issued a manifesto whose language was moderate on major issues, that is, effectively stopping military action and calling for 'ending the occupation', and accepting a Palestinian state on the 1967 borders. All these gestures fell on deaf ears. Regional and international contexts remained unreceptive to Hamas, rejecting the new democratic transformation of the movement. On the contrary, Israel and the USA, in cooperation with factions of Fatah in the Gaza Strip, joined efforts to bring down the Hamas government. The movement felt betrayed and frustrated that even when pursuing political and democratic course it continues to be rejected.

GAZA TAKEOVER, ANOTHER SURPRISING SUCCESS – 2007

The military takeover of the entire Gaza Strip in 2007, detailed in the introduction to the Second Edition of this book, was also unplanned in the way that it eventually manifested. From a military and power politics perspective, the move was a complete success that brought Hamas full control over the Gaza Strip. Like the 2006 victory (and, later, the October 7 attacks), it was surprising, swift and unexpectedly exceeded the 'initial plan'. It also brought about mixed fortunes to the movement. Hamas officials told me in 2009, and in 2012, that the immediate and short-term objective at the time was to 'punish the Preventative Security Apparatus' of the PA that strived to undermine Hamas's government and the movement's security in the Gaza Strip after Hamas won the elections. When Hamas assumed power in 2006, it found itself toothless as the Palestinian Authority Security Forces remained under the control of President Mahmoud Abbas, effectively creating a two-headed power structure. The United States supported the efforts of some security leaders of the PA to weaken Hamas's government, with the aim of exposing the movement as incapable at governance.* Hamas decided to strike pre-emptively and hit the PA security forces that was causing most of the trouble. Its immediate success in doing so, and the lack of efficiency of the security forces under Abbas' control, tempted Hamas fighters to expand their operation across the entirety of the Strip, ending with the dismissal of all PA security forces and the imposition of Hamas military control instead. This swiftness and efficiency and the lack of effective defence on the other side, leading to the ad hoc expansion of the operation, show the hallmarks of Hamas's later October 7 attacks.

The scale of the surprising and unplanned 'achievement' gave Hamas short-term success, yet without resulting in larger political gains. Instead, a bitter internal Palestinian division took place with Hamas controlling the Gaza Strip, while the PA under Abbas retained control over the West Bank. Israel immediately imposed land, sea and air blockade on the Gaza Strip. International and regional powers joined Israel in imposing diplomatic isolation on Hamas, refraining from recognizing it as an official government in Gaza. All parties, however, acknowledged the new reality and dealt with it indirectly via some UN agencies and NGOs. Hamas's military success brought about an unexpected burden as it found

---

* David Rose, 'The Gaza Bombshell', *Vanity Fair*, April 2008, www.vanityfair.com/news/2008/04/gaza200804.

itself the de facto ruler of a besieged Gaza Strip, responsible for delivering services and governance to its 2 million Palestinians.

GOVERNING THE GAZA STRIP

A third costly success has been Hamas's retention of control over Gaza since 2007, despite Israeli and other efforts to remove it from power. The movement managed to create an effective government, particularly in internal security, that had been lacking in the Strip in the years 2005–2006, after Israel withdrew its troops from Gaza. Prior to Hamas' control over the Strip, insecurity and chaos made the lives of Palestinians very difficult due to the PA's inefficient and multiple security forces, and the emergence of several militant groups that made Gazans' life unsafe. Over the subsequent years, Hamas's performance in some civil services and provisions fared relatively better than that of the PA, notwithstanding the impositions of the blockade.

However, the conditions of the populated Gaza Strip, the largest open-air prison on earth, continued to deteriorate. Israel's strategies against Hamas combined suffocating the population economically to provoke internal strife and revolt against Hamas, and deploying successive wars to weaken Hamas' military under the notion of 'mowing the lawn' (see Chapter 13). Those wars killed thousands of Palestinians, wounded and maimed tens of thousands more, and rendered the Strip unliveable. Creating miserable conditions laid the ground for the coming explosion. Israel was held as ultimately responsible for Gazans' misery, but part of the blame was also directed towards Hamas and its government.

At the Palestinian national level and throughout the 16 years of Hamas's rule of Gaza, the movement faced continuous pressures and accusations of being the cause of the Palestinian division. Hamas claimed to have offered more reconciliatory overtures to the PA/PLO to end the Palestinian split. Successive rounds of talks and agreements proved to be futile, with each party blaming the other for failure. In 2021, the movement went the extra mile in agreeing to hold 'engineered elections' where Hamas would participate in a calculated manner (avoiding winning a majority) and refraining from challenging Mahmoud Abbas in the presidential elections. The idea was to form a national unity government after the elections. Yet, three weeks before the date of the elections, Abbas decided to backtrack and cancel them, fearing unexpected outcomes considering the fragmentation and lack of discipline within the [Fatah] movement – his own party. Hamas denounced the decision but, once again, remained caged in the Gaza Strip. The potential outlet for relieving some of the pressure was closed off.

While Hamas and the PA shared responsibility of the failure to end the division, a reunification was indeed vetoed by Israel and the USA. Both controlled the financial means of the PA and threatened to end it if Hamas became part of the official system. The regional and international context remained, again, unreceptive of the idea of Hamas being part of the Palestinian system. Hamas' achievement in controlling the Gaza Strip turned into a sour reality, as the perpetuation of a split effectively served – and was fed by – Israel.

During the blockade years, Hamas attempted to create some cracks by announcing a revisited political vision and crystalizing its new moderate positions. In May 2017, the movement issued 'A Document of General Principles and Policies' – or its 'new Charter'.* The main element was the renewed acceptance of a Palestinian state in the 1967 borders. Israel's response was categorical rejection, with Benjamin Netanyahu tearing up a copy of the document in a televised theatrical act. These attempts at moderation, once again, faced a deadlock.

---

* For the entire text of the document, see the official English translation on Hamas's website: 'A Document of General Principles and Policies', Islamic Resistance Movement: Hamas, 1 May 2017, https://web.archive.org/web/20170510123932/http://hamas.ps/en/post/678/.

OCTOBER 7, THE COSTLY MILITARY SUCCESS

In the view of many military experts, the strike of October 7 was an astonishing military success, which inflicted the deadliest attack in recent history on the mightiest army in the region. The surprising success that came with subsequent heavy cost aligns with the pattern of temporal successes without long-term gains. The attack must be seen as the explosive culmination of long boiling conditions of humiliation and impasses the Palestinians at large, particularly in Gaza and along with Hamas, had been facing during the years of the blockade and well before. Specifically on the operation, its magnitude and timing, there was an anticipation that the strike could be part of a larger regional plan involving Iran, Hizbullah and the 'resistance axis' whose subsequent phases would follow. This was proven wrong as both Iran and Hizbullah denied any pre-coordination with Hamas. All parties, both foes and allies, were caught off guard by Hamas's move, seemingly including its leadership outside of Palestine.

Hamas outlined two immediate objectives of the strike: to stop Israeli incursions and violations into Al-Aqsa Mosque and the Haram al-Sharif area in Jerusalem, hence the name of the operation Al-Aqsa Flood; and to capture Israeli soldiers to exchange them for more than 6,000 Palestinian prisoners held in Israeli jails. The limited plan of capturing soldiers expanded unexpectedly. The ease of infiltrating Israeli military posts and the lack of initial Israeli military response, tempted Hamas fighters to expand their operation, as confirmed by senior Hamas leaders. News of the surprise military success spread across the Gaza Strip encouraging hundreds of non-military people to cross the borders to the fighting sites, turning the planned operation to a messy one that included killing civilians. Matters went out of control according to Hamas. Chaos multiplied when the Israeli army, awakened from the initial shock, activated its *Hannibal directive* that allows the killing of one's own people if captured by the 'enemy' along with killing the 'enemy' themselves. The main point to be made here is the contextualization of October 7 within the *longue durée* of the Palestinian struggle: a coming explosion that had been brewing for many years. The specific aspects of the attacks are dealt with in Chapter 15. However, similar to the previous episodes in 2006 and 2007, Hamas achieved unexpected and temporal success, the consequences of which the movement was unprepared to handle – internally, regionally and internationally.

In conclusion and by way of placing this event within the broader trajectory of the Palestinian struggle for liberation as offered by Hamas, I highlight what I think is an informative and contextualizing speech of Yahya al-Sinwar, who was Hamas's leader in the Gaza Strip at the time of the attacks and most likely the one who gave them the green light. After the assassination of Ismail Haniya, the head of Hamas's political bureau in Iran, on 31 July 2024, al-Sinwar, in his hideout in the Gaza Strip, was elevated within Hamas ranks and replaced Haniya. Until he was killed by the Israeli army while fighting in Rafah in October 2024, al-Sinwar was considered as the most influential leader in the movement (and the most wanted by Israel).

On 26 May 2021, al-Sinwar gave a prescient speech on Al Jazeera that could be seen as a precursor of what was coming on October 7, which went unnoticed by Western media (see Postscript). The long, televised address, in the wake of the 11-day Israeli war on Gaza in that month (see Chapter 13), featured al-Sinwar as a powerful leader whose ideological strength and political pragmatism were coherently integrated. In tandem with stressing Hamas's principles and uncompromising stances, he frequently advocated a non-violent resistance. Referring several times to international law and UN resolutions, he called upon the USA and the West to put pressure on Israel to implement those resolutions. He reiterated Hamas's acceptance of a Palestinian state within the 1967 borders in line with what has been acknowledged internationally and agreed upon by the PLO. On the use of military strategy, al-Sinwar's emphasis that this strategy is the last resort for Hamas and the Palestinians is striking. He stressed that Hamas and the Palestinians were left with no option because Israel, the USA and the whole world didn't listen to the Palestinians when they used non-military methods. Detailing Palestinian peaceful resistance means including the March of Return of 2018, which were all faced with brute Israeli force, al-Sinwar said, 'We prefer to resist this occupation by peaceful and popular means. This is our preference. But if the enemy continues its crimes and crosses red lines, we have no choice but military resistance. Our number one option is to achieve the goals of our people by peaceful means.'*

On the incompetence of the world in stopping Israeli occupation and aggression, al-Sinwar stated in the same speech:

Today there is a chance before the world to exert pressure on Israel to adhere to international law and international [UN] resolutions ... my message to Biden is one sentence: pressure the [Israeli] occupation to implement international law and resolutions, and we offer a long-term truce of four or five years or more. If the world compelled Israel to withdraw from the West Bank, dismantle the settlements there, withdraw from East Jerusalem, release our prisoners, end the blockade on the Gaza Strip, allow us to hold elections in Jerusalem and establish our Palestinian state on part of our land, we will commit to a long-term truce that postpones the conflict and creates stability in the region.

The above ideas were offered by the man whom Israel (and the USA) spared no vilifying adjective in describing. The backbone of Israel's discourse and its allies about Hamas is the designation of the movement as a terrorist organization. The same discourse was used against Fatah and other PLO factions in the past.

---

* Yahya al-Sinwar, 'Hamas Leader Says Group Won't Touch Gaza Reconstruction Aid', *Al Jazeera Network* (Qatar), 26 May 2021, www.aljazeera.com/news/2021/5/26/hamas-leader-says-group-wont-touch-gaza-aid.

Although it is harmful at the international level, scaring off state and non-state actors from interacting with Hamas, this labelling holds little relevance for the Palestinians. They, and many others, see Israel and the USA as lacking the moral standing to apply such labels. Factually, and throughout its political existence, Hamas has refrained from engaging in military activities beyond the borders of Palestine or directing its resistance towards targets other than Israeli ones, in contrast to its designation as a terrorist organization. While Hamas, like other liberation movements, has surely made mistakes, it remains firmly integrated within the Palestinians as a resistance movement. Caged for many years in the Gaza Strip with its more than 2.3 million Palestinians in increasingly boiling conditions, the anticipated explosion was only a matter of time.

1
Hamas's History

ISLAMISM AND THE PALESTINIAN STRUGGLE

How are Islam and Palestine interrelated?

Over the centuries, Islam and Palestine have been intimately linked in the imagery and history of Muslims. Palestine has been bestowed with Islamic holiness, as well as religious significance for Christian and Jewish people, for a host of reasons and historic events. Jerusalem, and in particular Al-Aqsa Mosque (the furthest), is the first place to which Muslims directed their prayers when the Prophet Muhammad started preaching Islam in Arabia in the early seventh century. *Bait al-Maqdes*, or Jerusalem, is the third holiest place in Islam after Mecca and Medina in Saudi Arabia. It is frequently referred to in the Quran and is given numerous mentions in the *Hadith* – the sayings of the Prophets. Most of the stories about God's messengers as related in the Quran have specific geographical references to Palestine. One full chapter in the Quran, surat *al-Isra*, is dedicated to the Prophet Muhammad's journey from Mecca to Jerusalem, and his ascension there to heaven to meet God. This is a chapter passionately embraced by Muslims the world over as one of the most astonishing divine stories. On the very rock where the Prophet set off on his journey to heaven, the Dome of the Rock was built, next to Al-Aqsa Mosque and adjacent to the spot where the Jews say the Old Temple of Solomon was built.

The Christian and Jewish religious significance of Palestine is also recognized in Islam. Jesus Christ, who was born in Palestine, and Moses, who migrated to it, are considered by the Quran and Muslims to be two of the five most highly regarded prophets of God (the other three being Muhammad, Ibrahim and Ismail). Added to its religious sacredness, Palestine has long occupied a geostrategic position, linking the African and Asian parts of the Middle East, offering a long coast and a rich passage on the Mediterranean between the Arabian Peninsula, Egypt and Greater Syria. Because of its religious and strategic significance, Palestine was destined to be the field of wars, invasions and rivalries between powers. Muslims conquered Palestine and brought it under their control in 638 AD. Since then, Islam has been a central feature of the political, cultural and emotional foundation of this ancient tract of land.

The Western Crusaders from 1097 AD, onwards for two hundred years, fought war after war to gain control over Palestine, and in particular Jerusalem, and bring it within Christendom. Unlike most of the dominant powers of the time, the Muslims, who at that point already had ruled Palestine for over 400 years, had long allowed people of other religions to live in peace in their lands. Muslims had long welcomed pilgrims of all religions and had made accessible all of the historical shrines of religious significance to themselves and others: Christians, Jews, Persians, Orthodox Christians, Copts and many others. Palestine was part of an ancient area, sacred to many people.

After centuries of open exchange, and to the humiliation of Muslims, the Crusaders ruthlessly took Jerusalem in 1099 AD, slaughtered its Muslim inhabitants and succeeded in ruling there for 88 years. When Saladin defeated the Crusaders in 1187 AD, he entered the imagination and history of Islam as one of its most prominent heroes, whose successes signified the end of Muslim disgrace and defeat. The name of Saladin brings to Muslims and Palestinians memories of glory and, for many of them, it emphasizes their inevitable will and capacity to rise from the ashes. Perceived as brutal foreign invasions launched by European Christians, the Crusades are still seen by many Arabs and Palestinians as the original blueprint for the Zionist invasion, which also had its roots in Europe.

What is the relationship between Islam and Palestine within the Arab–Israeli conflict?

In the consciousness of many Muslims, the identity of the ruler of Palestine indicates the strength or weakness of Islam and Muslims. If Palestine is ruled and controlled by foreigners and non-Muslims – from the Crusaders of the medieval ages to the Zionists of the twentieth century and the present – then Islam and Muslims perceive themselves to be weak and defeated.

After the final defeat of the Crusaders in 1291, Palestine remained under Muslim rule for over six centuries, until the break-up of the Muslim Ottoman Empire which had ruled Palestine, in the aftermath of the First World War. The collapse of this declining Turkish empire, which had sided with the German allies in the Great War, was met with scant specific regret and loyalty by many in Palestine and the rest of the Arab world, because of the brutality in the last decades of its reign. However, the Ottoman foundation in Islam had kept Palestine firmly fixed within the Arab and Muslim world.

With the complete political collapse of the Ottoman Empire in the wake of the armistice, Ottoman territories in the Middle East were carved up into temporary protectorates controlled by the European victors, until more permanent political configurations could be concluded. A temporary British Mandate was set up over Palestine from 1922 to 1948. While the centuries-long roots of Islamic heritage and allegiance in Palestine were self-evident, strong currents of Zionism had long infiltrated British thinking. In 1917, the Balfour Declaration was issued by the British government expressing the British Empire's support for a Jewish national homeland in Palestine. Since then and until the creation of Israel in 1948, Britain sponsored and backed the Zionist plan in Palestine, helping the Jews to build a state within the state. The

Zionist Movement mobilized and accelerated Jewish immigration into British-administered Palestine; and with the surge of Jewish refugees fleeing increasingly larger Nazi-controlled parts of Europe this immigration escalated throughout the 1930s and 1940s. Meanwhile, Britain itself and the United States closed their borders in the face of those persecuted Jews.

Fighting what were clearly perceived to be colonial powers, Arab liberation movements across the former Ottoman territories united with their assorted versions of Islam, Arabism and rising country-based nationalism, and attempted to maximize the mobilization capacities of all tenets. In Palestine, Palestinians revolted against the British Mandate during the 1920s and 1930s under just such a blended Islamic/Arabism banner.

But the fate of Palestine would be irrevocably compounded by factors beyond the simple struggle between colonizers and the colonized. By 1948, Britain's control over Palestine was severely compromised by its own state of economic depletion following the Second World War and, ironically, by the relentless intensity of Zionist terrorist attacks. With mounting international sympathy for Jewish settlement in Palestine, the United Nations proposed a partitioning scheme in November 1947, that gave the Jews 56 per cent of Palestine. In May 1948, an exhausted Britain withdrew from a Palestine that had already been falling to the Zionist strong mini-state at the expense of the Palestinian majority. A Jewish state of Israel was declared almost immediately, then instantly recognized by the United States. Palestinians had been dumped into an abyss of chaos in their own land.

One of the most popular rebellion movements against the British, often recalled with pride by Palestinians, is the Izzeddin al-Qassam movement of the early 1930s. Sheikh al-Qassam was a religious scholar who launched armed resistance against the colonial British and their allies, the increasingly militarized European Zionist settlers who by then were flooding Palestine. For al-Qassam, there was no difference between the British and the Zionists, and 'From the very first, Qassam preached against

British imperialism and Zionist settlement in Palestine. His message was unequivocal: holy war, *Jihad*, against ... was the only means of removing the invaders from Arab Palestine.'* Decades on, in the early 1990s, Hamas's military wing would be named after Sheikh al-Qassam.

When the Zionist intentions became evident of creating a Jewish homeland in Palestine, with the strong support of the European powers, Palestinians tried as early as the beginning of the 1920s to mobilize their Muslim brethren the world over to defend Jerusalem and its holy places. In the year 1938, the first conference to defend *Bait al-Maqdes* was convened in Jerusalem, with delegations from Muslim countries as far distant as Pakistan and Indonesia. Muslim organizations and activities intensified in Palestine in parallel with the increase of activities and the militarization of the Zionist organizations and their settlers.

With the creation of Israel in 1948, a wide shock of humiliation reverberated across the Muslim world. The Jews occupied more than half of Palestine and Jerusalem and were but a few steps from the Al-Aqsa Mosque. The Arabs had been outmanoeuvred by Zionist might and its British collusion. This defeat was astounding, and the disgrace cut deep into the psyche of Palestinians, Arabs and Muslims. Islam was immediately called upon as an indigenous ideology entrenched throughout Muslim society, which could be used as a rallying point of mobilization in the battle against the enemy and its state as erected in Palestine.

In the 1950s and 1960s, Arabs and Palestinians were strongly influenced by pan-Arab nationalist and Marxist ideologies in their campaign to fight Israel and liberate Palestine. As a result, in Palestine and the surrounding countries bordering Israel – Egypt, Syria and Jordan – as well as in more distant countries such as Iraq, Libya and Algeria, Islamist movements were sidelined and Islam as an ideology of mobilization was relegated to the back seat.

---

* Nels Johnson, *Islam and the Politics of Meaning in Palestinian Nationalism* (London: Routledge, 1982), 40.

Another, even more mortifying, defeat was looming for the Palestinians and the Arabs in 1967, when Israel launched devastating attacks on Egypt, Syria and Jordan, annexing more land from all of them: Sinai and the Gaza Strip from Egypt, the Golan Heights from Syria and the West Bank with East Jerusalem and the Al-Aqsa Mosque from Jordan. With this collapse of the Arab armies, nationalist and Marxist ideologies started to give way to the gradual rise of Islamist movements and political Islam. Starting from the mid-1970s, Palestinian Islamists, in the current usage of the word, started establishing stronger footholds in Palestinian cities. With the victory of the Iranian Revolution in the late 1970s, and the defeat of the PLO in Lebanon in 1982, the Palestinian Islamists were steadily on the rise. Their main nationalist rival, the National Movement for the Liberation of Palestine (Fatah), had started its long decline. Islam was once again being recalled to the heart of Palestinian politics.

THE MUSLIM BROTHERHOOD ROOTS OF HAMAS

Who are the Muslim Brotherhood?

In its original creation and intellectual make-up, Hamas belongs to the realm of Muslim Brotherhood movements in the region. These were first established in Egypt in 1928 on the eve of the collapse of the Ottoman Empire. As the major Islamist movement, the Muslim Brotherhood could be considered to be the 'mother' of all movements that comprise political Islam in the Middle East (with the exception of Iran). Over the past eight decades, the Brotherhood have branched out in almost every Arab and Muslim country, blending religion and politics to the greatest degree. The Palestinian branch was set up in Jerusalem around the mid-1940s, two years exactly before the creation of the state of Israel.

Although the Muslim Brotherhood was initially mainstream and relatively moderate, many radical small groups have sprouted from it in the last two decades. The influence of its main thinkers, mainly Sayyid Qutb (1906–1966), has had an enormous impact on various strands of political Islam the world over. The main objective of the individual Muslim Brotherhood movements is to establish Islamic states in each of their countries, with the ultimate utopia of uniting individual Islamic states into one single state representing the Muslim Ummah.

The Muslim Brotherhood (MB) movements, and groups that share the same intellectual background and understanding, are presently the most powerful and active political movements in the Middle East. Robustly represented on the political scene, their members enjoyed parliamentary legitimacy and government posts, before the 2010–2011 popular revolutions (Arab Spring) in countries such as Egypt, Jordan, Yemen, Kuwait, Morocco, Algeria, Iraq and Bahrain. In post-revolutions times, they shortly rose to power or shared power in Egypt, Tunisia, Libya and Yemen before the tide of counter-revolution sidelined most of them. They are also strongly represented in the outlawed opposition in countries such as Syria, the United Arab Emirates and Saudi Arabia. Although they share the same background and sources of teaching, these movements are greatly coloured by their own national and country-based concerns and agenda. There is no obligatory hierarchical organizational structure that combines all of the MB groups into one single transnational organization.

Islamist movements, historically and currently, differ greatly in their understanding and interpretation of Islam. In any discussion of the Hamas movement, the two major issues that need to be distinguished are the differing perceptions of various Islamist movements concerning the 'ends' versus the 'means'. The 'ends' issue denotes the extent to which politics is ingrained in Islam, whereas the 'means' issue reflects the controversy on the use of violence to achieve the 'ends'. The spectrum of such interpretations tends to vacillate between two extremes. At one end, there is an understanding of Islam that politicizes religion and renders it the ultimate judge in all aspects of life, including public affairs and politics. At the other end, there is an apolitical understanding of Islam, shifting the focus to morals and religious teachings away from politics and state-making, and adhering to peaceful means as the sole accepted ways of conveying the word of Islam.

Along the spectrum of Islamist movements, the Muslim Brotherhood occupies almost the centre of the continuum in terms of 'ends' and 'means'. The Muslim Brotherhood believes in politicized religion and religious politics, hence its strong conviction that eventually Islamic states must be realized, whose real form and substance have proven difficult to identify. Broadly speaking, peaceful means were adopted and declared to realize this end, and so had been stressed by the movement's founders back in the Egypt of the 1930s. Yet, over the following decades, groups affiliated to the Muslim Brotherhood adopted violence and clashed with governments in Egypt (in 1950s) and Syria (in 1980s). The late 1980s and 1990s onwards have witnessed an overwhelming adherence to peaceful means, even when confronted with extreme oppressive measures, as was the case with the Tunisian Islamist movement in the late 1980s and afterwards. This had links to the post-Cold War global democratization tide that impacted the Middle East, and consequently left a moderation measure on ideological parties including the Islamists.

On one side of the Muslim Brotherhood's centre position on the ends–means continuum, there are groups such as al-Qaeda and ISIS which embrace violence wholeheartedly in their pursuit of their political aims. Hamas also lies somewhere on this side of the continuum, but closer to the Muslim Brotherhood than to al-Qaeda or ISIS, by virtue of its unique specificity of using violence only against foreign occupying powers and not against national governments. On the other side of the Muslim Brotherhood, there are groups that distance themselves from politics, such as *al-Dawa wal Tabligh*, which believes only in spreading religious teaching and morality, and *Hizb al-Tahrir*, whose politicization of religion is perhaps stronger than that of the Muslim Brotherhood, but it believes neither in violence nor in political participation in existing systems; instead, the fight for this party is purely intellectual.

What are the links between the Muslim Brotherhood, Palestine and Hamas?

Hamas represents the internal metamorphosis of the Palestinian Muslim Brotherhood, which took place in the late 1980s. Officially, the Palestinian branch of the Muslim Brotherhood was founded in 1946 in Jerusalem, although its presence and activities in Palestine go back to 1943–1944 in Gaza City, Jerusalem, Nablus and other cities. The aims, structure and outlook of the Palestinian Muslim Brotherhood were drawn along the main lines of thinking of the mother organization in Egypt, where the Islamization of society is the prime goal. At this time, there was no Israel, and Islamists like all Palestinians were facing the British Mandate and the growing power of the Zionist movement.

There is no record of the Palestinian Muslim Brotherhood fighting against British troops in Palestine during the mandate period. The Egyptian Muslim Brotherhood, however, took part in the 1948 war against the Zionist armed organizations by sending hundreds of volunteers to fight alongside the then-weak Egyptian army. After the creation of the State of Israel in 1948, the Palestinian Muslim Brotherhood was physically divided into two parts: one in the West Bank and East Jerusalem, which was annexed to Jordan and where the Palestinian Brothers joined the Jordanian Branch of the Muslim Brotherhood; and one in the Gaza Strip, which was left under Egyptian administration, and thus the Palestinian Muslim Brotherhood there became very close to and influenced by the Egyptian Muslim Brotherhood.

By the war of 1967, new political and geographical realities were brought into being when the entire area of historic Palestine, including the West Bank, East Jerusalem and the Gaza Strip (as well as the Egyptian Sinai desert and the Syrian Golan Heights) fell under Israeli control. The two wings of the Palestinian Muslim Brotherhood, the Gazan and the West Banker, became closer and developed unitary structures over the years. In the 1970s and 1980s, the Palestinian Muslim Brotherhood amassed strength and established footholds in all major Palestinian cities. On the broader Palestinian political scene and by virtue of adopting resistance against Israel, nationalist and leftist movements had been outpacing and outpowering the Muslim Brotherhood in both Gaza and the West Bank from as early as the 1940s up to the late 1980s. In particular, the Fatah movement (the Palestinian National Movement for the Liberation of Palestine) and the PLO (the Palestine Liberation Organization), which is the wider umbrella of the national Palestinian movements, dominated Palestinian politics over those decades.

The 1980s witnessed a rapid growth in the power of the Muslim Brotherhood. In December 1987, a popular Palestinian uprising, the intifada, against the Israeli occupation erupted first in the Gaza Strip, then in the West Bank. On the eve of that uprising, the Palestinian Muslim Brotherhood decided to undertake a major transformation within the movement. It established Hamas as an adjunct organisation with the specific mission of confronting and violently resisting the Israeli occupation.

Are there other Islamist movements in Palestine?

There have been, and still are, Islamist movements other than Hamas in Palestine. The most important one is the Islamic Jihad Movement in Palestine, established in the early 1980s, at least five years before the emergence of Hamas. The Islamic Jihad was formed by discontented former members of the Muslim Brotherhood, Fatah and other nationalist and leftist Palestinian factions. Inspired by the victory of the Islamic revolution in Iran in 1978–1979, the idea of the Islamic Jihad was to create a bridge between Islam and Palestine, which were separately represented by the Muslim Brotherhood on the one hand, and the nationalist camp (the PLO) on the other hand.

When the Palestinian Muslim Brotherhood, the mother organization of Hamas, was immersed in its religious programmes in the first years of 1980s, the Islamic Jihad offered new dimensions to Palestinian nationalism, which incorporated Islamist armed struggle against Israel into the very heart of Islamic discourse and practice. From 1982 to 1987, the Islamic Jihad posed a serious challenge to the Muslim Brotherhood because of its adoption of military resistance against the occupation. It also posed an equal challenge to the nationalist factions whose main criticism of the Muslim Brotherhood concerned its deferment of confrontation with the Israeli occupation. If the PLO was nationalist enough, but lacked an Islamic dimension, and if the Palestinian MB was Islamist enough, but lacked a resistance/nationalist dimension, the Islamic Jihad combined both components and had ended what it had seen to be a disconnection between Islam and Palestine.

In the second half of the 1990s, and during the second Palestinian uprising in the year 2000, the Islamic Jihad carried out many suicide attacks. At certain periods, it outpaced Hamas and other factions in this practice. However, the Islamic Jihad grew weaker in membership and networking compared with Hamas, and perhaps this had created little enthusiasm for future elections in 1996 and 2006. Elections absorb national energy that should be directed towards resisting the Israelis, so has been the movement's justification. In the 1990s, whenever the Islamic Jihad took part in even minor elections for student unions or trade unions, its results ranged between 4 and 7 per cent compared with 45 to 55 per cent for Hamas.

Another Islamist movement with a certain visible presence in Palestine, with a narrower political relevance, is *Hizb al-Tahrir* (the Liberation Party). It was founded in 1952 as a splinter group of the Muslim Brotherhood in Jerusalem, and then branched outside Palestine. Its main belief is that the source of all sins in Muslim societies is the disappearance of Caliphate, an overarching pan-Muslim rule, and that all efforts should be focused on restoring Caliphate. Once in power, the Caliph (the leader representing the supreme Islamic authority) can mobilize Muslims by virtue of his appeal, and his power if necessary, and direct them to work for any cause. The failure of Muslims (including Palestinians), Hizb al-Tahrir concludes, stems from their overlooking this premise. Grassroots efforts and gradual Islamization are fruitless. Change should be undertaken from above, and when the Caliph is in power, many problems that face Muslims will be solved. Regarding the Palestinian question and confronting the Israeli occupation, the Hizb al-Tahrir Party maintains a passive approach which has lost its popularity and leverage among Palestinians. The party opposes all forms of political participation, such as elections, and, in the absence of the Caliph, it opposes a resort to violence against either national governments or Israel.

THE FORMATION OF HAMAS

When, why and how was Hamas founded?

Hamas came into being officially on 14 December 1987, declaring itself in an official communiqué a few days after the eruption of the *Intifada*, the Palestinian uprising, on 8 December. The decision to establish the Islamic Resistance Movement (Hamas) was taken on the day following the Intifada by top leaders of the Palestinian Muslim Brotherhood, Sheikh Ahmad Yasin, Abdul 'Aziz al-Rantisi, Salah Shehadeh, Muhammad Sham'ah, 'Isa al-Nashar, 'Abdul Fattah Dukhan and Ibrahim al-Yazuri (the first three were assassinated by Israel in later years).

Hamas was formed by the Palestinian Muslim Brotherhood itself, in order to respond to a number of factors pressing upon the organization. Internally and by the time of the Intifada, the rank and file of the Palestinian Muslim Brotherhood were witnessing intense internal debate on the passive approach to the Israeli occupation. Two main opposing views contended over the way forward. One pushed for a change in policy towards confrontation with the Israeli occupation, thus bypassing old

43

and traditional thinking whose focus was on the Islamization of society first. The other view clung to the classical school of thought within the Muslim Brotherhood movements, which adhered to the concept of 'preparing the generations for a battle' which had no deadline. When the Intifada erupted, the exponents of the confrontational policy gained a stronger position, arguing that Islamists would suffer a great loss if they decided not to take part in the popular and collective uprising, definitively and equally with all the other participating Palestinian factions.

Nationally, hard living conditions for Palestinians in the Gaza Strip, which had been created and exacerbated by the Israeli occupation, reached an unprecedented state. Poverty combined with feelings of oppression and humiliation charged the Palestinian atmosphere with the ripe conditions for revolt against the occupation. The uprising was the flashpoint. The explosion reflected the accumulation of past experiences and suffering more than any specific event that triggered things on the first day of the uprising. Strategically speaking, it was the golden opportunity for the Palestinian Muslim Brotherhood to heed (and be seen to lead) the uprising. It did just so by creating Hamas.

There was also the factor of the rivalry at this time from a similar Islamic organization, the Islamic Jihad Movement. As discussed above, the Islamic Jihad had been on the rise during the few years preceding the Intifada. The very incident that triggered the Intifada itself involved Islamic Jihad members who freed themselves from an Israeli prison and engaged in a shoot-out with the Israeli soldiers. Feeling envious of the Islamic Jihad and its members, who emerged as heroes in the eyes of the Palestinians after the incident, the Palestinian Muslim Brotherhood felt the danger of losing ground to its small, yet more active, competitor. The presence and activities of the Islamic Jihad partly compelled the Muslim Brotherhood to speed up its internal transformation.

Why did the Palestinian Islamists only start their armed struggle against Israeli occupation in 1987 when this occupation started in 1967?

In the thinking of the Muslim Brothers, both in Palestine prior to the creation of Hamas and in other countries, the failures of Muslims – their backwardness, weakness and their defeat by their enemies – were the results of their deviation from the true path of Islam. Therefore, the proper process for redressing all of these failures, including the defeat in the wars against Israel, was first to educate Muslims about Islam and make them committed to their religion. Transforming people from ignorant Muslims into adherents would rehabilitate all of Muslim society and prepare it for the fight with its enemies, from the certainty of standing on strong ground. In the rhetoric of the Muslim Brotherhood this was called 'preparing the generations'.

The Palestinian Muslim Brotherhood had a deep conviction in this principle, which they consistently used to justify their non-confrontation policy against the Israeli occupation during the 1950s, 1960s, 1970s and up until 1987. Against mounting accusations by other Palestinian nationalist and leftist organizations of cowardice or even of being indirectly in the service of the Israeli occupation, the Palestinian Islamists clung to their strategy of 'preparing the generations' for a long time. They argued that it was a fruitless effort to fight Israel (and its Western backers) with a 'corrupt army'; instead, one should build a devoted and religiously committed army, then engage in war against Israel.

This strategy came under continuous attack. For Palestinian nationalists and leftists, such an approach was a mere justification for refraining from joining the national armed struggle. It was also criticized as naive on two levels: the first being the association of an individual's capacity and genuine intention to fight the occupation with his or her level of religious commitment; and the second being the contrast between the open-ended abstraction of 'preparing the generations' with the daily imperative of engagement with the enemy. The true preparation of people to fight for their national rights and liberation, critics argued, is to fully engage in the struggle, where people learn and empower themselves as they advance and suffer. Moreover, Israel was understandably happy with the Islamists' concept of 'delaying the struggle' until the Palestinian generations were spiritually and morally well prepared and ready.

Hamas's supporters retrospectively defend the earlier thinking of their mother organization. They say that it was just exactly this strategy that guaranteed a strong beginning for Hamas and its continuous achievements on the ground in the years which followed. For them, the need for gradual and patient preparation was actually justified because in the 1960s and 1970s the Islamists were militarily and organisationally very weak, and had they involved themselves in fruitless confrontation against Israel then, they would have been crushed easily, serving neither Palestine nor Islam.

Regardless of their rationalizations, the Islamists paid a high price during the decades (the 1950s, 1960s, 1970s and most of the 1980s) when they opted for a non-confrontational policy. They provided the opportunity for their national rivals to outpace them and put themselves in a disadvantageous position. More importantly, they deprived the Palestinian struggle against the Israeli occupation of the participation and contribution of that significant segment of the Palestinian population who came under the influence of the Palestinian Muslim Brotherhood and its thinking.

2

Hamas's Ideology, Strategy and Objectives

THE DEFINITION OF HAMAS, ITS IDEOLOGICAL DRIVE AND WORLDVIEW

What is Hamas, and is it driven by religious or political convictions?

One informative answer to this common question can be found in a self-definition that Hamas once produced by way of introducing itself to a European government, years prior to its assuming power in 2006. In this document, Hamas states its aims and strategies in addition to its long-term view for the solution in Palestine. In this lengthy but worthy of quoting statement, Hamas describes itself as follows:

> The Islamic Resistance Movement (Hamas) is a Palestinian national liberation movement that struggles for the liberation of the Palestinian occupied territories and for the recognition of the legitimate rights of Palestinians. Although it came into existence soon after the eruption of the first Palestinian Intifada (uprising) in December 1987 as an expression of the Palestinian people's anger against the continuation of the Israeli occupation of Palestinian land and persecution of the Palestinian people, Hamas' roots extend much deeper in history. The movement's motivation for resistance has been expressed by its founder and leader Sheikh Ahmad Yasin: 'The movement struggles against Israel because it is the aggressing, usurping

and oppressing state that day and night hoists the rifle in the face of our sons and daughters.'

Hamas considers itself to be an extension of an old tradition that goes back to the early twentieth century struggle against British and Zionist colonialism in Palestine. The fundamentals from which it derives its legitimacy are mirrored in the very name it chose for itself. Hamas, in the Islamic language, means that it derives its guiding principles from the doctrines and values of Islam. Islam is completely Hamas' ideological frame of reference. It is from the values of Islam that the movement seeks its inspiration in its mobilisation effort, and particularly in seeking to address the huge difference in material resources between the Palestinian people and their supporters on the one hand and Israel and its supporters on the other. ...

The forms of resistance adopted by Hamas stem from the same justifications upon which the national Palestinian resistance movement has based its struggle for more than a quarter of a century. At least the first ten articles of the Palestinian National Charter issued by the PLO show complete compatibility with Hamas' discourse as elaborated in its Charter and other declarations. Furthermore, the same justifications for resistance had, prior to the emergence of Hamas in December 1987, been recognised, or endorsed, by a variety of regional and international bodies such as the Arab League, the Islamic Conference Organisation, the Non-Aligned Movement and the United Nations. It is clearly recognised that the Israeli occupation of the West Bank and Gaza in 1967 is illegal in UN Security Council Resolutions 242 and 338. ...

In spite of the overwhelming militant image it has in the minds of many people in the West, Hamas is not a mere military faction. It is a political, cultural and social grass roots organisation that has a separate military wing specialising in armed resistance against Israeli occupation. Apart from this strategically secretive military wing, all other sections within

Hamas function through overt public platforms. The military wing has its own leadership and recruiting mechanism.

Hamas's social and educational activities in the Occupied Territories have become so interwoven within the Palestinian community that neither the Israelis nor their peace partners in the Palestinian Authority have been able to extricate them one from the other. The fact of the matter is that Hamas, contrary to Israeli assessment, acts as an infrastructure to the numerous cultural, educational and social institutions in Gaza and the West Bank that render invaluable and irreplaceable services to the public. In other words, it is Hamas that gives life to these institutions and not the reverse. The Israelis have repeatedly told the PA to close them down. The PA has tried but failed. A crackdown on these institutions amounts to a declaration of war not against Hamas but against the Palestinian community as a whole.

It must be pointed out that the above text identifies Hamas with the Palestinians' struggle to liberate their land only. There is no implication, either explicit or tacit, of any intention to establish an Islamic state in Palestine in the future, or any similar goals advocated by other Islamist organizations. There is further discussion of this below.

What is Hamas's ultimate aim? Is it to establish an Islamic state in Palestine?

The vague idea of establishing an Islamic state in Palestine as mentioned in the early statements of the movement was quickly sidelined and surpassed. Even when it was repeated by members of Hamas, it never amounted to any really serious proposal with thoughtfully considered details. If anything, the early reluctant existence of references to an Islamic state, followed by almost complete disappearance in Hamas's documentation and discourse, reflected the tension in the minds of Hamas's leaders between the political and the religious. On one hand, there is the subconscious urge to remain sincere to the pure pre-Hamas religious utopia, where the dream of an Islamic state sought to fulfil the goals of the long-distant future. On the other hand, the over-simplification and naivety of this dream exposed the extent to which Hamas needed to become aware of the realities and priorities of what the Palestinians were dealing with, on the ground, day after day. In this light, the Hamas dream of an Islamic state was practically embarrassing, but the realization of this developed a more sophisticated Hamas that is engaged with the actual needs of a Palestinian people under siege. Palestinians across the spectrum of political convictions have struggled desperately for more than a century to extract even minimal legitimate rights, first from British occupiers following the 1922 Mandate, and then from 1948, when Britain withdrew from Palestine, leaving the Zionist organization to declare the Jewish State of Israel. The new state has essentially been occupying and colonizing not only those parts of Palestine 'allocated' to it by the UN 1947 division plan, but even large areas of Palestine that were not. After all these decades of struggle, the maximum that the Palestinian leadership has struggled to achieve, without success, has been the retention or recovery of no more than one-eighth of the historic land of Palestine.

The Islamic state put forth in early Hamas literature was visualized to include the whole of Palestine from the River Jordan to the Mediterranean Sea. The question became, would Hamas wait in hope for full liberation of all historic Palestine, or would it seek to impose a temporary Islamic state in just the West Bank and the Gaza Strip, if they were ever returned to the Palestinians? What kind of state would this be, and how would it deal with its surroundings, with Israel, with the world? On what basis would it do so? And so forth. These were part of the endless intractable questions surrounded this idea of establishing an Islamic state; thus, it eventually ended in complete trivialization, with Hamas dropping the idea altogether.

If not the formation of an Islamic state, then what now is Hamas's ultimate goal? A plain answer, suggested by the movement's formal declarations, might be the simple total liberation of the historic land of Palestine from the River Jordan to the Mediterranean Sea. However, similar to the utopian religious goal of establishing an Islamic state, this utopian nationalist goal, measured against present harsh realities for the Palestinians, tends to be mentioned less frequently in Hamas's documents and verbal statements. In fact, the longer Hamas functions, the less of a maximalist discourse it adopts on what many see as the 'ultimate goals'. Hamas has developed over time into a movement that is increasingly preoccupied with current and immediate, and medium-term goals.

In the course of taking power after the elections of 2006, Hamas's election campaign and its post-win discourse explicitly focused on resisting the illegal Israeli occupation while implicitly, if reluctantly, accepting the principle of a two-state solution. Neither an Islamic state nor the total liberation of Palestine have been emphasized. The ultimate goals, thus, have been postponed or replaced with short- and medium-term ones, which are more pressing and more realistic.

What is Hamas's strategy?

To confirm its move out of the realm of far-fetched dreams, Hamas started to advocate more achievable goals in both the short and medium term. It not only sought immediate relief and benefits for Palestinians on the ground now, but it also pursued goals that could be comprehended by regional and international audiences. Minimizing the religious in its use of language, Hamas's discourse has become more aware, embracing legal jargon and basing itself on the norms of international law. Yet Hamas still struggles to keep alive the principle of the 'liberation of Palestine' as a whole, in the mildest way possible, within the context of the immediate challenges faced by the movement and Palestinians at large. In the few years after the 1987 Intifada, Hamas developed its strategy considerably and departed from the initial raw statements mentioned in its Charter. Marking a turning point, an 'Introductory Memorandum' that was published in Palestine in 1990, elaborates 'The Movement's Strategy':*

Hamas constructs its strategy for confronting the Zionist occupation as follows:

- The Palestinian people, being the primary target of the occupation, bear the larger part of the burden in resisting it. Hamas, therefore, works to mobilize the energies of these people and to direct them toward steadfastness.
- The field of engagement with the enemy is Palestine, Arab and Islamic lands being fields of aid and support to our people, especially those lands that have been enriched with the pure blood of [Islamic] martyrs throughout the ages.
- Confronting and resisting the enemy in Palestine must be continuous until victory and liberation. Holy struggle in the name of God as our guide, and fighting and inflicting harm on enemy troops and their instruments rank at the top of our means of resistance.
- Political activity, in our view, is one means of holy struggle against the Zionist enemy and aims to buttress the struggle and steadfastness of our people and to mobilize its energies and that of our Arab Islamic nation to render our cause victorious.

In this strategy, Hamas confirms the 'boundaries' of the armed conflict, stating clearly that it wishes to undertake no military steps outside Palestine: 'the field of engagement with the enemy is Palestine'. Hamas reiterates this conviction in its strategy to assure

---

* For the full text, translated from Arabic, see Khaled Hroub, *Hamas: Political Thought and Practice* (Washington, DC: Institute of Palestine Studies, 2000), 292–302.

the outside world that attacking any Western or even Israeli targets outside Palestine is not on the agenda of the movement.

It is worth mentioning that these guidelines were outlined 13 years before Hamas came to power and took control of the Palestinian Authority in January 2006. These broad proclamations of Hamas's strategy were drawn with very little expectation, if any, of where political and military developments concerning the Israeli–Palestinian conflict would lead the Palestinians. Surely it was beyond the imagination of the people who drafted the above strategy that Hamas would one day be allowed to win free and fair democratic elections to control a limited self-rule authority created according to peace agreements between the PLO, Hamas's rivals, and Israel.

This new situation has brought the cornerstone of Hamas's strategy – 'military resistance' to the Israeli occupation – under close scrutiny. In taking over a government of besieged and weakened authority, Hamas was overwhelmed by the numerous issues relating to the simple daily living of Palestinians. Any thought of military resistance appeared for a while to be a luxury that the movement could not afford. As was noted above, Hamas had pragmatically recognized earlier that the immediate welfare of the besieged Palestinian people was as important as any more long-term ideological ideals. It has managed to save face as the party of resistance by adopting the standard line that 'political activity ... is itself one of the means of struggle', a line echoed in the statement often made by its leaders that military resistance is not an end in itself, but a means to an end. Thus, being consumed in government undertakings and serving the Palestinian people on a daily basis can easily be linked to the broad parameters of resistance.

How does Hamas perceive the world?

Hamas's immediate world, as explained in its literature, comprises three concentric circles: the Palestinian core, the larger Arabic circle, and the larger still embracing the Islamic circle. Beyond those circles lies the rest of the world. The question of Palestine is, for Hamas, the fundamental determinant in shaping the relationship between those three circles and the rest of the world. The movement's Charter and Introductory Memorandum state that:

Hamas believes that the ongoing conflict between Arabs and Muslims and Zionists in Palestine is a fateful civilizational struggle incapable of being brought to an end without eliminating its cause, namely, the Zionist settlement of Palestine.

The West is charged not only with the responsibility of having illegally created Israel but also with bringing devastation and dismemberment to the region as a whole:

This enterprise of aggression [on Palestine] complements the larger Western project that seeks to strip this Arab Islamic nation of its cultural roots to consolidate Western Zionist hegemony over it by completing the plan of greater Israel and establishing political and economic control of it. Doing so implies maintaining the [current] state of [physical] division, backwardness, and dependency in which this Arab Islamic nation is forced to live. The conflict as described is a form of struggle between truth and falsehood, which obligates Arabs and Muslims to support the Palestinians in bearing the consequences of a holy struggle to extirpate the Zionist presence from Palestine and prevent it from spreading to other Arab and Islamic countries.

Of the circles surrounding Palestine, the first one is Arabic, the second is Islamic and the third is the rest of the world. Naturally more affinity and intimacy are felt towards the closer Arabic and Islamic circles. There is a considerable amount of dismay, criticism and attack against the indifference that the outermost circle comprising the 'world' has exhibited concerning the suffering of the Palestinians. The western world is typically criticized and accused not only of 'transplanting' Israel in Palestine – at the heart of the Arab region – by force, but also for its continuous support of the usurping and aggressive Zionist state, which has sought even to exceed the borders of the original illegal foundation.

In its very early stages, Hamas thinking was skewed by a dichotomy that bisected the world into the 'truthfulness' represented by Muslims and believers, and the 'falsehood' represented by non-Muslims and particularly Westerners and Jews. This naive perception later almost disappeared from the movement's discourses. In tandem with Hamas's rise in influence, the expansion of its regional and international relations and its realization of the complexity of reality and politics at ground level, Hamas has rehabilitated its worldview and effectively abandoned the dichotomy based on believers–nonbelievers. The notion of political support for the Palestinians and their just cause, as well as pragmatic considerations, have prevailed as the defining parameters by which Hamas assesses world players and where they stand. At the present, and indeed ironically, Hamas has no official links with prominent Muslim countries such as Saudi Arabia and United Arab Emirates, while enjoying high-level reception in Moscow and Beijing, the former leading Communist world powers.

What is the Hamas Charter, and is it relevant?

There has been much talk about Hamas' Charter that was published in August 1988, nine months after the emergence of Hamas. Hamas has grown out of the primitive ideas and statements pronounced in that Charter. The movement issued dozens of documents that meant to elaborate its more mature outlook, leading to the 2017 'Document of Principles and General Policies' (see Chapter 14) and which could be considered as Hamas' new Charter. Still, the original Charter merits close analysis despite being rendered irrelevant for the movement. The 'Charter' was published with the aim of introducing the new movement first to its immediate, then to broader, constituencies. It was meant to be the founding treatise: the embodiment of Hamas's objectives, vision and beliefs, and the movement's guidelines for its strategy and worldview. The main emphasis of the Charter is to assert that Palestine is an Arab and Muslim land that should be liberated from Zionist domination, and that Israel is a 'usurper' and an alien entity which was 'transplanted' in Palestine only with the support of Western superpowers. Perhaps unsurprisingly, the Charter failed to maintain a central position in Hamas's political thinking; a few years after its publication, it was shunted onto the margins with little reference to its content. It was deemed by many Hamas leaders, both inside and outside Palestine, to be simplistic and overloaded with claims and arguments that would reflect a naive, rather than a sophisticated, image of Hamas. Over more than 30 years of following Hamas' political conduct and politics, I have never heard one of its leaders quoting a single line of the Charter. Rather, in several interviews over the years, I have been told by a number of Hamas figures that the Charter never reflected the movement's thought and ideology, as it was written by one leading personality in the Gaza Strip, then hastily distributed without enough prior consultation.

The Charter is a long and not a well written text in Arabic that, in English, runs to 24 pages, comprising 5 chapters with 36 articles which tackle a wide array of issues and positions.* The general language of the Charter is distinctively polemic and characteristically religious, unlike the more politically nuanced language that Hamas has adopted in subsequent years. All the chapters are infused with Quranic verses, Hadiths, quotations from prominent religious people, ancient and contemporary, and sometime

---

* For the full text of the English-translated version of the Hamas Charter of August 1988, see Khaled Hroub, *Hamas: Political Thought and Practice* (Washington, DC: Institute of Palestine Studies, 2000), 267–91, from which all the quotations and references from the Charter in this chapter are taken.

classical Arab poetry. A considerable measure of obscurity and a generic Islamic bent in the Charter has produced a de-Palestinized discourse, which makes it less easy to understand the specifics or relevance of certain statements or discursive engagement in the text. Modern references are also made, especially to European anti-Semitic discourse blaming the Jews for all the sins and catastrophes in the world.

The Introduction the Charter is as follows:

This is the Charter of the Islamic Resistance Movement (Hamas), showing its form, revealing its identity, stating its position, clarifying its expectations, discussing its hopes, and calling for aid, support, and a joining of its ranks, because our struggle with the Jews is long and dangerous, requiring all dedicated efforts. It is a phase that must be followed by succeeding phases, a battalion that must be supported by battalion after battalion of the vast Arab and Islamic world until the enemy is defeated and the victory of God prevails.

The first chapter of the Charter is the 'Introduction of the Movement', where the text is anxious to declare that Hamas is a branch of the Muslim Brotherhood chapter in Palestine, emphasizing that the 'Islamic perspective' of the Brothers is the same as that of Hamas. This chapter goes on to outline the 'Structure and Essence' of Hamas, where little and only general abstractions are given, such as that it comprises Muslims who are devoted to God and worship Him verily: 'The historical and geographical dimensions of the Islamic resistance movement where Islam is confirmed as the "origin" of the movement and where its geography extends to wherever Muslims are found.' In the sections 'Differentiation and independence' and the 'Universality of the Islamic resistance movement', the first signs of bold 'Palestinianism' emerge in the Charter, which states that 'Hamas is a distinct Palestinian movement', similar in some ways to but different in others from other movements.

Chapter 2, the shortest in the Charter, deals with Objectives, and stipulates that:

The goal of Hamas ... is to conquer evil, crushing it and defeating it, so that truth may prevail, so that the country may return to its rightful place, and so that the call may be heard from the minarets proclaiming the Islamic state. And aid is sought from God.

Achieving this goal is described in Chapter 3, the longest in the Charter, through 'Strategies and Methods'. The opening statement of this chapter affirms that:

The Islamic resistance movement believes that the land of Palestine is an Islamic land entrusted to the Muslim generations until Judgement Day. No one may renounce all or even part of it. No Arab state nor all Arab states combined, no king or president nor all kings and presidents, and no organization nor all organizations, Palestinian or Arab, have the right to dispose of it or relinquish or cede any part of it.

The chapter moves on to discuss Nation and nationalism from the point of view of the Islamic resistance movement, considering nationalism as 'part and parcel of religious ideology'. Then it emphasizes the role of jihad in fighting the occupiers: 'If an enemy invades Muslim territories then Jihad and fighting the enemy becomes an individual duty on every Muslim. Jihad is the only way to restore rights: There is no solution to the Palestinian problem except through struggle [jihad]. As for international initiatives and conferences, they are a waste of time, a kind of child's play.'

Further 'strategies' are laid down by elaborating the 'three circles' that should be engaged in the liberation of Palestine: 'the Palestinian circle; the Arab circle; and the Islamic circle', each of which has its contribution to the 'battle'. In order to prepare the

Palestinians and other Muslims to engage in this battle, a process of 'Islamic education and training' should be undertaken, as the text points out, where the 'role of Muslim women', the 'role of Islamic art in the battle of liberation' and 'social solidarity' are given specific attention.

Perhaps the most embarrassing part of the entire Charter in the eyes of today's Hamas is the less-than-one-page section under the title 'Forces Abetting the Enemy'. Here the Charter paints a picture of the global conspiracy that was behind the establishment of Israel. It states:

> The enemies have planned well to get where they are, taking into account the effective measures in current affairs ... with money they financed revolutions throughout the world in pursuit of their objectives. They were behind the French Revolution, the Communist Revolution, and most of the revolutions here and there that we heard about and are hearing of. With wealth they established clandestine organizations all over the world, such as the Freemasons, the Rotary and Lions Clubs, etc., to destroy societies and promote the interests of Zionism. These are all destructive intelligence-gathering organizations ... let us speak without hesitation: They were behind the First World War in which they destroyed the Islamic Caliphate ... monopolized the wealth and got the Balfour Declaration. They created the League of Nations through which they could rule the world. They were behind the Second World War ... There was no war that broke out anywhere without their hands behind it.

Chapter 4, 'Our Position', is devoted to Hamas's positions regarding a number of immediate and pressing issues (and parties). It starts by offering amicable gestures towards 'Other Islamic movements' (hinting at Hizb al-Tahrir in Palestine and the Islamic Jihad Movement; the latter was amassing popularity to a degree considered 'alarming' by the Palestinian Muslim

Brotherhood at the time of the emergence of Hamas). Then the text outlines Hamas's position regarding 'patriotic (secular) movements in the Palestinian arena', confirming that 'it will lend its support to them as long as they do not give loyalty either to the communist East or the crusading West'. Regarding Hamas's relationship with the PLO however, the Charter attempts to carefully describe a position that shows an appreciation of the organization, but remains far from acknowledging it as the representative of the Palestinian people, using the excuse of the secular nature of the PLO: 'despite our respect for the Palestine Liberation Organization and what it might become, and not reducing its role in the Arab–Israeli struggle, we cannot exchange the Islamic nature of Palestine for the secular ideology [of the PLO]'.

Chapter 5, which is a short conclusion, is meant to inject hope and steadfastness into Hamas's followers by means of citing the 'Historical Proof: Facing the Enemy Throughout History', as the title of the chapter goes. Here the text reaches another peak in its polemics, declaring that 'Palestine is the heart of the earth, the meeting of the continents, the object of greed for the avaricious since the dawn of history'. Then it refers to the current 'Zionist invasion of Palestine' as a passing phase that will only follow previous failed phases:

The current Zionist invasion has been preceded by the many invasions of the crusading West and others, such as the Tartars from the East. The Muslims confronted those invasions, prepared for fighting, and defeated them. They should be able to confront and defeat the Zionist invasion.

Now that I have outlined the main themes addressed in the Hamas Charter, it is important, however, to reiterate that the significance that is given to the Charter in much anti-Hamas literature, even until the time of writing this edition of the book, is in fact unjustified. Also, the often-repeated charges that the Charter explicitly calls for the 'destruction of Israel' or the 'termination of the Jews' are not accurate; no such literal phrases occur in the Charter. There is no doubt, however, that the Charter with its rhetoric and unlimited generalizations has inflicted much damage upon Hamas. But the movement's literature since 1990 has become far more sophisticated than what was initially presented in the Charter (see Chapter 10). As explained elsewhere in this book, Hamas's more current discourse is politically driven, unlike the Charter's heavily religiously riddled language. To change or replace the Charter, however, would be a very difficult and delicate step, and it is one that Hamas has lacked the courage to take. Hamas leaders fear that such a step would be construed by many as giving up on the basic principles of the movement. What Hamas has resigned itself to do, thus far, is to let the Charter die on its own, moving on and leaving it behind; hoping it will just go away. Yet the cost of simply downplaying its existence remains high, as all that is stated in the Charter is still formally taken to be representative of Hamas.

HAMAS: A NATIONAL LIBERATION MOVEMENT OR A RELIGIOUS MOVEMENT?

What are the nationalist elements and religious elements in Hamas's thinking and practice?

Hamas is a blend of national liberation movement and Islamist religious group. By virtue of such a nature, its driving forces are dual, its daily functioning is biaxial and its end goals are bifocal, where each side of the binary serves the other.

The dual driving reasons for Palestinians to join Hamas are to actively engage in the liberation of Palestine by resisting the Israeli occupation and whatever else that may take, and to serve Islam and spread its word. The word 'and' is pivotal here and cannot be replaced by the word 'or', though the balance between the two motives need not be equal or the same in everyone. Hamas considers that its power is to be found in this link, the strengthened alloy of these two separate strands of Palestinian political activism: the national secular liberation movement that has confronted Israel, and the Islamist religious movement that largely has not. The desired thinking is that in struggling for the liberation of Palestine, an individual is serving Islam and, in strengthening the call of Islam, this individual serves the liberation struggle. When it comes to the broader support of Hamas beyond its official membership, that support from many Palestinians, Arabs and others is directed to Hamas's resistance to the Israeli occupation and not necessarily to its social and religious aspects.

Still, however, the link between resistance and Islam remains a major underlying explanation for the continuous rise in support and popularity of Hamas. People with strong nationalist feelings and the drive to struggle against Israel, and with a traditional Islamist background, tend to choose Hamas as their natural movement. Others, with strong religious sentiments and who also want to be active against Israel, also join Hamas. Indeed, it is to be expected that both driving forces will occupy the mind and soul of the Hamas membership, but certainly their strengths differ at the level of individuals. For example, members of the Muslim Brotherhood organization who became de facto members of Hamas when the former was transformed into the latter tend to nurture a stronger religious drive than those members who joined Hamas in later stages and after defecting from other nationalist factions.

The day-to-day operations of Hamas are therefore spread along the axis of religious and nationalist activities. It devotes considerable efforts to educating its membership according to Islamic ideals, as understood and interpreted by the organization, including steadfastness and discipline in times of war. Mainly by using mosques, Hamas has built a strong generation of young people who are adherents of Islam. From committed daily prayers and reciting Quranic verses to fighting what it considers to be anti-religion practices in the street, Hamas members cohere to the finest details of Islamic rituals. The other part of the daily function of Hamas is the struggle against Israel. It is deeply believed in Hamas's thinking that the more devout the individual is, the more self-sacrificing on the battlefield he or she will be. In this way, religious teaching strengthens the liberation front.

The ultimate goals of Hamas are also dual: the liberation of Palestine and the Islamization of society (*en route* to the establishment of the, vaguely defined, future Islamic state). In the early Hamas thinking and among rigid Palestinian Islamists, these two goals can never be reached simultaneously, but must come in sequence. For them, it would be futile to try to liberate Palestine before achieving a satisfactory degree of Islamization in Palestinian society. To their way of thinking, only religious and Islam-disciplined individuals would be able to defeat Israel. What Hamas has done within that traditional thinking is to break such an imagined sequence and argue that both processes can be fought for in parallel. In this, Hamas attracts both those who want to liberate Palestine, and those who want to Islamize Palestinian society.

How far are the nationalists and the religious reconciled with Hamas?

During Hamas's lifetime, the movement has shown a reasonable degree of reconciliation between its nationalist and religious sides. This was helped by the fact that it was in opposition and never faced the serious practical contradictions until its fortunes had dramatically changed in 2007 when it controlled the Gaza Strip. Since then, as will be explained in coming chapters, maintaining harmony between religious ideals and national politics dictated by necessities and governance proved to be unattainable.

From the nationalist perspective, the religious aspect of the movement Hamas had mixed fortunes. It maintained extraordinary discipline and a high level of sacrifice from the movement's rank and file in the struggle against Israel. This was the basis for the movement's social solidarity work, which benefited wider Palestinian constituencies, especially in the face of extreme hardship and poverty in refugee camps and deprived areas. Yet, at the same time, the religious aspect has sometimes taken over the political and nationalist aspect of Hamas at the grassroots level. The major controversial religious practice that Hamas has adopted, directly or indirectly, is the perceived imposition of religious moral codes on Palestinians. In parallel to its rise in influence, a quasi-intimidating atmosphere was created particularly in the Gaza Strip, where people felt indirect pressure to comply with Hamas's dictates on moral issues. This issue is discussed in detail in Chapter 5, but the relevant point here is that moves to the forced Islamization of society provoked anger and condemnation among some, at the expense of Hamas's nationalist appeal.

From the religious perspective, the nationalist aspect of the movement also brought Hamas mixed fortunes. In the first place, it gave Palestinian Islamists an immensely needed legitimacy, which automatically originates and multiplies once a movement stands firmly in resisting and confronting the Israeli occupation. Thus, upon its transformation from the former non-confrontational mother organization (the Muslim Brotherhood) to a resistance movement, Hamas became bestowed with an additional appeal to reach out to more potential followers and recruits. Moreover, the heavier involvement in the nationalist confrontational effort has broadened the perspectives and experiences of Palestinian Islamists, and brought them to the fore of political realities. This, of course, propelled the movement to mesh its religious understanding, by way of issuing fatwas – religious justifications of successive political and even pseudo-military actions – with the rapid pace of the nationalist struggle and its political requirements. However, the nationalist element was seen as sometimes and in certain ways preaching to or overriding the province of the religious. This has taken place under the surface, in areas such as striking alliances with leftist groups, and participation in politically concerted efforts that could involve agreeing politically on matters that would be disapproved of from the religious viewpoint. For example, in 1996, Hamas boycotted the elections for the legislative council, however, in 2006, they not only participated in the elections, but also won them. This change was faced with some internal religious disapproval. A minority of voices considered these elections to be *haram* (forbidden) because they involved a compromise over the 'Islamic land of Palestine and Islamic sovereignty over it'.

In summary, Hamas managed to keep its nationalist and religious components somewhat harmonious before taking power in the year 2006. In the post-election era and with Hamas in power, the tension between the religious and the nationalist political dimensions within the movement started to surface publicly. Immense pressure was thrust on the political leadership of Hamas when, upon unexpectedly winning the elections, it found itself faced almost overnight with hitherto unexperienced challenges. Hamas's government came under immediate international siege, led by the United States and the European Union and involving even the United Nations, not to mention Israel, and this required creative and fast political initiatives. The luxury and time available for formulating every single political step to appease every faction of the internal membership, and for presenting those policies in an appealing format to the outside world as well, have come to an end. I argued in the first edition of this book (2006) that: 'It is safe to say that the longer Hamas remains in power, the more tensions will appear between its religious and nationalist constituents, with the probable pragmatic outcome of pushing the movement to a more politicized nationalist leaning.' Hamas's reigning years over the Gaza Strip from 2007 to 2023 had shown sufficient evidence supporting this point. We will see examples of Hamas's overriding pragmatism in the coming chapters, particularly concerning its alliances with other political actors inside and outside Palestine.

3
Hamas, Israel and Judaism

Is Hamas an anti-Semitic movement?

To start with, the term 'anti-Semitic' is highly problematic when it is used to describe Palestinian and Arab perceptions of Jews and Judaism, because Palestinians and Arabs are Semites themselves. Since it is indeed self-contradictory within an Arab context, a more accurate term to describe certain Palestinian and/or Arab attitudes towards Jews might be 'anti-Jewish'.

In their historic context, the indigenous Muslims, Christians and Jews of the Middle East lived together with a remarkable degree of harmonious coexistence, particularly when compared with the lack of religious tolerance and the predominance of religious fanaticism in medieval Christian Europe. Jews in particular enjoyed a 'golden era' of centuries-long peaceful living under Islamic rule in what is known now as the Middle East and North Africa, and particularly in Andalusia. Tolerance towards Jews and Christians in Islamic tradition and societies is underpinned by the Quran, where the common roots of Islam, Judaism and Christianity in the Old Testament are acknowledged, and respect for Jews and Christians by Muslims is required. Moses and Jesus are highly revered and of course acknowledged as prophets of God. Thus, in principle there is no theological basis for religious (as well as ethnic or racial) discrimination that could lead to European-type anti-Semitism and its manifestations.

Ironically, the strong anti-Jewish feelings that crept into the Middle East by the start of the twentieth century originated in

66

Europe, from European ideas compounded by European actions. Since the early twentieth century, European Zionism exploited the ever-growing European desire to resolve the 'Jewish question' (a question astoundingly and notoriously exacerbated by the events of the Second World War in Nazi-occupied Europe), ultimately by exporting the Jewish populations outside Europe and marrying the solution with the Jewish aspiration of creating a Jewish state in Palestine. With the establishment of Israel by diktat and at the expense of the indigenous Palestinians, who had peaceably occupied their lands for over 2,000 years, Jews and Zionists, and Judaism and Zionism, became conjoined. With half of the Palestinian people forced out of their homes and lands on the eve of the formation of Israel in 1948, the Western-exported Jewry forcibly replaced them, all under the approving eye of Europe and the United States. Thus, the Jews/Zionists came to be seen in the eyes of Palestinians and Arabs as a form of colonial military occupation, consequently destroying the peaceful coexistence of Muslims and Jews that had prevailed in the region for centuries.

The spurious anti-Semitic book *The Protocols of the Elders of Zion* (which also originated in Europe) described the Jews as masterminding a global conspiracy to control the world. Its claims suddenly found a receptive climate in Palestine and the Arab region because of the creation of Israel in the Palestinian homelands in 1948. This date ended the peaceful period of coexistence between Muslims and Jews, and unfolded a new chapter of bloody relationships and hatred. Over centuries, hundreds of thousands of Arab Jews coexisted in the region, in the Levant in Syria, Iraq and Yemen, and in North Africa in Libya, Tunisia, Algeria and Morocco. Never had the idea of a mass immigration to Palestine dominated Arab Jewish communities, at times when many of them could have immigrated to Palestine if they wished to do so. This idea was exclusively formed in Europe as a colonial idea by its Zionist Jews.

Unless this background is taken into account, a deep understanding of the explicit or implicit attitudes towards the Jews in

Hamas and even across the region is unlikely. Intrinsically and religiously Hamas could not be anti-Jewish. By virtue of Islamic religious teachings, Hamas, or any other Islamic individual or group, is prohibited from inflicting any harm on Jews simply because they are Jews (or Christians, or any other group for that matter). So to be factually correct, Hamas is strongly anti-Zionist, not anti-Jewish, with the term Zionist defined as 'a person or group whose focus is the establishment of a Jewish state in Palestine'. Although in the early years of its inception Hamas made little effort to differentiate between Judaism as a religion and Zionism as a political movement, in later and more recent years, Hamas has completely clarified its thinking on this issue. It is anti-Zionist, not anti-Jewish.

But surely Hamas's Charter is full of 'anti-Jewish' statements?

It is true that many 'anti-Jewish' statements do exist in the Hamas Charter of 1988. However, it also true that eight years later these statements were rendered irrelevant to the present Hamas party, and that the Charter itself has become largely obsolete. As discussed in Chapter 2, the Charter was written in early 1988 by one individual and was made public without appropriate general Hamas deliberation, revision or consensus, to the regret of Hamas's leaders in later years. The author of the Charter was one of the 'old guard' of the Muslim Brotherhood in the Gaza Strip, completely cut off from the outside world. All kinds of confusions and conflations between Judaism and Zionism found their way into the Charter, to the disservice of Hamas ever since, as this document has managed to brand it with charges of 'anti-Semitism' and a naive worldview.

Hamas leaders and spokespeople have never referred to the Charter or quoted from it, which is evidence that it has come to be seen as a burden rather than an intellectual platform that embraces the movement's principles. The sophisticated language of the Hamas discourse on the eve of its assuming power after the 2006 elections, as well as its 2017 Document of Principles, are so distinct in their language and discourse to the Charter of 1988, that they almost appear to describe two completely different political movements.

Indeed, just two years after the publication of the 1988 Charter loaded with anti-Jewish rhetoric, Hamas published the 'Introductory Memorandum' in 1990 (see Chapter 2), distancing itself from what had been included in the Charter. Emphasizing that its struggle has been merely against Zionists and Zionism, not against the Jews and Judaism, it drew a clear distinction between the two:

> The non-Zionist Jew is one who belongs to the Jewish culture, whether as a believer in the Jewish faith or simply by accident of birth, but ... [who] takes no part in aggressive actions against our land and our nation ... Hamas will not adopt a hostile position in practice against anyone because of his ideas or his creed but will adopt such a position if those ideas and creed are translated into hostile or damaging actions against our people.*

Discussing this differentiation with the author, one of Hamas's leaders went so far as to say that 'being Jewish, Zionist or Israeli is irrelevant, what is relevant for me is the notion of occupation and aggression. Even if this occupation was imposed by an Arab or Islamic state and the soldiers were Arabs or Muslims, I would resist and fight back.'

On the ground, however, ordinary people, Palestinians and Arabs including Hamas members, do use the terms 'Jew', 'Zionist' and 'Israeli' interchangeably. On the surface, mixing up these terms blurs the differences: clearly not every Jew is a Zionist, and not every Israeli is a Zionist. However regrettably imprecise the

---

* For the full text of the 'Introductory Memorandum', translated from Arabic, see Khaled Hroub, *Hamas: Political Thought and Practice* (Washington, DC: Institute of Palestine Studies, 2000), 292–302.

use of any of these terms interchangeably might be in common parlance, it is somewhat irrelevant in the face of the ongoing presence of an aggressive, illegal and non-Palestinian occupier, which whatever distinctions are made is identifiably Jewish (Zionist/Israeli). It is the aggression and occupation that is most relevant, whichever way it gets labelled in the heat of day-to-day confrontation.

Though this should be borne in mind, a type of undeniable anti-Jewishness has come to cut across Palestinian and Arab societies. It is not based on religious, racial or cultural hatred, as in the Western rubric 'anti-Semitism'. The roots of any anti-Jewishness in Arab society are entirely political, in response to aggression, and any other form of anti-Jewishness would be completely refuted from the perspective of Islamic theology. Certainly unjustified, military actions taken against 'Jewish' targets are taken against them as representatives of an illegal, aggressive occupier, and have nothing whatsoever to do with their creed, race or non-Islamic culture.

In Hamas's view, what would be the future of the Jews in Palestine?

Hamas's views on this question are rather vague. In Hamas's early years, a standard answer would have been that the Palestinian Jews whose forebears had lived on the land in peace and coexistence with its Muslim inhabitants for centuries would be welcome to stay on in a future Palestinian state. They are, after all, first and foremost Palestinians. Western and other foreign Jews, on the other hand, who had migrated to Palestine from all parts of the world, should return to their countries of origin. In fact, this view was commonly shared by Palestinians and Arabs for a long time after the establishment of the state of Israel in 1948, before it gradually faded away. This view has long since been realized to be unrealistic and has almost completely dropped out of Hamas's discourse. But Hamas has formulated no new answer to fill in the void.

The dilemma that Hamas – and the Palestinian intelligentsia at large – have faced concerning this issue is that generations of young Jews with Western and worldwide ancestry have been born on historically Palestinian soil as the years of this conflict have dragged on. Of course, this is an issue that is part and parcel of the larger 'demographic dimension' to the conflict, which worries both the Palestinians and the Israelis.

Population projections suggest that there are roughly equal numbers of Jews and Palestinians living in the historic land of Palestine. The spectre of demography, and in particular who will overrule whom in the not-so-distant future, concerns both parties. Israeli solutions have revolved around annexing the maximum amount of Palestinian land with the minimum Palestinian population on it, to preserve the Jewishness of the state in the long run. Palestinian solutions have been to fight to stay on their lands across all parts of Palestine, defying direct and indirect Israeli measures to force as many of them as possible to leave, and upholding the right to return for refugees whom the Israelis have managed to expel.

Hamas has attempted to break away from the limited thinking that can only imagine Palestinians and Israelis squeezed into 'Palestine/Israel'. A reluctant idea that appears now and then in Hamas's discourse is that Palestine in the future should be part of a wider union of Arab and Muslim territories. In this case, even if the Jews were the majority within the confines of whatever part of historic Palestine they might ultimately claim, they would lose any numerical superiority when the remaining territory of Palestine was merged with other Arab territories. The overwhelming Arab majority in the neighbouring countries, who would mix with the population in Palestine, would serve to neutralize the effects of any Jewish majority in Palestine.

A rather less far-fetched view that is, again reluctantly, talked about by Hamas is the one-state solution, based on equality and citizenship, but only if the (more or less 7 million) Palestinian refugees were given the right to return to their cities and villages in Israel. Israel takes no notice of this idea, saying that it would implicitly carry with it the death of the State of Israel by eroding once and for all its Jewish nature and majority. Hamas, it seems, will have to grapple for a while longer with the question of the future of the Jews in Palestine.

HAMAS'S VIEW ON ISRAEL

What is Israel in Hamas's eyes?

For Hamas, and in fact for the Palestinians at large, Israel is a colonial state established by force and resulting from Western colonialism and imperialism globally and against Arabs and Muslims before and after the turn of the twentieth century. To the left and right of this central view, there are other perceptions that feed into each other, and sometimes coincide with perceptions held by more secular Palestinian groups. In the early years of its formation, Hamas's view of Israel, as has already been established, was loaded with religious significance, holding that Israel was the culmination of a Jewish onslaught against Muslims and their holy places in Jerusalem. The establishment of Israel with the strong support of Western powers was seen as a renewal of the medieval Crusades.

The discourse of Hamas has, however, become more developed and adaptive to modern realities. Its views on Israel, accordingly, have been recast within the parameters of occupation– occupier, with the main drive of resistance against Israel directed against its aggression, not its religion. It would be inaccurate to suggest that this development in the discourse of Hamas has sprung from deep roots, or that is has completely replaced the old language, laden with religious antagonism to Israel. But, in general parlance, the political discourse that is delivered by the movement's leadership and included in its official statements and documents on Israel is now based mostly on the language of international law, and on political, not religious, assumptions.

Is Hamas planning the destruction of Israel?

The phrase 'the destruction of Israel', as often used by the media when referring to Hamas's 'ultimate goal', is in fact never used and has never been adopted by Hamas, even in its most radical statements. Hamas's ultimate slogan is 'the liberation of Palestine', which falls short of saying what would actually be done with Israel should that goal be achieved. In its old and rather obsolete Charter of 1988, which is crammed with rhetoric that is embarrassing to the Hamas of today, there are statements that could be interpreted as referring to the destruction of Israel. However, the entire document is of minimal present value, and hardly corresponds to any realities and thinking that Hamas lives and expresses currently.

Realistically speaking, the argument that 'Hamas's tacit and ultimate end is the destruction of Israel' bears no relevance. The realities on the ground speak in the opposite direction completely. Neither Hamas nor any other Palestinian or Arab party – or even state for that matter – has any dream of having the ability to destroy Israel. Israel enjoys military capabilities, both conventional and nuclear, that would enable it to destroy all of its neighbouring countries in the Middle East in a matter of days. It is an uncontested fact that there is no threat to the existence of Israel in either the medium or the long term, but there certainly is one against the Palestinians posed by Israel. The Israeli destruction and genocide war on Gaza in 2023–2024 is a fresh evidence to this. Hamas can and did incur harm on Israel, as it has done through the decades. But stretching this fact to depicting Hamas (and the Palestinians) as a party that will bring Israel to destruction is more of political propaganda and sensationalism that intends to garner more material and diplomatic Western support.

In recent years, Hamas has grown out of its early naive discourse of the late 1980s, and today's Hamas projects are more nuanced and its pronouncements more realistic. The dominant theme of its political and military discourse is resistance against the occupation of illegally seized lands and driving the occupiers out of the West Bank and Gaza Strip. Since Hamas took control of the Gaza Strip in 2007, its leaders have avoided the ill-considered rhetoric and slogans of the Charter.

In summary, any suggestion that Hamas plans or aims to destroy Israel is obviously naive. For Hamas to be able to achieve such a goal it would have to remain in power for decades, bringing all the Palestinian groups, including those opposing Hamas, to join forces with the movement towards that goal. It would also have to build a massive Palestinian army in the West Bank and the Gaza Strip over decades, with Israel unconcernedly looking on. It would have to import tanks and jet fighters from sympathetic international sources that do not exist, and train hundreds of thousands of soldiers on the tiny strips of non-contiguous land it would control. For such a 'plan' to succeed, Hamas must convince Arab neighbouring countries to support it by abolishing peace treaties between them (Egypt, Jordan and the some of the Gulf states) with Israel, and also facilitate Hamas's steps. Meanwhile, the USA, Europe and other supportive states of Israel must keep quiet and stand on the fence watching! How could Hamas possibly defeat Israel militarily, let alone destroy it, when all other Arab countries collectively have failed to do so in the past half-century?

Despite what euphoria Hamas has seemed to enjoy at its high peaks, both militarily in its waves of successful suicide attacks in the heart of Israeli cities during the second Intifada (2000–2004), politically in its election victory in 2006, its performance against the successive Israeli wars on Gaza (in 2008–2009, 2012, 2018 and 2021), and in its surprising strike against Israel on 7 October 2023, Hamas remains defensive rather than offensive. The structural confines that limit Palestinians in general apply to Hamas as well, and even more so because of the Islamist specificity of the movement (such as the lack of international support, as was the case with the PLO). Wary of its difficult position, Hamas's engagement in politics and world affairs is mostly driven by defensive mechanisms. One could say that the movement's ultimate goal from 2007 to 2023 was simply to preserve its own existence and avoid destruction – not to destroy others. The gamble strike of October 7 had changed its fortunes perhaps for ever, as we will see in later chapters.

Would Hamas ever recognize Israel and conclude peace agreements with it?

It is not inconceivable that Hamas would recognize Israel. Hamas's pragmatism and its realistic approach to issues leave ample room for such a development. Yet most of the conditions that could create a conducive climate for such a step lie in the hands of the Israelis. As long as Israel refuses to acknowledge self-determination and the basic national rights of the Palestinian people in any end result based on the principle of a two-state solution, Hamas will find it impossible to recognize Israel.

Despite the often-cited rhetoric in Hamas's discourse about the impossibility of recognizing Israel, there actually is a visible thread of thinking that offers just such a possibility, though only if Israel reciprocated positively. After assuming his post in early April 2006, after Hamas formed its post-election government, Hamas's foreign minister Mahmoud al-Zahar sent a letter to Kofi Annan, the then Secretary-General of the United Nations, declaring that his government would be willing to live in peace, side by side with 'its neighbours', based on a two-state solution. However, other statements attributed to Hamas leaders have implied that the issue of recognizing Israel should be one of the goals of negotiations, not a prerequisite to them.

If Israel shows no interest in dealing with Hamas and insists on 'unilateral measures' that perpetuate the occupational status quo,

Hamas will never recognize Israel. If this were to be the only proffered political climate, the maximum that the movement could accept would be a long-term truce, and it would avoid and evade recognizing Israel to the end.

That a peace treaty could be concluded between Israel and the Palestinians at large including Hamas, however, is not implausible. Hamas enjoys influence, legitimacy and political and resistance capital among the Palestinians, furnishing it with the authority and capability needed to negotiate with Israel. Attempting to find some leeway between its past declarations about non-recognition of Israel and the pressing realities at hand, the movement has created a distinction between the government of Hamas and Hamas as an organization. Implicitly, this means that Hamas's government, or an inclusive Palestinian government that Hamas joins, could be ready to go beyond the standard and well-known declarations of Hamas as a party. Yet again, the extent to which Hamas could go down the course of negotiating with Israel is strongly contingent on the positions offered by the latter, as well as creating a unified Palestinian leadership that represents all parties including Hamas.

To reconcile the extreme of the liberation of the entire historic land of Palestine with the realities of the existence of Israel on the ground, Hamas has suggested resorting to a national referendum on the final settlement to be concluded by Israel and the Palestinians. The democratically elected Hamas, if this was the case at the time of referendum, would abide by whatever the Palestinian people decide freely and democratically concerning their own fate. By Hamas's way of thinking, the referendum idea is a decent solution to the theoretical and practical impasse that could result, and be exclusively, if wrongly, put down to Hamas's refusal to recognize Israel and accept the principle of a two-state solution. If peace talks led to the drafting of a peace treaty that required the 'negotiating parties' to recognize each other (and it was a treaty in which Palestinian rights were acknowledged and granted in a manner likely to be satisfactory to the Palestinians), then Hamas would accept any decision taken by the people on such a treaty via the mechanism of a referendum. Hamas as an organization says publicly that under such conditions it would have no choice but to respect the will and decision endorsed by the Palestinian people.

4

Hamas's Resistance
and Military Strategy

FORCING UNCONDITIONAL ISRAELI WITHDRAWAL

What is Hamas's 'programme of resistance'?

'Resistance as a concept is the most central principle in the thinking and formation of Hamas; it is even part of its very name, 'The Islamic Resistance Movement'. When Hamas was established in late 1987, the Palestinian and Arab political climate was still absorbing the shock created by Egypt's recognition of Israel and the peace treaty concluded by both countries in 1982. Negotiation, rather than armed struggle, was being put forward emphatically as a means to achieve political goals, including the restoration of occupied land. In the same year of 1982, the PLO was defeated by Israel in Lebanon and consequently all Palestinian guerrillas and their leadership were forced to leave the country and move to Tunis. The logic of using armed struggle to liberate Palestine had thus suffered two major blows in one year. Since then, and with the new North African PLO base very far from Palestine, a strategy of peace negotiations and initiatives started to dominate over the armed struggle approach. The PLO itself became far more lenient than before on the issue of negotiation with Israel and the principle of a two-state solution.

By contrast, in reiterating and reaffirming the concept of 'resistance', Hamas was declaring its position against any negotiated settlement with Israel and injecting new blood in a somewhat fading concept. The only way to regain Palestinian rights, Hamas vehemently suggested with rising confidence, was through resistance against the colonial occupation and wresting back rights from the enemy. Hamas's logic came down to the idea that wherever a military occupation exists, a military resistance should be expected. Such resistance, in all its various forms, would only stop when the occupation ended.

All Hamas's conduct, policies and actions emanate from and are justified by this conviction. However, there have been few specific details offered about how matters would proceed beyond this concept, particularly on how the 'withdrawal' of the occupying troops would take place, or what would follow it. Hamas's leaders have kept repeating: 'Withdraw first, then we take things as they come.'

This 'strategy' of Hamas, which in effect spells out no long-term strategy, might appear on the surface to be futile and shallow. Yet, at a more fundamental level, it has proved successful and pragmatic for the organization over many years. First, its plain terminology and uncompromising simplicity have been hard to argue against; second, this same single focus and simplicity conceals Hamas's theological arguments, which are more difficult to sell; third, it provides an uncomplicated theoretical umbrella under which Hamas's military and non-military actions of resistance can easily be conducted.

Throughout Hamas's lifetime, various forms of resistance have been deployed, ranging from popular uprisings, mobilization, strikes, and military attacks against the Israeli army and settlers, to executing suicide bombings in the heart of Israeli cities, ending at the time of writing with the October 7 attacks in 2023. These have been deployed either in combination or separately but, in all cases, using whichever method has corresponded to the specific political environment prevailing at the time. The ultimate aim of any combination of all sorts of resistance, in Hamas's thinking, is to force unconditional Israeli withdrawal. The struggle of all Palestinian organizations, including of course the PLO and its factions, and the Palestinian Authority, which was established in the West Bank and Gaza Strip in 1993–1994, has been focused on achieving such a withdrawal. However, Hamas wants it without surrendering any other Palestinian rights in return, and without the recognition of Israel. The PLO and some other Palestinian factions have come to terms with a reciprocal recognition with Israel based on the two-state solution. Hamas did not accept this, yet might accept a formula that tacitly recognizes the de facto existence of Israel but without formally recognizing any right of Israel to exist. This is because regardless of whether the withdrawal resulted directly from peace talks or by force, Hamas could logically insist that it was achieved without compromising any additional Palestinian rights, or issues such as sovereignty over East Jerusalem, the position of borders and the right of Palestinian refugees to return.

How has Hamas's 'programme of resistance' materialized on the ground?

Hamas believes that the unilateral Israeli withdrawal from the Gaza Strip in 2005 validates its strategy of resistance. Various declarations by Hamas representatives have stated that the withdrawal was the result, to a large part if not fully, of the continuous resistance and long-term pressure on the Israeli troops and settlers in the Strip, which left Israel with no option but to yield and withdraw. Other Palestinians, however, refute this view and call into suspicion Israel's real purpose and intention in taking this step. They fear that Israel has withdrawn from the Gaza Strip, which has no strategic or religious value to the Jewish state, in order to concentrate and consolidate its occupation, settlement expansion and control over the West Bank and Jerusalem, where the true battle between the Palestinians and the Israelis lies.

In the West Bank, too, Hamas believes that carrying out cycles of confrontation against the occupation will make the toll of the Israeli presence there unsustainable; that multiplying Israeli costs in terms of human loss, draining of resources, mounting internal tension and deteriorating image worldwide will eventually bear fruit. When the Kadima party, upon winning the Israeli elections in March 2006, made public its intention to undertake unilateral partial withdrawals from certain areas in the West Bank, Hamas claimed part of the credit. It argued, again, that had there been no resistance with costly consequences to Israel, any withdrawal, however small, would have only been undertaken in return for excessive Palestinian concessions.

It is worth mentioning that Hamas points to the experience of the Lebanese party Hizbullah, which was perceived to have forced Israel to withdraw unconditionally from south Lebanon in 2000. At that time, the Israeli step was taken for a variety of reasons, including the diminishing chances of the Israeli occupation in that area achieving any strategic objectives, and the mounting questioning of the value of that occupation by Israeli decision makers and the Israeli public as well. That, of course, was in addition to the continuous, conspicuous and highly emotive daily losses, notably on the side of Israeli soldiers. Hizbullah naturally chose to focus on this last factor exclusively, to vindicate its 'resistance strategy'. Likewise, Hamas has underlined the same factor, calling Palestinians to emulate Hizbullah in exerting extreme pressure on the Israeli occupation to force unilateral withdrawal.

What is the Intifada (in 1987 and 2000)?

Intifada is the Arabic word for a popular uprising. Within the Palestinian context, it evokes sentimental connotations, since popular uprisings, or *intifada*s, typically and historically marked certain turning points in the course of the Palestinian national struggle in the past decades. During the British colonialism over Palestine (1922–1948), Palestinian uprisings were directed against the British, with the most significant one occurring in 1936.

In the era of the Israeli occupation, intifadas were almost the only effective means at the disposal of the Palestinians. Apart from small-scale uprisings and forms of resistance, the two major Intifadas erupted in 1987 and 2000. The 1987 uprising took place initially in the Gaza Strip on 8 December, then the spark moved to the cities of the West Bank. The causes that led to the Intifada were multifold and fed off each other. They were the escalation of brutality by the Israeli occupation, and the growing anger among Palestinians in response to the humiliation of the occupation – not only politically, but also in the very real way that the occupation had reduced those areas to soul-destroying poverty – and the rising power of the Islamists, who were compelled to adopt a new confrontational policy against Israel, as has been discussed earlier in the book.

The immediate causes that actually ignited the Intifada were a series of events linked to the escape of a number of Palestinian prisoners who hid in one of the refugee camps, then killed an Israeli settler. In response to the killing, an Israeli truck ran down some Palestinian workers, killing four and wounding nine others. Consequently, angry Palestinians took to the streets of the Gaza Strip in the following days in unprecedented mass demonstrations. If the early days of the Intifada were spontaneous with no organizational planning behind them, the following days witnessed heavy engagement and even rivalry between the Palestinian organizations, including the newly established Hamas, to co-spearhead the Intifada and keep it going.

The 1987 Intifada was mostly a non-armed confrontation, relying instead on mobilizing people, mass demonstrations and throwing stones at Israeli soldiers. Hence, it was called the 'stones revolution'. Erratically waxing and waning, the Intifada lasted roughly until 1993 when the Oslo Accords were signed between Israel and the PLO, resulting – for the first time – in a Palestinian form of authority in the West Bank and the Gaza Strip.

The second Intifada took place in September 2000. The causes behind this Intifada were somewhat different and similar. After seven years of the Oslo Accords with Israel, which had vaguely promised the Palestinians a sovereign and independent state by the end of the year 1999, the Palestinian public lost confidence in the process and became frustrated. Through those Accords it had been hoped that an interim period of five years, starting in 1994, would end in resolving the major issues of the conflict including Jerusalem, the control of borders, dismantling the Israeli settlements in the West Bank and the Gaza Strip, and the status of refugees.

Contrary to those expectations, all evidence pointed to the fact that the Israeli occupation was tightening its grip, and that the newly set-up Palestinian Authority was being restricted in effect to administrating much of the occupation – from the prosaic daily services of the population, to actually maintaining the security of Israel and its settlers from Palestinian attacks. The size and population of Israeli settlements on land that was supposed to have been returned to the Palestinians almost doubled during the years following the Oslo Accords. The status of Jerusalem, a major issue of the conflict yet to be resolved in negotiation, was swept under heavier Israeli control. By the eve of the second Intifada, the peace process brought about by the Oslo Accords was witnessing the first signs of its own demise.

The immediate spark of the 2000 Intifada was a provocative visit by Ariel Sharon, the Israeli leader of Likud opposition at the time, to the Al-Aqsa Mosque area the holiest Muslim site in Jerusalem, which infuriated Palestinians. Against much advice, Sharon decided to make a point for political purposes against the ruling Israeli Labour party, that even the holiest of Muslim places in Jerusalem were under full Israeli control and jurisdiction.

Although it started as a popular uprising with no use of weapons, the second Intifada quickly turned into an armed confrontation. Palestinians across the political spectrum supported the Intifada: the ruling PA organizations, such as Fatah and other PLO factions, stood side by side with Hamas and other opposition factions.

83

Will Hamas disarm itself voluntarily or be disarmed at all forcibly if needed?

'What you get from anyone, or on a negotiating table should match your strength on the ground', Sheikh Ahmad Yasin, the founder of Hamas, was once quoted as saying. 'Strength' is interpreted in all forms, with the military figures on the top. Thus, since its inception in late 1987, Hamas (and other Palestinian factions) have tried to amass as many caches of weapons as possible, mainly in the Gaza Strip but also in the West Bank. These include machine guns, bombs and home-made rockets with a range of a few kilometres and capable of striking Israeli settlements if launched from parts of the Gaza Strip.

In terms of quality, quantity and military effectiveness, Hamas's weapons – and all other Palestinian weapons combined for that matter – have never amounted to a level of being able to pose an existential threat to the State of Israel. These weapons could only inflict harm in the form of guerrilla attacks, quick and short shoot-outs and suicide bombings. The main source for acquiring weaponry is Iran and Hizbullah; and Hamas has managed to smuggle weapons via tunnels through the Sinai desert (against the policy of the Egyptian government, of course). A less significant source is buying Israeli weapons from 'black markets' and from discontented individuals in the Palestinian security forces, who were armed officially by the Palestinian Authority. Hamas has also developed local manufacture of primitive weapons, notably bombs and short-range rockets, based on domestic material. The scale of locally manufactured weaponry has proven to be large and impressive, as shown in Hamas' performance and resilience in the 2023–2024 war. After more than a year of relentless and ferocious Israeli war, with the firepower dropped on the Gaza Strip exceeding more than four times of the power of a Hiroshima atomic bomb, the cut-off Hamas continued to show remarkable military resistance and fight back.

84

During and after the second Intifada of 2000, it was obvious that Hamas's military power had reached new peaks, particularly in the Gaza Strip, paralleling that of the Palestinian Authority. On the eve of its landslide victory in the January 2006 elections in the West Bank and the Gaza Strip, it was believed that Hamas's arsenal of weapons could furnish the movement with the enormous leverage that goes hand in hand with its political and popular influence.

There had been a measured consensus among observers that Hamas's weaponry, used and supervised by its military wing Al-Qassam Brigades, is under the tight control of the movement. The October 7 attacks made many observers change their view, seeing that military wing taking the initiative while the political leadership took a passenger seat, even if temporarily. Generally speaking and apart from a few factional incidents where Hamas members used weapons, their use is strictly limited to the struggle with Israel. Also, this weaponry has clearly provided Hamas with a deterrent against other Palestinian rivals, mainly the Fatah movement and the Palestinian Authority.

The situation in the Gaza Strip from 1987, the year of the first Intifada, to 1993–1994, the year when Oslo Accords were concluded had been marked by increasing Israeli crackdowns and suppression, security chaos and a multiplicity of Palestinian voices and centres of power. Relative accessibility to arms had created a hard-to-control situation for Israel, and factional rivalry among the Palestinians. When the Palestinian Authority was established in 1993–1994, one of its main responsibilities – pressed on it by Israel under the Oslo Accords – was to control the chaotic situation and unify the 'Palestinian arms' under its control. Stridently Hamas refused any proposal to hand in its weapons to the Palestinian Authority, or any suggestion in the direction of giving the Palestinian Authority the slightest supervision over its weapons.

Ironically, when Hamas came to power after winning the elections in 2006 and becoming itself the Palestinian Authority, it called upon other factions to unite their armed wings under one unified control under the supervision of Hamas in its new PA role. As was to be expected, Fatah's military wing and other factions refused Hamas's call.

Hamas is unlikely to disarm voluntarily, as it did not in the past, nor would it in the future; and it is inconceivable that other parties (primarily Israel) could completely disarm the movement forcibly. Hamas keeps repeating its position that its arms are there to defend the Palestinian people and their rights; and insofar as Israeli continues to occupy Palestinian land and those rights are not realized, then armed struggle and all it entails should stay at the heart of Hamas and part of the official Palestinian strategy.

SUICIDE ATTACKS

When and why has Hamas adopted suicide bombing as a strategy?

From roughly the mid-1990s until 2005, Hamas adopted the tactic of conducting suicide attacks against Israeli targets, be they military or civilians. Those attacks were justified by Hamas as being reciprocal actions, done in response to the Israeli killing of Palestinian civilians and would end immediately once Israel stopped doing the same to Palestinians. Offers by Hamas to neutralize civilians from both sides were met with categorical refusal from Israel on the grounds of not dealing with terrorists.

Hamas waited until 1994 to adopt the tactic of suicide attacks against Israel. The first wave of these attacks was carried out in retaliation for the Hebron massacre, in which a fanatic Israeli settler killed 29 Palestinian worshippers in the Abraham Mosque in February 1994. Hamas vowed to take revenge and it did so by blowing up Israeli soldiers, settlers and civilians in the heart of Israeli cities. At that point, Hamas discovered the spectacular effect this kind of attack had on the public imagination and embraced it. Realizing that targeting civilians deliberately can be a dangerous strategy, Hamas has been careful to link any suicide bombing that it has undertaken to specific Israeli killings of Palestinian civilians, stressing it was an eye-for-an-eye practice.

Prior to 1994, Hamas's policies were clear in attacking only military targets. The major shift to targeting civilians, even with the justification of only retaliating for a civilian killing with another civilian killing, has nonetheless incurred heavy costs to Hamas. Defying Israel's violent retaliation against Hamas, epitomized by the Israeli strategy of assassinating its leaders, the movement geared up its use of suicide operations over the following years. It realized that although these operations rallied the international community against Hamas and distorted somewhat the image of the legitimate Palestinian struggle, they provided the movement with an aura of strength and popularity. The Palestinians started to look at Hamas as an organization capable of inflicting damage on the Israelis and taking revenge for any Israeli killing of Palestinians.

Lacking any effective means to defend its civilians against these suicide attacks, Israel was devastated by them. The horror of a potential bombing that could take place in any bus, shopping centre or restaurant brought Israeli cities at certain periods of time nearly to a complete state of terrifying suspense. Israel not only mobilized its military might to stamp out Hamas's infrastructure in the Gaza Strip and the West Bank, but also brought to bear all sorts of pressure, including external pressure. On more than one occasion, Israel hinted, via unofficial mediators, that it was ready to talk to Hamas with a view to stopping these attacks. However, Hamas adhered to its declared position: 'Stop killing Palestinian civilians and we will stop killing Israeli civilians.' Israel repeatedly refused this offer.

Sheikh Yasin, the movement's founder, succinctly articulated Hamas's policy on suicide bombings in September 2003. When asked whether the attacks would continue irrespective of circumstances, he replied in the negative, and explained, 'If we perceive that the atmosphere favours such a decision, we stop. And when we perceive that the atmosphere has changed, we carry on.' In general, the wider the gap between the peace strategy and the attainment of Palestinian rights, the more room Hamas would have to pursue its resistance strategy.

Politically and strategically, Hamas became aware that, at certain junctures and particularly in the years 2000–2004, using suicide attacks had become its strongest card in the conflict with Israel, as well as with its rivalry with the Palestinian Authority and its Fatah movement. Relinquishing this card would only be considered if there was really a possibility of a worthy return. Continuous Israeli military efforts, coupled with repetitive crackdowns on Hamas by the security forces of the Palestinian Authority, failed to destroy Hamas's capability in undertaking these attacks. Political and diplomatic pressures were also exerted on Hamas by Egypt, Jordan and even by some indirect European channels in order to compel the movement to stop these attacks, at least temporarily. In finding itself on the receiving end of much high condemnation for the suicide bombings, both regionally and internationally, Hamas discovered that the exact same attention regionally and internationally was also furnishing them with further leverage.

On several occasions, Hamas has shown flexibility in temporarily halting its attacks, either to avoid straying from a collective agreement among Palestinian factions, or to prove its pragmatism. In late 1995, it stopped suicide attacks for months, only to resume them after the Israeli assassination of one of its military leaders, Yahya Ayyash. Similar halt–resume 'tacit agreements' took place during the second Intifada (2000–2005) for short periods of time, but all of these failed because Israel would waste no opportunity to assassinate one Hamas leader after another.

How many Israelis has Hamas killed? And how many Hamas members have the Israelis killed?

Hamas's suicide attacks have given the movement a bad name by enabling Israel to succeed in selling an image of Hamas as a mere 'terrorist organisation' whose sole purpose is the killing of innocent Israeli civilians. The justness of the Palestinian cause has paid a high price because of them, as Israel has exploited the attacks by reducing the nature of the Palestinian struggle to an issue of 'terrorism and counter-terrorism'. The worldwide condemnation of the Palestinian killing of Israelis is gravely uneven compared with the mild condemnation of similar Israeli killings of Palestinians.

The United Nations Office for the Coordination of Humanitarian Affairs in Jerusalem compiles data of Palestinian and Israeli casualties resulting from the military occupation and confrontations.* From early 2008 to mid-2024 (excluding the casualties of the 2003–2004 war), the death toll was 6,936 Palestinians and 330 Israelis, and the number of injured were 158,632 Palestinians and 6,465 Israelis. These figures yield the following ratios between the two parties: there were 21 Palestinians killed for each Israeli killed; and 24 Palestinians injured for each Israeli injured. From the years 2000 to 2005, the peak time period of suicide attacks, the ratio was four Palestinians to each Israeli killed.

During the second Intifada, from roughly 2000 to 2005, the aggregate figures of the statistics provided by the Israeli human rights organisation B'Tselem show that 1,426 Israelis, military personnel and civilians were killed by Palestinian factions, compared with 5,050 Palestinians killed by Israel during those years.** Of those casualties, there were 137 Israeli children (or under 18) killed against 998 Palestinian children of the same age group.

What is the truce (hudna) that Hamas offers?

Hamas's defiance of both continuous Israeli attacks and mounting international criticism against its suicide operations has been

---

* 'Data on Casualties', The United Nations Office for the Coordination of Humanitarian Affairs in Jerusalem, www.ochaopt.org/data/casualties.
** B'Tselem, The Israeli Information Center for Human Rights in the Occupied Territories, www.btselem.org.

accompanied by the offer of a *hudna* – the religious Islamic concept of the classical notion of a truce, with the aim of easing pressure. The *hudna* is a rather flexible traditional Islamic war practice, which was first used by the Prophet Muhammad in the famous Hodaibiya *hudna*, when, in 628 AD, he concluded with his enemies a ten-year truce, during which people of the two parties were to live in peace. Later in Islamic history, *hudna* were used by different rulers to achieve different goals, hence the flexibility and broad meaning of the concept. The debate remains open among Muslim scholars whether the *hudna* concept is merely a tactical ceasefire or a more sophisticated practice which lays the groundwork for non-violent solutions.

Bound by its religious roots, Hamas has felt the need to justify its adoption of any controversial policy on Islamic religious grounds. Hamas's offer of a truce would seem to contradict its leading principle of jihad – military struggle – against Israel. Similarly, refraining from military struggle was the approach that was officially adopted by the PLO and the Palestinian Authority and which ended in peace negotiations with Israel which were, in turn, strongly opposed by Hamas. To yield to a ceasefire Hamas would be seen to be simply following in the footsteps of its rivals, risking the loss of its distinctiveness.

Thus, by offering the *hudna*, Hamas has been very keen to distinguish this concept from the practice of the PLO and the Palestinian Authority, which has always been described by Hamas as capitulation. There are two main distinctions that Hamas draws between a ceasefire and a *hudna*. The first is that a *hudna* is only an agreement on halting hostilities, not a peace treaty which could comprise concessions; and the second is that a ceasefire has lately come to imply an open-ended agreement whereas the *hudna* is limited by a period of time that is agreed between the belligerent parties. If the PLO and the Palestinian Authority are ready to abandon armed struggle and promote a lasting ceasefire, Hamas is not ready to do the same. The furthest that it could do, the *hudna* argument runs, is to agree on 10 or 20 years of ceasefire without compromising on Palestinian rights. The *hudna* would calm down the situation, end the violence and save the blood of civilians. The question, of course, is what would happen after the *hudna*? Hamas's answer is that the next step would depend on the acceptable behaviour of Israel and its intentions: the *hudna* could be renewed or ended.

On several separate occasions, Hamas has offered a *hudna* to Israel. The late Sheikh Ahmad Yasin was the first to suggest the idea back in 1993. Since then, Hamas figures have repeated the offer, sometimes changing the period of time that it included (10, 20 or even 30 years). Israel has always ridiculed the offer, yet some Israeli politicians conceive it to represent a pragmatic element in Hamas that should be encouraged. When Hamas came to power and controlled the Palestinian Authority in January 2006, it renewed its offer of a *hudna* to Israel for from 10 to 20 years.

5

Hamas's Political and
Social Strategy

HAMAS'S POSITION ON THE VARIOUS PEACE PLANS
WITH ISRAEL

Why does Hamas reject the peace agreements reached by the
PLO and Israel in 1993–1994, known as the Oslo Accords?

The original Palestinian position concerning the creation of
Israel in 1948 was a complete Palestinian consensus to reject
any proposal that would situate Israel on any part of the historic
land of Palestine. This position remained almost unchanged
until 1988, when the Palestine Liberation Organization (PLO)
publicly declared its readiness to accept the concept of a two-
state solution: Palestine in the West Bank and Gaza Strip (on 22%
of historic Palestine) and Israel in the rest of the land (78%). By
then Israel would not even entertain the proposal, and none of
the major Israeli parties accepted the idea of a Palestinian state as
envisaged by the PLO. Some discounted versions of the vaguely
defined two-state solution were however reluctantly talked about.
In these versions, East Jerusalem is excluded, major Jewish settlements blocs in the West Bank will be annexed to Israel, borders
adjusted, Jordan valley either neutralized or kept under remote
Israeli control, and the future state being demilitarized while
the sovereignty over the space between the River Jordan and the
Mediterranean remains in Israel's hand.

Over decades, the balance of power has constantly favoured
Israel, which has always enjoyed American and Western unre-

served support. Israel was thus under no pressure to even acknowledge the resolutions issued by the United Nations supporting the two-state solution and calling on Israel to withdraw from the territories it has occupied since the 1967 war. The Oslo Accords in 1993–1994 offered the Palestinians limited self-rule but only over the Palestinian population – with no jurisdiction over Palestinian land – for five years, as a testing period. Should the Palestinians show 'good behaviour' then negotiations would be initiated to settle the major issues of the conflict, such as the fate or division of Jerusalem (which both 'states' claim as their rightful capital), the status and plight of millions of Palestinian refugees, the dismantling of illegal Jewish settlements, control of borders and full sovereignty. From the Palestinian viewpoint, throughout the 'test period', the situation surrounding all the major contested issues has been exacerbated deliberately by Israel so that the resulting confrontational disorder would fail to meet the minimal requirements for any restitution of Palestinian rights. From the Israeli perspective, the Palestinians have failed to prove that they are fit to be a 'partner' in peace, and thus no advancement should be undertaken to jointly solve the conflict.

Hamas's view has been that the Oslo Accords, and any peace talks for that matter, are worthless as long as their design is built around a balance of power where the fulfilment of Israeli demands tops the agenda. According to Hamas, these are capitulation treaties, not peace agreements, and they are doomed to inevitable failure. The movement outlined its detailed position as follows:

Oslo proponents claimed for months following its signing that it would bring an end to the occupation [of Palestine] and that, therefore, the Palestinians need no longer exercise an armed struggle against the Israelis. But eight years after Oslo, the following have been the dividends of peace:

1. The territories occupied in 1967 are still occupied.
2. More than ever, the West Bank and Gaza have been carved up, mutilated and turned into isolated islands of human con-

centrations, or cantons, administered on behalf of the Israelis by the Palestinian Authority.

3. Existing illegal Jewish settlements continue to expand and new ones have been erected.

4. Jerusalem is being expanded and de-Arabised.

5. Large areas of land have been confiscated to allow for the construction of bypasses for the exclusive use of Jewish motorists and especially settlers who illegally live on confiscated Arab land.

6. Thousands of Palestinians continue to be detained in Israeli prisons.

7. Various forms of collective punishment continue to be adopted by the Israelis including the demolition of Palestinian homes, the closure of entire areas and the enforcement of economic blockades, the destruction of Palestinian infrastructure and the uprooting of trees and crops.

8. The economic situation for Palestinians is more dire than ever before. In other words, the peace process has not improved by one iota the conditions of Palestinians under occupation and does not seem to promise any better future. The claim that armed struggle was no longer necessary (it should be noted here that no one within the Palestinian camp ever agreed that resistance was illegal) has been refuted by reality, giving credence to the Hamas argument (which is no different from the argument adopted before Oslo by the nationalist movement as a whole and that continues to be adopted by a score of Palestinian factions opposed to Oslo) that armed struggle is the only real means of liberation.

Hamas claims that by refusing ill-designed peace processes it upholds Palestinian rights and remains their defender. Hamas's opponents and critics in Palestinian circles and beyond say that the movement has not only offered no alternative but was partly, if not mostly, responsible for the failure of the peace process when it continued its military attacks against Israel.

POPULAR REFERENDA AS A POLITICAL PROGRAMME

The political dilemma that Hamas has faced emanates from a realistic assumption: what is the reality if the majority of Palestinians accept a peace treaty with Israel that is still rejected by Hamas? If Hamas is adamant in staying true to its own principles, which consider peace treaties predominantly predicated on Israeli terms as akin to surrender, it is equally anxious to remain connected to and representative of the desires and aspirations of the majority of Palestinians. The solution to this dilemma was offered by Hamas through the idea of a referendum. This would mean that any form of final solution based on a negotiated settlement should be reached through a Palestinian consensus, which is achievable only by holding a referendum for all Palestinians inside and outside Palestine under international supervision.

In calling for a referendum, Hamas wants more than to just rally the general Palestinian public into becoming strongly involved in deciding their own destiny; the movement is more concerned that at some point it will face the hard choice between continuing the armed struggle against the general mood of the Palestinian public, or becoming a purely political party. The referendum idea gives legitimacy to any future decision on the part of Hamas to abandon its armed activities. At the same time, a collective popular vote on the final settlement would work to place the negotiating process and its results or compromises under bold popular scrutiny. This scrutiny, Hamas could then be assured, would surely be based on the preservation of Palestinian rights.

ELECTIONS, DEMOCRACY AND MOBILIZATION

Is Hamas genuinely democratic?

This is a standard rhetorical question which is always waved in the face of Islamist movements (including Hamas) in the Middle East and elsewhere. One implicit accusation in this question charges Islamist parties of being cunning in agreeing on a democratic process that they would exploit to arrive to power, then to rule with authoritarianism. The Islamists believe in, as their critics and opponents argue, in one man, one vote, one time. There is little historic experience upon which these accusations could be confirmed or refuted. The Arab revolutions of 2010–2011 brought to power Islamist parties in Tunisia and Egypt, both faced powerful counter-revolution forces, nationally and regionally, which managed to eventually remove them from power. Thus, the lack of actual long history could allow some benefit of the doubt. In the Middle Eastern context, the question applies equally to all parties regardless of their political ideology, Islamists and non-Islamists. Democratic practice is visibly in short supply and, in the postcolonial era in the region, there have been almost no fully fledged democracies. In Arab republics, nationalist and socialist parties have come to power, by either election or military coups, and have never relinquished power peacefully. In Arab monarchies, changing the system by democratic means has been out of the question. Thus, questioning how authentically democratic the Islamist movements are, in an environment that lacks democracy, implies considerable accusation as a starting point. In all the cases in the Middle East, where ruling parties rejected democracy or dismissed the results of elections because an opposition party won the majority, the intransigents were non-Islamist parties.

In an early interview with Jerusalemite Arabic newspaper *Al-Nahar*, on 30 April 1989, Sheikh Ahmad Yasin, the founder and leader of Hamas for many years, spoke about his movement's views and the Palestinians aspirations. He responded to questions about the stance of his Hamas in the event that the majority of the Palestinian people desired a solution, supported a strategic vision different from that of Hamas, or voted for a party other than Hamas. The question was about the nature of the state Hamas sought (after liberation). The gist of Yasin's answers was the same, 'I will respect and honour the desire and will of the Palestinian people.' He emphasized his acceptance of what the Palestinian people would decide, in response to a provocative question in the same interview about his and Hamas's stance if the Palestinian Communist Party won elections in Palestine. Yasin stated at that time: 'I would respect the wishes of the Palestinian people even if the Communist Party won ... If the Palestinian people were to express their rejection of an Islamic state, I would respect their will and honour their wishes.' From these insights of Sheikh Yasin transpired the idea of a referendum in Hamas' political thought that was later proposed by the movement. This idea meant to offer a practical bridge between Hamas's high bar of liberation of all Palestine and the possibility of achieving a Palestinian state in 1967. Or could be seen as a pragmatic way to descend from the high tree it climbed.

Therefore, Hamas is as genuine in its democratic conviction as any other political party, in a region inexperienced in this form of governance. There are, however, certain specifications in the make-up of Hamas that could help in exploring the level of its democratic credibility. Internally, the movement has embraced democratic practices in choosing its leaders. These practices have been well established and have even stretched less practicably to areas where democratic consensus might not have brought about ideal results. For example, when Hamas was in the process of forming its government in March 2006 after winning the elections, the prime minister and all the cabinet ministers were elected by the rank and file: in the process, Hamas's cabinet ended up with a team of ministers that was not necessarily composed of the best people for their responsibilities. Instead of mandating the prime minister to form his government as a working unit based on professional and political considerations, all of the individual ministers were imposed on him in a democratic but perhaps more shambolic fashion from the party floor.

As far as clinging to power once elected by abolishing the democratic structure and process that allowed them to rule, a couple of arguments merit contemplating here. It must be remembered that Hamas has always defined itself as a resistance movement, essentially preoccupied with confronting the Israeli military occupation of Palestine. This occupation, with all its military resources, has always held the upper hand in this conflict, and controls every aspect of sovereignty over what has been left of any Palestinian state. All internal Palestinian politics take place under that control, and being voted in to take charge of a Palestinian government that functions under ultimate Israeli rule is hardly a great enticement to Hamas.

Specifically because of the parameters of this foreign military control, Hamas never aspired to, or planned to, win a majority in any Palestinian elections, since this would have forced it into such an awkward position. Hamas's victory in the 2006 elections caught the movement by surprise, and it is hard to imagine Hamas wishing to cling to this awkward position by blocking or manipulating any coming elections. Given the 'siege' of protest and censure that Hamas-in-power (in 2006–2007) had faced regionally and internationally, the movement's biggest challenge was to avoid total collapse and finish its four-year term in government with the least possible losses. Any scenario that suggested Hamas would deploy its efforts and manoeuvrability to remain in such a compromised position of power by force had proven to be unrealistic.

Within the Palestinian polity, especially in the immediate years after the death of Yasser Arafat in 2004, the Palestinian political environment was hardly receptive to any kind of authoritarian rule. The centres of power have been fragmented and Hamas stood at loggerheads with its rivals, particularly the Fatah movement. If Hamas decided to remain in power contrary to democratic practices, the immediate internecine result would be severe. A prevailing general sentiment at that time suggested that the diversity of Palestinian society, the high level of education, and the general envy of the 'Israeli democracy' next door, had narrowed down any possibility of the development of an undemocratic Hamas. Secular, leftist and liberal lines of thought have been historically engraved all over Palestinian society, no less upon the powerful Palestinian Christian community, which is highly politicized and active. Thus, even if Hamas wanted to opt for any undemocratic form of politics, the surrounding internal circumstances would abort such a choice.

What is the significance of Hamas's winning the Palestinian elections of January 2006, and why did Palestinians vote for Hamas?

Hamas's triumph in the 2006 elections was a complete shock for all parties concerned, including Hamas itself. Hamas's plan was to win a large enough number of seats, around 40–45 per cent, to enable it to play the role of the guardian of the Palestinian people's rights but without bearing the direct and ultimate responsibility of the government, which, because of the Israeli control, was highly undesirable. The general thinking was that, by winning this share of seats, Hamas would easily form coalitions with other smaller leftist opposition groups and would be capable of blocking any future compromises made by Fatah. The 'dirty' business of day-to-day governing would still have been left to Fatah, but it would have been hobbled politically in its negotiations with Israel. The outcome of the elections, however, was a landslide victory, with Hamas winning almost 60 per cent of the seats. The defeat of Fatah was resounding.

The reasons behind the Hamas victory are multiple. In the first place, the movement harvested long years of devoted work and popularity among Palestinians. At least half of the voters supported Hamas outright for its programmes and declared objectives; the other half were driven by other forces. The failure of the peace process combined with the ever-increasing Israeli brutality had left Palestinians with no faith in negotiating a peaceful settlement with Israel. The balance in the debate surrounding peace talks versus resistance was teetering, as the date for the elections came nearer and nearer. The notion of 'peace talks' was clearly losing ground, but there was no clear and definite support for the '*résistance*' concept. The latter was vague, and many Palestinians were wary about its meaning and mechanisms. But the frustration of the peace talks took its toll and contributed largely to the defeat of the Fatah movement, the main force behind and upholder of the Oslo Accords and all that resulted from them.

Another major factor that helped Hamas in winning these elections was the failure in almost all areas of the Fatah-led Palestinian Authority. Not only did it fail externally in the peace talks with Israel, but it also failed miserably internally, in managing the daily lives of the Palestinian people. Mismanagement, corruption and theft were the 'attributes' that came to be used to describe top leaders, ministers and their high-ranking staff. As unemployment and poverty reached unprecedented levels, the extravagant lifestyle of senior Palestinian officials infuriated the public, and it was the elections that empowered the people to punish those officials. Thus, the elections proved to be the reaping season for both Hamas in its victory, and Fatah in its defeat.

It is easy to refute any suggestion that the Palestinian people voted for Hamas primarily on religious grounds. There was certainly no overnight popular conviction in favour of Hamas's religious or even political ideology. Christians and secular people voted for Hamas in various constituencies side by side with Hamas members and exponents. Hamas members also supported Christian candidates and won them seats in the parliament. Hamas itself appointed a Christian to its cabinet as the minister of tourism. The diverse nature of Hamas's voters confirmed that people were voting for Hamas as the nationalist liberation movement that promised change and reform on all fronts.

The victory itself is of paramount significance not only for Palestinians but also for Arabs, Muslims and beyond. At the Palestinian level, it is a historic turning point, where a major shift in leadership seemed at the time to have taken place democratically. For the first time in more than half a century, an Islamist group –

grounded in national liberation – has moved into the driver's seat, replacing the secular leadership that had controlled Palestine's destiny and national decision-making process for decades. This fundamental change, furthermore, was realized through peaceful means and without violence, giving Hamas and all Palestinians a great sense of pride that they have embraced democracy and respect its outcome. It also gave them the chance to revisit the strategy over the conflict with Israel, which had been designed and pursued by the Fatah movement. For Hamas, this victory had represented the greatest challenge that the movement has faced since its inception up until that time. Almost overnight, all Hamas's ideals and slogans have been brought down to face the realities on the ground. It could be safely said that the post-elections Hamas had become considerably different from the one before them.

At the Arab and Muslim level, Hamas's victory has been almost unique in that an Islamist party in the region finally gained power – and in a democratic way. Islamist movements in the region were jubilant over Hamas's triumph and considered it as their own victory as well. Arab and Muslim regimes, on the other hand, have watched the rise of Hamas to power with worry and suspicion, fearing that such a victory could encourage their local Islamists to pursue power more vigorously. Secular groups and individuals in the region have been divided. They supported the nationalist liberation side of Hamas but were anxious over its religious and social stance.

At the international level, a Palestinian government led by Hamas was regarded as a highly unpalatable fruit of democracy. The West in particular was caught in the dilemma of having to either accept such an undesirable result in order to show the Arab and Muslim world that its call for democracy in the region had been sincere or be seen to cynically partake in an Israeli effort to bring down Hamas's government and risk losing any credibility.

HAMAS'S ECONOMIC OUTLOOK

What is Hamas's economic thinking?

Except for extra emphasis on religious values against greed, corruption and the likes, Hamas has offered no distinct economic ideology or national programme that is any different from the mix of free market and state regulation that dominates the region. This mix used to be the foundation of the Palestinian economy after the creation of the Palestinian Authority in 1994. Weak and fragile by the standards of a medium-sized capitalist state, the crippling Israeli limitations and control have made it almost impossible for this economy to prosper. Realistically speaking, a Palestinian economy that is tightly controlled by Israel will never prosper, whether it is market-oriented or state-controlled. Unlike the Palestinian leftists, whose strong stamp of socialism colours their economic thinking, Hamas puts forth no ideologically led economic programme. Hamas as a party has never offered a comprehensive vision of a so-called 'Islamic economy', which is sometimes referred to by individual Hamas figures, and frequently mentioned in the literature of other Islamist parties.

By and large, the movement seems to be content with the capitalist mode of economy which is based on free enterprise. It subscribes to the widespread belief within the circles of Islamist movements that Islam encourages free enterprise and enshrines the right to hold individual property. Therefore, the very basics of any 'Islamic economy' are close enough to the underlying tenets of capitalism. Yet, the morality of such an 'Islamic economy' is closer to socialism – where, at points, Islamist thinkers theorized about the so-called 'Islamic Socialism'. Many religious notions, such as a deep interest in justice and equality, obligatory systems of helping the poor, curbing monopolies and the prohibition of the unfair accumulation of fortunes, all echo the essences of socialist thought.

In practice, although Hamas's bulk membership includes the working and middle classes, it also includes merchants, businesspeople and the rich. They have always been looked on with respect and admiration because of their continuous donations to the movement. Outside Palestine, rich Muslim businesspeople in the Gulf countries and other Muslim places represent one main source of Hamas's funding. Therefore, Hamas's experience of 'capitalism' and 'capitalist' people is somewhat positive. In recent years, however, there has been scattered criticism by some Hamas writers of the international economy and the monopolies of globalization, but these appear only in the margins of discussions of other major issues, such as the global hegemony of the United States.

In an attempt to secure a confidence vote from the Palestinian parliament in March 2006, the governing Hamas statement showed perhaps too much eagerness to emphasize its interest in encouraging foreign investors to come to Palestine and explore economic opportunities. Hamas's government statement vowed that:

it would build the economic institutions of the country on foundations that will attract investment, raise the rates of growth, prevent monopoly and exploitation, protect workers, encourage manufacturing, increase exports, develop trade with the Arab world and the world in general, and in ways that serve our Palestinian interests and strengthen our self-capacities, by issuing laws that are appropriate for all of this.

GRASSROOTS SOCIAL WORK

What is the role of Hamas at the grassroots level in Palestinian society?

Grassroots work has always been one of Hamas's strongest aspects. Its unstoppable rise over the 20 years prior to the eventual triumph over other Palestinian factions is largely attributed to its success in social work. This work takes the form of providing structured educational, health and welfare services and help to the poor. Since 1987 and through powerful pervasive networks of charities, mosques, unions, schools and sport clubs, Hamas's assistance and care of needy people have been felt personally by hundreds of thousands of Palestinians. The provision of these services has been mostly clean-handed and transparent, which equally has always been compared with the corrupt performance of the Palestinian Authority from 1994. The popularity of Hamas and its victory in the 2006 elections is at least partially an outcome of its sustained devotion to helping the poor. Hamas was known to give monthly help even to people who worked for the Fatah Palestinian Authority when their income was considered to be below the poverty line.

Known to be Hamas's major strategic strength, the Islamic charities and institutions run by the movement have always been targeted by Israel from 1987 to 1994. For years, Israeli attacks aimed to close down these charities, block their funds and mobilize international campaigns against their external donors. Israel has tried to claim that Hamas's social work organizations in the West Bank and the Gaza Strip channel funds to Hamas's military activities. However, the real intention behind the continuous harassment and closure of these charities and facilities, either by Israel or later by the Palestinian Authority, was the popularity they bring to Hamas.

After the New York attacks of 9/11 in 2001, the pressure on Hamas and its activities multiplied. Israel succeeded in mobilizing the United States and the United Kingdom to take measures against a number of Islamic organizations accused of sending funds to Hamas's charities. The United States also pressured the Palestinian Authority to act against Hamas's social activities, which included providing monthly stipends to the families of 'martyrs' to the cause of liberation, such as suicide bombers. This particularly was seen as an indirect encouragement for the future recruitment of bombers, who would rest assured that their families would enjoy protection and support.

At various periods of time, Hamas's social work was really hindered or crippled by Israeli or official Palestinian efforts, yet it would gather momentum again and resume its operations. In the years 2003–2004, the Palestinian Authority yielded to Israeli/ American pressure and took harsh measures against Hamas's charities, including freezing the bank accounts of 12 charities in the West Bank and 38 in the Gaza Strip. The Islamic Society, which has nine branches in the Gaza Strip, was a particular target. Protesting against these measures, thousands of Palestinian families took to the street in November 2003, throwing stones at the premises of the Legislative Council. According to local field workers, there were 120,000 Palestinians receiving monthly financial help from those charities. Thirty thousand more benefit from them on an annual basis.

Closing those charities did not help in either lessening Hamas's military attacks or reducing its popularity. Despite all the ruthless measures against them, not only by Israel but also by the Palestinian Authority, these charitable organizations remained functioning, serving hundreds of thousands of poor Palestinians in the Gaza Strip and the West Bank.

At one point, there was a remarkable show of power by Hamas against the combined efforts of Israel, the United States and the Palestinian Authority to block Hamas's funds. Hamas wanted to show that it could solicit funds from ordinary Palestinians to support its organizational and military activities, and that it did not need to rely on its impounded funds, nor would any international blockade against external sources of funding destroy it. Thus, it organized a one-day fundraising campaign in the Gaza Strip on Friday, 9 April 2004. During and after Friday prayers, Hamas appealed to the Gazans to donate to the movement and specifically to its Al-Qassam military wing (not to any outfit or charity affiliated to it). Canvassing all the mosques and public places across the Gaza Strip, Hamas collected huge sums of money. According even to independent local sources, around US$1.2 million was estimated to have been collected on that day. Hamas's own estimate was more than double that figure.

Does Hamas's social programme include imposing Islamic symbols such as the hijab and other notions of sharia law on the Palestinians?

Ironically, within the sphere of Hamas's social work – its most powerful strategic asset – lies one of the weakest aspects of the movement: its heavily religious societal outlook. As was discussed in Chapter 2, Hamas is a blend of liberation movement and religious party. The religious drive within Hamas is indeed visible and powerful, prompting many Palestinians to ask whether the movement would be willing to impose its own views and understanding of Islam on Palestinian society in the event of taking power.

Hamas's often-declared position is that it will never impose any religious practice on the Palestinians. Addressing detailed questions about the movement's stance regarding the hijab, alcohol, segregation between males and females and applying certain aspects of sharia law, Hamas's spokespersons are unanimous in negating the possibility of Hamas imposing such things on the Palestinians against their will. However, there is a social dynamism and reality in the West Bank, and even more evident in the Gaza Strip, that reflects indirect practices or influences that contradict these official declarations. Because of the heavy presence of Hamas and the efficiency of its social activities, an atmosphere exists which has to some degree precipitated the indirect imposition of Hamas's norms on the Palestinians they support and help. Receiving continuous help and teaching from Hamas, many poor Palestinians would not only give their votes to Hamas in any coming elections, but in many cases would also adhere to the religious traditions and practice propagated by Hamas. And this does not simply follow out of gratitude or agreement. A woman that doesn't wear hijab, for example, would not think to apply for help from Hamas before wearing it in the first place. This could be considered to be an indirect 'benign or paternal' imposition of practices.

More worrying examples surface, from time to time, of more 'malignant' impositions of practices. These include very direct and harsh interference by Hamas members specifically in the Gaza Strip against certain behaviour or events that are deemed 'immoral' in their eyes (partying, drinking alcohol, not wearing the hijab, mixed swimming and so forth). One infamous incident of this kind, which greatly embarrassed Hamas, was the murder of a Palestinian woman in her fiancé's car at the beach in Gaza by Hamas gunmen, and the beating up of her fiancé until he bled. Although an official statement of Hamas condemned the incident and compensated the family of the woman, the justification provided by her killers was based on 'moral reasons and the fight against corruption'.

Throughout its years in power over the Gaza Strip since 2007, Hamas has indeed grappled with the idea of imposing a 'religious moral code'. The more power and popularity the movement acquires, the more tempted it is to use its leverage to impose its social and religious ideals. There is visible confusion about Hamas's temptation to use its popular and political capital in creating and imposing its religious morality. Some of Hamas's figures would convey the message with conviction that Hamas has the right to invest its resistance capital in empowering an ideological social (or religious or cultural) vision on society. Other voices in Hamas opposed this publicly. Understandably, not all Hamas supporters agree with its religious outlook. Palestinian society at large is very diverse, with secular and religious people, Muslims and Christians, who have been living side by side for centuries without adhering to any rigid form of social or religious structure.

The potential misuse by Hamas of its 'resistance capital' in the religion/morality stakes is rooted in its self-perception of the role it has played. There is a valid claim made by Hamas that it has helped diminish certain negative phenomena in Palestinian society, such as the use of drugs, as well as its considerable contribution to social services and aid to thousands of poverty-stricken families. Yet, this has often been in tandem with propagating ideas like the sorting of the social fabric into 'moral' and 'immoral' classifications. Such potentially inflexible or divisive classification in the Palestinian case, and in any resistance situation, only complicates matters and makes things more dangerous, and pushes the national movement away from its all-inclusive character.

There is tension here between what pertains to 'resistance' and what concerns 'society'. Hamas is facing the same choice that many movements before it have done, of linking its social agenda (the Islamization of society) with its resistance programme. It should acknowledge that achieving the former goal might result in the loss of the latter. The experience of the broader Palestinian national movement shows that a pluralist national and social approach, which includes different moderate versions of religiosity, is the most successful in mobilizing the widest sections of the Palestinian people.

In the months that followed Hamas's control of the Palestinian Authority in March 2006, the confusion within Hamas's government on where to start and where to stop on 'imposing' moral religiosity was still apparent. The ministers of culture, media and women's affairs (all members of Hamas) have made scattered statements on issues that could involve 'moral imposition' and censorship, such as movies and the contents of plays and other material. However, judging by Hamas's government conduct in the Gaza Strip since 2007, one could argue that Hamas's performance on imposing social and religious morality, directly or indirectly, had been one of its weakest aspects.

What is the position of Hamas on women?

Hamas is no different from other mainstream Islamist movements in the region and beyond whose ideas and practices with regard to women draw on the experience and thought of the Muslim Brotherhood. This means adhering to a conservative outlook on women, but not necessarily very restrictive. It is a viewpoint and practice that is not as narrow-minded and rigid as that of extreme groups such as the Taliban of Afghanistan or even as limiting as in the Wahhabi attitudes that dominated Saudi Arabia before the rise of Crown Prince Mohammed bin Salman in 2015. Specifically, women in the Hamas movement are politically active especially in universities and graduate sectors (with syndications of engineers, doctors and so forth). They have their own committees at a local and national level, with their main areas of interest being the rather traditional spheres of women, charities and schools. Hamas's female activism reaches high peaks at the time of elections, when female members of Hamas are fully mobilized to reach out to Palestinian women and attract their votes. Whether these elections take place at the level of student unions or parliament, the power of the 'female voters' is paramount to putting Hamas in the lead. Thus, women are very central to Hamas at the level of functioning in the field and mobilization, that is to say, for Hamas's own political interests.

At other levels in Hamas, mainly in leadership, women disappear. Since it was founded in 1987, not a single female has been elevated to a public political leadership position, barring the late appointment in March 2006 of Myriam Saleh to Hamas's cabinet as (rather predictably) minister of women's affairs. The female membership of Hamas consists mostly of university graduates who were active in their university years but have been sidelined after marriage and family life. Their role is limited to familial and social affairs that are bound by geographical areas. Compared with the broader Palestinian national movement, where many female figures have left a political impact at the public and leadership level, Hamas's women are almost invisible to the outside world.

The widely believed conviction among Hamas's male membership is that the responsibility of women is mainly to look after home and family affairs. This view is popular as a matter of preference, but not as a diktat that could prohibit active women from pursuing other paths in their life. Hamas women work in schools, hospitals, companies, the media and other sectors. But they stop short of pursuing leading positions and avoid competing with men at those levels.

Within the 'resistance project' against the Israeli occupation, Hamas women play a significant mobilization role. They provide logistic and emotional support to the youth, and the mothers show a startling level of steadfastness when their boys are killed by the Israeli army. A very limited number of females from Hamas have carried out suicide attacks. Hamas leaders, ever adopting the 'benign paternal authority role', insist that they are not short of men to carry out these attacks.

When Hamas ran for the elections in the year 2006, it had on its list 13 females out of 66 candidates, with 6 of them ending up winning contested seats. By comparison, there were eight women from Fatah list (the main nationalist and secular competitor of Hamas) that had also won seats. When Hamas formed a Palestinian government by virtue of winning the majority, it only included one woman in the cabinet, Myriam Saleh. To the disappointment of many Hamas supporters who were hoping that the movement would show more openness, the portfolio that was assigned to Saleh was the ministry of women's affairs, a step that in effect perpetuates the traditional view that women's affairs are separate and should be administered by women.

In more than one way, Saleh's credentials which recommended her to that post reflect the profile of many of Hamas's women: young, educated females who divide their time between family responsibilities and organizational activism. Saleh holds a doctorate in Islamic studies and taught at Palestinian universities for years prior to assuming her new job. Married, with seven children, she is a devout mother, yet very engaged in Hamas activities: she is the founder and head of several women's organizations in the West Bank. In her view, 'women represent not only half of society, but actually its foundation'. Responding to questions about whether the Hamas government will impose the hijab on Palestinian women, she said:

> We assure all women that we will not force anybody to wear the hijab ... we only present our ideas by suggestion and with good intention. The majority of Palestinian women wear the hijab with full conviction and without coercion from anyone.

6

Hamas and the Palestinians

HAMAS'S POPULARITY

How popular is Hamas in the West Bank and Gaza Strip?

Hamas's landslide victory in the 2006 Palestinian Legislative Council (PLC) elections shows a clear measure of its popularity. The movement's election Platform for Change and Reform, along with four independent candidates supported by Hamas, reaped almost 60 per cent of the votes, with a turnout of 78 per cent of eligible voters. The victory stunned everyone, including Hamas members themselves. Yet, when scrutinized at a deeper level, the share of votes that Hamas won far exceeds Hamas's real power, and it merits closer analysis.

Over the many years prior to the 2006 PLC elections, Hamas's results in all kinds of elections, including those of student unions, professional associations and municipalities, averaged between 35–45 per cent. The ups and downs in the number of votes given to Hamas at various times corresponded to the political environment at the time of the particular elections. When people have been more hopeful in peace talks with Israel, Hamas's 'programme for resistance' tended to generate more doubt, and a drop in Hamas supporters followed. By contrast, when frustration with fruitless talks has been mounting and exacerbated by continuous Israeli humiliation of Palestinians, in such a charged atmosphere, Hamas has tended to gain more support in any elections held. The level of frustration and anger among the Palestinian electorate at the time of the 2006 PLC elections was unprecedented. The conjunction of unstoppable Israeli arrogance and military aggression against the Palestinians, coupled with the failure of the corrupt Fatah-led Palestinian Authority, furnished Hamas with the extra support that was added to its original hardcore constituency.

Therefore, the 60 per cent victory that Hamas achieved in the PLC elections was not reflective of its clear-cut strength, but rather represented a coming together of two separate voting segments, what might be called 'genuine support' and 'conjunctural support'. Hamas's solid genuine popularity is the constant support that it enjoys regardless of the fluctuations of the political situation, either at the level of the conflict with Israel or in internal Palestinian affairs. The bedrock popularity of Hamas ranges between 30–40 per cent of the entire Palestinian constituency. Any additional support to this share comes effectively from the conjunction of public reaction against the blunders and failures of Hamas's rivals, public frustration or outrage at ongoing humiliations from Israel, and the unforgivable corruption within.

This assessment of Hamas's support was somewhat confirmed four months after its PLC election victory, when it had to face the first critical test regarding its popularity. Hamas supporters ran for the student union elections of Bir Zeit University, the biggest and most politicized Palestinian higher education institution in the West Bank, near the city of Ramallah. Historically, Bir Zeit University has been the stronghold of secular and leftist Palestinian groups. From the early 1990s, Hamas started to fiercely contest the leadership of the student union. In April 2006 elections, in an intensified electoral battle against the Fatah platform, Hamas won a majority of 23 seats out of the 51 being contested on the student council, leaving Fatah with only 18 seats, with the remaining 10 divided among other factions. Hamas's Bir Zeit victory of 45 per cent of the votes is a much more accurate indicator of Hamas's real power on the ground than the inflated 60 per cent of the 2006 PLC victory and is historically consistent as well.

From 2007 to 2023, the years of Hamas's control over the Gaza Strip, polls over the years have shown fluctuations in Hamas's support reflecting the degree of satisfaction of its performance in resistance and governance. Perhaps unsurprisingly, Hamas's support in the West Bank and within the Palestinian diaspora is stronger than in the Gaza Strip. The latter area has witnessed all forms of hardships including blockade, continuous Israeli wars, high levels of poverty and unemployment, and eventually the genocide of 2023–2024. The following are some periodical poll results produced by the respected Palestinian Center for Policy and Survey Research (PSR) in Ramallah, which allow deeper understanding of the situation over time.* A survey in June 2024 conducted by the PSR concluded that a rise in supporting armed struggle to 54 per cent, rise for Hamas by 6 per cent to 40 per cent, while Fatah, Hamas's rival, led by President Mahmoud Abbas stopped at 20 per cent support. One month before the October 7 attacks, the results were as follows: Hamas leader Ismail Haniya wins a presidential election against Mahmoud Abbas, 58 per cent and 37 per cent respectively; Hamas receives 34 per cent votes in PLC elections, while Fatah receives 36 per cent. The September 2018 results showed that Haniya would receive 45 per cent of the votes in a presidential election against 47 per cent for Mahmoud Abbas; while Hamas scores 27 per cent of the PLC against 36 per cent received by Fatah.

How much influence does Hamas have among the more than 7 million Palestinians who live outside Palestine (in the Arab countries and the rest of the world)?

Unlike the situation in the West Bank and the Gaza Strip, there has been little visible presence of Hamas within the Palestinian communities abroad, barring the refugee camps in Lebanon and Syria. This situation did not change after Hamas's victory in the PLC elections, and it is certainly difficult to draw an accurate assessment of Hamas's outside popularity. There have been few electoral processes outside Palestine with Hamas-affiliated

---

* Palestinian Center for Policy and Survey Research (PSR), www.pcpsr. org/en/.

groups partaking whose results could offer reliable indications of Hamas support and influence among Palestinians worldwide.

In general, the political orientations of the expat Palestinian communities vary and are sometimes influenced by place and conditions of residence. Tentatively, it could be said that the closer to Palestine and the harder the living conditions for a Palestinian community, the more supportive to Hamas it could be. Also, the more the Palestinians who live in various countries are exposed to the influences of local Islamist movements, the more support they tend to show to Hamas. Thus, Hamas is notably popular in the refugee camps in Lebanon, Syria and Jordan. These are the places closest to Palestine, where not only is the daily 'hot news from home' followed in detail, but also these countries themselves unavoidably feel the pressures of the conflict constantly. In Jordan, in particular, where the majority of the population is Palestinian or of Palestinian origin, and the influence of Jordanian Islamists is paramount, Hamas's popularity matches the levels of the West Bank and Gaza Strip. As an indirect indicator, many Palestinians who are supposedly Hamas supporters typically vote for the Jordanian Muslim Brotherhood, whose average share of the Jordanian Parliamentary seats ranges from 30–35 per cent. The Palestine issue and support for the Palestinian struggle against Israel normally figure on the top of any electoral platform of the Jordanian Islamists.

By contrast, Palestinians who live in the United States, Europe and other places far from Palestine are relatively less supportive of Hamas. Yet again, there is no concrete evidence that could be used to identify general trends for the extent to which those Palestinians support Hamas, or Fatah for that matter. Many Palestinians have been living in these areas well before the establishment of Hamas, leading secular and non-religious styles of life. It is safe to suggest that the observance of religious teachings, which is a pivotal underpinning in supporting Hamas, is visibly less in evidence among European and US-based Palestinians than among those who live in Palestine or the Arab countries. Thus,

Hamas's popularity within the former communities lags behind its levels within the latter.

How much influence does Hamas have on Palestinians inside Israel proper?

Inside Israel, that is to say, outside the West Bank and the Gaza Strip, there are about 2.1 million Palestinians, who represent about 21 per cent of the Israeli population. They remained on land within what became the new Israeli borders during and after the 1948 war, and officially became Israeli citizens. Largely displaced from their original homes and villages, these Palestinians managed to resettle in less desirable areas within Israel, and have since suffered much discrimination, in spite of their nominal citizenship status. In terms of level of education, achievement, careers and freedoms, they lag behind the bulk of Israeli society. Their inherent allegiance has always been questioned and seen by the Israeli establishment as a 'fifth column', working for the enemy. Their identity has been torn between officially being citizens of the State of Israel, which was established on their own land, and their own 'Palestinianism'. Prevented from serving in sensitive areas or assuming high-ranking positions in the government, the 'Arabs of Israel', as they are usually called, have never been given the same privileges as other Israelis in relation to their political, linguistic and legal rights. Israelis look at them with deep suspicion. However, Palestinians everywhere consider them part and parcel of the Palestinian people. They live in almost exclusively 'Palestinian' cities and villages, with little mixing with the larger Jewish population.

Other than a minority of Israeli-Palestinians who have joined major Israeli parties, the politically active members of this community have created their own parties, spanning leftist, nationalist and Islamist leanings. These parties compete against each other in local municipalities to represent and defend the rights of Palestinians in Israel on legal grounds and without the use of violence.

Since the mid-1980s, a strong Islamist movement has spawned within the 'Israeli Arabs', challenging all the other Arab parties. This took place almost in tandem with the emergence of Hamas in the West Bank and the Gaza Strip. The religious affinity between these movements is definitely strong, but they operate differently. The leaders and members of the 'Islamist movement' in Israel function in Israel within Israeli law, but Hamas functions in the West Bank and Gaza and is against Israel altogether. There are no organizational links between the two.

By and large, the 'Islamist movement' in Israel has been morally and politically supportive of Hamas. During the 1980s and 1990s, the Islamist movement in Israel was accused of being active in channelling funds to charities affiliated with Hamas. In 1996, the Islamist movement was divided into two groups. The Islamist Movement in the North that since then is seen as the 'radical' one and the Islamist Movement in the South that has been perceived as 'moderate'. Hamas's appeal and activities have rained mixed fortunes on the two groups of the Islamist movement in Israel. On the one hand, Hamas has inspired its members to mobilize more strongly against the Israeli authorities, and to strengthen the 'Islamist' ideals within their constituencies. On the other hand, Hamas's suicide attacks in Israeli cities from the mid-1990s to 2004 have greatly affected them negatively. Somewhat caught in the crossfire, both figuratively and at times literally, these Islamists as well as many Palestinians in Israel have felt unable to support Hamas publicly. At the high peak of the suicide bombings, leaders of both wings of the Islamist movement, which had by then split into two, publicly condemned Hamas's operations.

By and large, Hamas has little political leverage either on the Islamists Israel or on the overall Palestinian constituency there. Supporting Hamas would bring down heavy security and legal bearings upon the Arabs of Israel, thus, even any emotional support they might offer is almost hidden. The most that Hamas can aspire to get from the Islamists inside Israel is support for its charities and campaigning against the deArabization of Jerusalem. Because these Islamists and the Arabs of Israel in general are official Israelis, they can move in and out Jerusalem freely, thus they are able to mobilize themselves to protest about Israeli measures to eradicate the Arab nature and places of the city.

HAMAS AND SECULAR PALESTINIAN MOVEMENTS

What is Hamas's view of and relationship with the Palestine Liberation Organization (PLO)?

The PLO was established in the mid-1960s and has since evolved to embody the Palestinian national movement. It is an umbrella of all Palestinian factions, left, right and centre, with the Fatah movement being its backbone and leading force. Established before the 1967 war and the fall of the West Bank and the Gaza Strip to Israeli occupation, the PLO was originally created to liberate Palestine: that is, the land on which Israel was formed after the 1948 war. Yet, by the early 1980s, the aim of the PLO became to liberate the West Bank and the Gaza Strip, and establish a Palestinian state with implicit acknowledgement of the State of Israel. In 1988, the PLO recognized Israel and, in the following years, from 1991 to 1993, it engaged in peace talks with Israel in the hope of realizing its 'new' aim of a Palestinian state. The Palestinian Authority that was established according to the Oslo Accords was only responsible and could only speak in the name of the Palestinians in the West Bank, the Gaza Strip and East Jerusalem. The Palestinian refugees and non-refugees outside these areas (i.e. in the diaspora and inside Israel) were left outside the Oslo framework and thus remained represented by the PLO. Formally speaking, the PLO is the ultimate political leadership of all Palestinians, and is placed higher than the PA.

Hamas was bound to compete with the PLO since its emergence in the late 1987. It rejected the 'secular' nature of the organization and condemned its continuous concessions to Israel. In contrast to the later PLO conviction that Palestinian goals would only ultimately be realized through a negotiated settlement with Israel, Hamas advocated a resistance approach, which was justified all along the way by the obvious futility of the peace talks. Because of the secularity of the PLO and its 'capitulating' approach as perceived by Hamas, Hamas refused to join the PLO. Because of its immovability on this point, Hamas has always been accused of functioning at a distance from the collective national effort, and thus harming it. Not only that, but it has also been accused of undermining the PLO by not recognizing it as the sole and legitimate representative of the Palestinian people. Because the PLO fought hard against regional players, such as Israel, Jordan and Syria, to exact the status of the sole and legitimate representative of the Palestinians, it accused Hamas of indirectly undermining Palestinian legitimacy and representation.

Hamas, for its part, was inflexible on the issue of recognizing the PLO as the sole representative of the Palestinians. The most that it would acknowledge was that the PLO is 'a representative', not 'the representative', of the Palestinian people. Hamas also suggested that it might join the PLO if it was represented by 40–50 per cent of the PLO leading hierarchy. Hamas has continued to express its readiness to discuss joining the PLO, yet it has put forward terms completely unacceptable to Fatah, the central force of the PLO.

The Fatah movement has been fully aware of the challenge that Hamas has represented. As the PLO/Fatah continued its peace talks approach, almost from 1988 onward Hamas has travelled alongside with its resistance approach. With the continuous erosion of PLO legitimacy because of the lack of success of the peace talks route, Hamas became more powerful and intractable in its rejection of joining the PLO. Finally, in 2005, Hamas and Fatah along with other Palestinian factions agreed on the principle of restructuring the PLO so that Hamas could join.

When Hamas won the elections of 2006, it dealt the greatest blow to Fatah and the PLO, this time challenging the status of 'the sole and legitimate representative of the Palestinian people' as it had never been challenged before. In its cabinet platform, Hamas refused, once again, to recognize the sole legitimacy and representation of the PLO, infuriating Fatah and many other Palestinians who have argued that the PLO is above factional rivalry. Hamas, however, was eager to form a national unity government and called upon Fatah, other factions and independent members of the newly elected parliament to join. They all rebuffed Hamas's offer because of its position on the PLO.

How has the Hamas–Fatah rivalry developed?

The general characteristic of relations between Fatah and Hamas ever since the latter was formed, and between Fatah and Hamas's mother organization prior to the emergence of Hamas, has been one of continuous competition and tension. Fatah, the Palestinian National Liberation Movement, was formally established in 1965. The origins of the movement, however, pre-dated that by almost a decade, with some of Fatah's roots partly branching out from the Muslim Brotherhood. Until the mid-1950s, the Palestinian Muslim Brotherhood (PMB) in the Gaza Strip and to a lesser extent in the West Bank enjoyed considerable strength, emanating from the then powerful position of its mother organization in Egypt (see Chapter 1), which was ruled by the pan-Arabist leader Nasser. In the second half of the 1950s, Nasser outlawed the Muslim Brotherhood in Egypt and mercilessly suppressed them not only in Egypt but also in the Gaza Strip, which was then under Egyptian administration, in a similar manner as the West Bank was under Jordanian administration after the 1948 war. Prominent figures of the PMB decided to leave the organization, for it was seen to be heavily involved in an unnecessary struggle with Nasser, and they wished to create a movement whose entire focus would be the Palestine issue.

In July 1957, Khalil al-Wazir, an active PMB member (he would eventually become the second and long-standing leader of Fatah until his assassination by the Israelis in Tunis in 1988) presented a proposal to the leadership of the PMB in the Gaza Strip. In it, al-Wazir suggested a new approach where:

The Palestinian Brotherhood should establish a special organization alongside their own which has no visible Islamic coloration or agenda but which has the stated goal of liberating Palestine through armed struggle. The new organization should have the responsibility for preparing for that struggle and should engage in armed struggle once the required capabilities are acquired.*

The PMB did not take Khalil al-Wazir's proposal seriously, but al-Wazir and his close colleagues went ahead with the project on their own initiative. The effort of those former PMB members in the Gaza Strip was coordinated with other groups of active Palestinians (both pan-Arabists and nationalists, among others) outside Palestine who advocated a similar line of thinking, and Fatah was gradually in the making. The idea of Fatah was to disentangle the Palestinian national effort from inter-Arab rivalries by creating an ideology-free movement that would accept the membership and support of any party or individual who believed in 'the liberation of Palestine', without any additional ideological package. Over the following years, initial Fatah cells succeeded in bringing together active Palestinians from different political backgrounds, including, of course, some former members of the PMB.

Soon after its formation, between its adoption of armed struggle as the only strategy to 'liberate Palestine', and its setting aside of all ideological differences and conflicts with 'reactionary Arab regimes', Fatah rose to capture the imagination and support of the vast majority of Palestinians. By the end of the 1960s, it was far ahead of any other leftist, pan-Arabist or Islamist Palestinian

---

* 'Abdullah Abu 'Azza, *Ma'a al-haraka al-Islamiyya fil-aqtar al-'arabiyya* [*The Islamic Movements in the Arab Countries*] (Kuwait: Al-Qalam Publishing House, 1992), 85–6.

faction. Parallel to Fatah's rise, the PMB receded to the margins, fearing Nasser's wrath and convincing itself that the Fatah project was hasty and doomed to failure. It watched the continuing ascendance of Fatah with envy and dismay; many of its leaders had to live with the harsh fact that a number of their juniors had become leaders of the new rival and more popular movement. In the PMB literature, the 1950s defection of some of its members to take part in the creation of Fatah is treated with bitterness and confusion. Sometimes old leaders of the PMB would regret not having controlled Fatah from the outset instead of letting it grow away from their influence. In the 1970s and most of the 1980s, the PMB was inactive on the front of fighting the Israeli occupation; instead, it was preoccupied with a 'preparation strategy' – a grassroots process of Islamization of young generations that would be ready to fight Israel in the future (see Chapter 1). During those 'idle years', Fatah accused the inactive PMB of merely serving the Israeli occupation.

As the PMB eventually transformed itself into Hamas in 1987, bringing with its change of stance a surprisingly swift increase in its strength, it entered into competition with Fatah for support at the Palestinian grassroots level. The charges against the PMB/Hamas changed from fence-sitting to trying to create an alternative to the PLO and trying to unravel the achievements of the PLO and its mainstay, Fatah. In the early 1990s, relations between the two factions deteriorated dramatically. One of the major arenas of conflict was inside the Israeli prisons, where Fatah and Hamas prisoners clashed bloodily. Hamas prisoners were not allowed by Fatah members, who had been in prison much longer, to form their own cell groups, and were forced to join the already existing system of grouping, which was exclusive to factions that belonged to the PLO. Thus, Hamas inmates had to go through the educational and indoctrination courses organized by other factions, which naturally led to disputes on ideology and views. The prison clashes spread outside, and the atmosphere was charged in many Palestinian cities and refugee camps, until late in 1992 when the

Fatah leadership agreed to give Hamas prisoners the right to form their own groups.

A new phase of rivalry came into being with the establishment of the Palestinian Authority (PA) in 1994, as a result of the Oslo Accords of 1993. The PA, led by Fatah, was supposed to prove that it was competent to run an interim administration for a period of five years, after which negotiations between Israel and the Palestinian Authority would begin, establishing the 'permanent solution' and the creation of a Palestinian state. Fatah saw in the agreement a chance to realize Palestinian rights, and concurrently stopped its armed struggle.

Hamas, by contrast, saw the Accords as a continuation of the Israeli occupation by proxy, and continued its armed struggle. The PA considered Hamas to be a spoiler and demanded that the movement stop its military attacks against Israel so that peace talks could be given a chance. Hamas considered daily Israeli measures to essentially be ignoring the Accords, as Israel continued not only its usual policies on the ground, but especially its relentless expansion of settlements. Thus, the major issue that drove both parties to intense friction from 1994 to the year 2000 was Hamas's persistence in carrying on its military attacks against Israeli targets at times when the Fatah-led PA was trying to conclude incremental peace deals with Israel.

The second Intifada of 2000 forced the two parties to downplay their differences and focus on the Israeli occupation and its incursions into Palestinian cities and refugee camps. Practically speaking, the Oslo Accords had failed and Israel's brutal measures were imposed on Palestinian activists regardless of their organizational affiliation. Israel effectively reoccupied all the areas that it had initially (if only partly) withdrawn from according to the Oslo terms. The president of the PA, Yasser Arafat, was besieged in his offices in Ramallah for almost three years, from February 2002 until his death in October 2004. It was reported that Arafat extended indirect help to Hamas and turned a blind eye to the further arming of Hamas. The time around Arafat's death, marked the period of least friction between Fatah and Hamas in the past few years.

In the post-2006 election period, when Hamas took the reins of the Palestinian Authority, Fatah attempted to bring down Hamas's government and started to play the role that Hamas used to play when it was in the opposition. While Hamas was anxious to buy time and bring calm to the Gaza Strip and the West Bank so that it could prove itself as a successful government, Fatah became the spoiler that Hamas had been in the past. The military wings of Fatah have always been difficult to control, even by the Fatah leadership itself. With large stocks of arms and separate armed groups which move chaotically without clear focus and aims, the possibility of the Palestinian situation drifting into civil war was becoming higher than ever before. Eventually, the civil war nightmare scenario that many Palestinians had feared became reality in mid-June 2007. At that point, Hamas violently used force to seize power over all the security services that had continued to be controlled by Fatah. Many Palestinians were killed or injured in the clashes. Ultimately, Hamas won over Fatah militarily as it had democratically in the January 2006 elections (see Chapter 10).

What is Hamas's view of and relationship with the Palestinian left?

The left wing has a long and nostalgic history in Palestine, with the first Communist Palestinian party being established in Jaffa in the 1920s. It also had a pioneering role in inspiring parts of the Arab left movement in general. In the decades after the establishment of Israel in 1948, especially during the 1960s and 1970s, the Palestinian left stood in the forefront of the struggle. Its relationships with the Palestinian Islamists and the Muslim Brotherhood during those decades were extremely toxic. The Islamists were seen as a backward social force which contributed nothing to the struggle against Israel. When Hamas was formed in the late 1980s, the Palestinian left was confused about whether to welcome the sudden decision by the Islamists (in the guise of Hamas) to become engaged in active confrontation with Israel, or to fear their definitely rising power.

Against this backdrop of historical suspicion and lack of common ideological ground, Hamas and the Palestinian left organizations developed rather limited relationships. They were mainly propelled by a collective rejection of Fatah's (and the PLO's) willingness to participate in the Madrid Peace Conference in 1991, and then in the Oslo Accords of 1993–1994. Hamas and other Palestinian factions formed an alliance against Fatah, The Ten Faction Alliance, and fanned the flames of the spontaneous people's Intifada in progress as the resistance alternative to the Fatah 'capitulating' approach. On the top of the leftist factions came the Popular Front for the Liberation of Palestine (PFLP), the Democratic Front for the Liberation of Palestine (DFLP), and the Palestinian National Initiative (Al-Mubadara). The Ten Faction Alliance never came to the stage of issuing joint statements and stopped short of any concrete joint political or military actions. Intrinsically, the Palestinian left rejected the 'religious content' of Hamas and kept pressing for more secular emphasis in the struggle against Israel. In recent years and given the maturation of shared experiences, Hamas and the leftist factions, mostly the Popular Front for the Liberation of Palestine, gave more space for cooperation and joint action at the expense of suspicion and ideological differences.

One of the major issues that have kept Hamas and the Palestinian left apart has always been Hamas's unreserved refusal to recognize the PLO as the sole representative of the Palestinian people, as discussed above. The leftist organizations thought that this constant rejection revealed Hamas's future intention to exclusively control the Palestinian leadership. For its part, Hamas despaired of the left because whenever and wherever Hamas clashed on the ground with Fatah, the left would either stay neutral or implicitly support Fatah. Hamas has felt that the left have been hypocritical, only paying lip service to an alliance with

Hamas against the political capitulation of Fatah. For its part, the left has always accused Hamas of shortsightedness and engaging in unnecessary political battles or field provocations.

After the elections of January 2006, Hamas's relationship with the Palestinian left have further deteriorated. None of the three small leftist groups (PFLP, DFLP and the Initiative), which won seven seats in total in the PLC agreed to join Hamas's government. Hamas blamed them for foiling its efforts to form a national coalition government. In March 2006, Mousa Abu Marzouq, Hamas's deputy head of its Political Bureau, publicly criticized the Democratic Popular Front for the Liberation of Palestine (DPF) for its refusal to join the government. He also predicted that this group would disappear completely from the Palestinian political scene if it did not acknowledge the 'new realities'. One of the 'new realities' that Abu Marzouq was pointing out to the DPF was the 'Islamic choice' that the Palestinian people had made when they elected Hamas, a choice which contradicted the DPF demand that Hamas state clearly that one of its government's objectives would be to 'secularize Palestinian society'. Abu Marzouq insisted that it was illogical of the DPF to put forward this demand when it had managed to get only one member elected to the parliament (out of 132), particularly in light of the fact that that Hamas itself, with its vast majority in parliament, had not called for the 'Islamization of Palestinian society'.

What is Hamas's view of and relationship with Palestinian Christians?

In its conduct towards the Palestinian Christians, Hamas has shown extraordinary sensitivity. Realizing that its views on non-Muslims and its dealing with them would always be brought under the spotlight because of Hamas's religious colouring, the movement has succeeded in establishing cordial relationships with Palestinian Christians. Bearing in mind that the vast majority of Palestinian Christians are not strictly religious in lifestyle, there have been in general few areas of potential friction with Hamas. Generally, convergences of the nationalist cause rather than the divergences of religious beliefs, tended to govern the relationship.

In its official documents, Hamas speaks with warmth about the sacrifices of the Palestinian Christians, who have shown steadfastness side by side with their Muslim counterparts in the face of the Israeli occupation and its atrocities. Hamas keeps referring with a deep sense of pride to the fact that Muslims and Christians and (pre-Israel) Jews have long lived in peaceful coexistence in Palestine, and Hamas would maintain that tradition. Also, the specificity of the Palestinian situation has compelled Hamas to adopt a consensual and cooperative approach towards other Palestinians, regardless of their religious or political affiliation.

In actuality though, many Christians have felt uncomfortable with the increasing rise of Hamas. The religious atmosphere that was created alongside Hamas's political ascendence undoubtedly brought about a somewhat discomfiting climate for Christians, as well as for secular Muslims. There have been views and research which argue that the rise of Hamas in Palestine has put extra pressures on the Palestinian Christians, pushing more of them to migrate abroad. That said, there have been no religiously driven sectarian friction or riots in Palestine during the lifetime of Hamas that could be linked directly to the movement.

Hamas's tension and/or cooperation with other Palestinian groups has been almost exclusively politically driven. Its main rivalry remained to be with the Fatah movement, which is predominantly Muslim. With the other two major, though smaller, groups – the PFLP and DFLP – Hamas has developed closer relationships, and both used to be headed for many years by Christians. Indeed, this fact has never affected Hamas's position towards these two leftist factions.

In its 2006 election campaign for the PLC, Hamas supported two independent Christian candidates, one in Gaza and another in Bethlehem city in the West Bank. When it had to form a cabinet, it included a Christian as one of its ministerial team. Although there are no organizational rules that prohibit a Christian from joining Hamas, the movement has failed to attract a single Christian to its membership. This failure embarrasses Hamas as it is the only Palestinian movement whose membership is exclusively based on Muslims, though not by diktat but by practical reality.

7
Hamas and 'International Islamism'

HAMAS AND MUSLIM COUNTRIES

What are Hamas's relationships with Arab and Muslim countries?

Hamas's relationships with different Arab and Muslim countries vary from one country to another depending on various factors. These relationships exist at two levels: at the cautious official level; and at the (usually) warm and more supportive popular level. Across the region, states that are known to have an outspoken, strong policy line against Israel, even if only verbally, are naturally closer to Hamas. This group included over decades, if at varying degrees, Iran, Egypt, Syria, Sudan, Saudi Arabia, Jordan, Lebanon, Tunis, Turkey, Qatar, Algeria, Mauritania, Malaysia and Libya, where Hamas has succeeded in establishing official links. Political developments in some of these countries and in the region have affected their relationship with Hamas, negatively or positively. For example, Sudan after 2019 and Saudi Arabia after around 2015 severed their relations with Hamas. Egypt, during the short term of the Islamists rise to power in 2012–2013 became the closest ally of Hamas, then was very hostile after the removal of the Islamists by the army in July 2013. Iran figures at the top of Hamas's allies, openly supporting the movement politically, financially and militarily, with Hamas enjoying almost full diplomatic status in Tehran. A similar diplomatic and political strong presence that Hamas enjoys has also been in Qatar and Turkey. In the other countries, Hamas has operated at a lower profile, sometimes granted offices, and other times spokespersons of the movement were allowed to function at the political and media level.

Before the Arab revolutions of 2010–2011 and their impact on regional political landscape, a closer look is merited on Hamas's relations with Egypt and the Gulf states, mainly Saudi Arabia, Qatar and Kuwait. These countries used to (and still are) well known for their non-revolutionary politics but they attempt to maintain a reasonable relationship with Hamas in order to counterbalance what was perceived to be a threatening Iranian/ Syrian influence on Hamas. Egypt was particularly keen to have strong links with Hamas and has mediated several times since the late 1990s between Hamas and Israel to reach a 'truce'. Egypt's interest was in having calm and security in the bordering Gaza Strip, and to keep the rise of Palestinian Islamism under check so that it does not spill over Egyptian territory. Within this same time-frame, Jordan has also maintained open channels with Hamas almost for the same reasons perceived by Egypt – security and future borders concerned with Israel, as well as to fend off Hamas's potential influence over the Palestinians in the kingdom.

Beyond the Arab region, Hamas has established varying levels of links with Pakistan, Malaysia, Indonesia and Turkey. Delegations from Hamas make frequent visits to these countries to appeal to their 'Muslim brothers' for support for Palestine and for Hamas. Governments of these countries have established calculated links with Hamas in order to make sure that Hamas's contacts in their countries are not taking place behind the back of the regime. The principal concern in most Arab and Muslim countries is to monitor Hamas and its contacts and extract the guarantee from the movement that it will have no activities in the country, and will only be a receiver of support and not become an inspiration or mobilizer of any disgruntled factions there. However, in the cases of Malaysia and Turkey, Hamas enjoys considerable contact and looks with high appreciation to the moderate Islamist ruling parties there.

In all countries, Hamas's eye has always been on nurturing strong relationships and presence among the people, through the political parties and Islamic associations. The wider Hamas strategy is based on engaging Arab and Muslim peoples in supporting the Palestinians. Reaching out to these particular populations is vital, for it explains the Palestinian suffering and solicits support in moral, political and financial forms. At the official level, Hamas has focused on acquiring political and diplomatic recognition and legitimacy. Hamas has been very keen to be accepted as a political organization that is received and respected by governments, so that it constantly tries to mitigate its image as a 'terrorist organization'. Official links also help in enhancing Hamas's aspiration of representing the Palestinians and speaking for them, against the wishes of the PLO, the officially recognized body for that purpose.

At the popular level, Hamas has succeeded in creating strong local relationships with Islamist parties, associations and individuals. Not only within the realm of Islamists, but also within the anti-Israeli and anti-American camps, Hamas has enjoyed warm relationships and support. These relationships have played a fundamental role in helping Hamas in fundraising and mobilization of public opinion in the Arab and Muslim world. Supporters of Hamas will convey its message and defend its views and practices in their areas, by political and media means. The sympathy for Hamas in the Gulf and other Arab and Muslim countries often reaches high levels, creating the much-needed atmosphere in which Hamas's local supporters, organizations or individuals are able to collect considerable funds for the movement.

HAMAS AND MUSLIM COUNTRIES IN THE WEST

What has been the impact of Hamas's rise on the growing number of Islamist movements in the world, especially in the West?

In the general realm of Muslims worldwide, Hamas's rise as an Islamist Palestinian movement has encouraged millions of

Muslims to further support the cause of Palestine. Muslim communities in the West are no exception. Palestine occupies a central and emotional place in the imagination and sentiment of Muslims. Hamas believes that with the adoption of a strong Islamic ideology, an additional level of power will be bestowed upon the call for support of the Palestinians. Ordinary Muslims would certainly feel more resonance with the Islamist discourse of Hamas than the secular discourse of the PLO. With the spread of Islamic political movements in the past three decades, Muslim communities in the West have become amenable to Hamas's call in particular. What Hamas has most wanted from them has been the propagation of the Palestine cause and funding of Hamas's charitable work. Almost simultaneously with the eruption of the first Intifada in late 1987, many Islamic organizations were established in Europe and the United States in order to help the affected Palestinians. Money poured into Islamic charities that were efficiently run by Hamas. Hamas reaped the fruits and amassed further popularity.

In more specific areas, Hamas influences Islamist movements worldwide by offering a 'jihad model' that is not controversial by nature of its just cause, but would not hesitate to use controversial means to serve that cause. Hamas's jihad is seen as directed against Israel, a foreign military occupation led by Zionist Jews against Muslim homelands and holy places. Because this particular jihad is not launched against a contentious Muslim regime or a despised government where Muslims would end up fighting Muslims, there is a near consensus among Islamists everywhere on the righteousness and justice of Hamas's struggle. Also, Hamas is considered to be a source of inspiration – an example of steadfastness in the face of tremendous pressures – because of its committed refusal to bow to the status quo and international forces and recognize Israel, as the PLO did.

On the other hand, Hamas's controversial means, specifically the suicide attacks (1994/1995–2004), have also influenced many Islamists and propelled many of them into adopting this tactic.

Although they were originally introduced into modern conflicts in the Middle East by Shii militants in Lebanon in 1982, against US-led multinational troops, suicide bombings had to wait until the early 1990s before they were freely adopted by Hamas. Despite the justifications made by Hamas to legitimize this controversial practice (see Chapter 4), the movement bears the responsibility for having promoted this kind of self-killing among modern Islamists as a manner of inflicting maximum harm on the side of the enemy. It could be said that the waves of suicide bombings conducted by radical Islamist groups across the globe in the 1990s and 2000s have been in part at least inspired by Hamas's conduct.

The activities of Hamas's supporters in the West have been restricted to informational, political and financial support. There purposefully has never been any military or armed action outside Palestine. Hamas has been vigorously strict on avoiding any direct or indirect engagement in armed activities in the West, or encouraging or approving any action in that direction undertaken by its supporters. As a result of this, many US and European judicial cases against organizations and individuals close to Hamas and charged with 'sponsoring the terrorism of Hamas' have failed. These organizations had been channelling money to thousands of poor Palestinians via Islamist charities, some of which were loosely associated to Hamas. All money transfers from the United States or Europe were undertaken via Western or Israeli banks, under the full monitoring of Western and Israeli intelligence as to where this money came from and to whom it was given. Hamas and its supporters abroad have been successful in maintaining a complete distance between the political, social and financial funding of the movement and its military branch and activities.

Is there either a visible or invisible presence of Hamas in the West?

There is no organizational structure for Hamas in the West. It has been felt that any such remote structure with any degree of party-strictness, however loyal it might be, would add an extra unnecessary burden on the movement in return for benefits that it already receives through the existing system of supporters. Thus, until the formation of Hamas's government in 2006, there was no official spokesperson or address for Hamas in any Western country. Yet, as outlined above, there has been an 'indirect' presence through Islamist networks and associations in the West that have shown support and solidarity to Hamas either directly or indirectly by virtue of their broader support of the Palestine question. Many of these associations have been established by Palestinians who are driven emotionally and politically to support their people. Within these circles of Western expat Palestinian societies and communities, more visible support for Hamas can undoubtedly be found.

What matters most, in an atmosphere charged by suspicion about Muslims and Arabs in the West, is that Hamas's invisibility in the West does not mean that it has an underground cellular network, armed or unarmed. Since it was established in 1987 and up to the present, there has not been a single incident where Hamas was proved to have operated any illegal action within or against any Western country or citizens. The eagerness that Hamas has always shown about having a future presence in the West was specifically directed to, and restricted to, the establishment of official contacts with Western governments. Succeeding on that front has always borne far more strategic significance for Hamas than recruiting individuals or setting up underground cells.

HAMAS AND ISLAMIST MOVEMENTS

Is Hamas part of a global network of 'international Islamism'?

The answer to the question of whether Hamas constitutes part of a global network of 'international Islamism', is yes – and no. If by 'international Islamism' we mean a coherent organizational structure, where various groups and parties worldwide belong to a single and unified 'umbrella' hierarchy, then the answer is no. If, however, the term denotes a loose common ground where Islam is considered the source of ideological convictions and guidelines, then the answer is yes.

Perhaps against the conventional thinking of many in the West, Islamist movements differ startlingly, one from another. First of all, there are political movements and non-political movements. The latter type of movement is hardly mentioned, as these function quietly and limit their efforts to charitable work, religious preaching and propagation of the call to Islam. The other type however, known as movements of political Islam, constitute a rising force not only in the Middle Eastern context, but globally.

Even within the groups affiliated to political Islam, the factors that separate them from each other perhaps override those that unite them. Some movements are engaged in fierce and armed conflict against their governments and are confined within their national boundaries. Their jihad aims to bring down these governments, which are seen as unIslamic, and to replace them with Islamic ones. Democratic means are rejected by these groups because they imply recognition of the non-Islamic status quo under which democracy is implemented. Examples of such political Islam groups existed in 1990s in Algeria, Egypt and Pakistan, yet they were not the mainstream Islamists.

Other movements conduct their protests against the ruling elites in their countries by peaceful means and, in many cases, through parliamentary political processes. The main groups in this category are the Muslim Brotherhoods that exist almost in every Arab or Muslim country. These groups abandon the use of violence altogether and prefer long and patient incremental reform within the system. Each group operates within the nation-state boundaries of its country.

Another generation of more recent and radical Islamist groups is 'stateless' in terms of the focus of their jihad. This means they are not bound to the confines of any certain country, and consider the very existence of many Muslim states as an abnormality to the 'supposed' one and unified single Muslim country. These groups are the force behind 'global jihad', where fighting is driven by the injustices suffered by Muslims, and against those who inflict these injustices, regardless of time and space. The West in general and the United States in particular is the number one enemy to this type of Islamist movement. Thus, Western interests in Arab and Muslim countries and elsewhere are their legitimate targets. Instead of fighting puppet leaders and governments installed by the West to maintain its interests in the region, they advocate that the fight be launched directly against the West, the principal culprit. 'By attacking the head, the tail falls off', these factions are fond of repeating.

Within this mishmash of Islamist movements, Hamas is somehow unique. Its fight is not against any national regime, but against colonial foreign occupation. Its national liberation substance is no less potent than its religious creed (see Chapter 2). In many cases, and within the realm of 'international Islamism', Hamas's nationalist concerns have overridden its religious affinities. One recent and unmistakable example was its dismissal of calls from its 'Chechen brothers' to cancel an official visit of a Hamas delegation to Moscow in February 2006. For the Chechens, the Russian leadership is criminal and guilty of killing thousands of Muslims in the 1994 war against Chechnya. Hamas, it was felt, as an Islamist brotherly organization should never shake hands with the criminals. Hamas dismissed this and thought that fostering relations with Moscow had far more value to the Palestine issue than showing solidarity with its Chechen brothers.

In conclusion, the concept of 'international Islamism' stops far short of any effective and concerted plan of action. It is only manifested in verbal solidarity, moral and perhaps material support, but does not amount to a coherent global force that would have any particular significance to Hamas.

What is the difference between Hamas and al-Qaeda and ISIS, and is there any cooperation between them?

There are big differences between Hamas and the two groups, in terms of the ends, means and battlefield, and also the very nature of each of them. Because of such differences, Hamas is indeed very anxious to keep itself well distanced from both, and certainly does not engage in any cooperation with them. In terms of the ends, Hamas's aims are focused on Palestine and national context, starting with the 'liberation of Palestine', then narrowing down later and refocusing on ending the Israeli occupation of the West Bank and Gaza Strip. The ends of al-Qaeda and ISIS are almost the reverse in type: vague and without focus, and expanding, with the ultimate goal being to establish Islamic rule over Arab and Muslim lands after ridding them of foreign troops and puppet leaders. They also include intermediate goals such as forcing American troops to leave Arabian land, fighting US and British armies in Afghanistan, Iraq and Syria, and bringing down puppet governments in the Gulf countries and elsewhere: all along the way, both groups implement a very strict interpretation of Islamic practices on any area and segment of any population that would come to control as had been witnessed in some parts of Syria and Iraq in the years 2014–2017.

To realize its end, Hamas is engaged in a 'resistance programme' which includes armed struggle and political conduct. Within its armed struggle, it has adopted the controversial tactic of suicide attacks, justified by the Old Testament as 'an eye for an eye', a stance that has currency it has to be said, in both Jewish and Muslim traditions. Yet, Hamas's leaders repeat that resistance is not an end in itself, hinting that they would be ready to adopt a purely political strategy when the time was right. Al-Qaeda and ISIS means include armed struggle in all its forms, engaging in conventional confrontation against combatants, but also conducting suicide bombings, targeting civilians without reservations.

Hamas limits its fight to within the borders of historic Palestine, and its enemy is Israel. Al-Qaeda and ISIS consider the entire world to be their battlefield and, although the principal enemy for them is the United States, the list of its enemies is open-ended. It includes those European countries that took part in the wars against Afghanistan and Iraq in 2002 and 2003, such as Italy, Spain and Poland. It also includes Muslim states that are seen as Western bases, such as Saudi Arabia, Pakistan and Morocco.

Hamas has never targeted Westerners either inside or outside Palestine. This is a strict policy by the movement that has been adhered to over years without a single exception. Al-Qaeda and ISIS, by contrast, consider Westerners as legitimate targets anywhere, be they combatants or civilians. Attacking the World Trade Center on 9/11 was the culmination of al-Qaeda thinking and practice, and demonstrates the extent to which al-Qaeda will go in implementing its indiscriminate strategy. Similar atrocities committed by al-Qaeda against civilians by bombing trains in Madrid and London in March 2004 and July 2005 fall far outside any thinking or strategy of Hamas; so also would the targeting of any other civilian groups of Westerners, such as blowing up tourists, hotels or residential complexes of Western expats. For ISIS, their brutal conduct during their control under the so-called 'the Islamic State' in Syria and Iraq was never condoned by Hamas.

The nature of Hamas is also completely different from other two groups. In the first place, Hamas is a Palestinian movement, and its membership, leadership and main base is Palestinian, unlike the international nature of al-Qaeda and ISIS. Further, Hamas is a multifaceted social and political organization thriving within defined national borders and parameters, unlike the other two organizations. The military provision of the Hamas movement is just one of its many other aspects. It has engaged in a political and democratic process, in 2006, like any other Palestinian party, publicly and with very well-known leaders. Al-Qaeda and ISIS, by contrast, are completely secretive and underground organizations. Both confine themselves mostly to military activities without any political or social programme, while democratic practices and peaceful means are ruled out completely.

Are we witnessing the rise of an 'Islamic and radical arc', starting from Iran, spanning Syria, Hizbullah and then Hamas?

When Hamas won the elections of 2006, Iran was on the rise, defying the United States and the world by enriching uranium, threatening to make the life and tasks of the American troops in Iraq very difficult, and supporting Syria and Hizbullah in Lebanon against US policies and allies. Iran was jubilant over Hamas's victory, and it started to talk about an 'axis of resistance' starting from Tehran, passing through Iraq where many of Iran's allies are, through Damascus to Lebanon's Hizbullah, and ending in Palestine with Hamas. Later on, after the failure of most Arab revolutions of 2010–2011 and beyond, Iran consolidated its influence over Syria and expanded to Yemen by supporting the Houthis. This defiant alliance was declared to be against the United States and Israel and their arrogant policies in the region. Initially, Iran's challenge to US policies in the region was tailored specifically to the US impasse in Iraq after the invasion of 2003. The eventual American withdrawal from Iraq in 2011 gave way to further Iranian leverage over Iraq. Beyond Iraq, Iran has indeed consolidated its dominance in the region and increased its support to Hizbullah and Hamas as well as other groups. Hamas benefited greatly from this support and from being part of this 'axis of resistance'. Iran's support was crucial for Hamas in all aspects during the movement's rule of the Gaza Strip (2007–2023). Hamas's military capabilities and training, as well as its performance against the successive Israeli wars on Gaza Strip owe much to Iran's support.

8

Hamas and the West

HAMAS AND THE WEST

Does Hamas see the West as an enemy?

In general, Hamas's perception of the West is negative. In common with prevailing thinking in Palestinian and Arab circles, Hamas holds the West – and particularly Britain, in the way that it handled both Zionist immigration in its mandate period administration and its pull-out in 1948 – responsible for the creation of Israel. This creation of a historically remote Jewish 'homeland' in 1948, in the heart of land that was and had been a solidly Arabic homeland for long centuries, resulted in endless wars and an intractable bloody conflict. Hamas also blames the West, particularly the United States at the present, for continuous and unconditional support for Israel, at the complete expense of the Palestinian people, who are the only ones who seemingly have no rights in this matter. The West is perceived by Hamas, and by Palestinians in general, to be the staunch backer and protector of Israel.

Over the decades since 1948, Western policies concerning the conflict in the Middle East have contributed to the cumulatively repulsive perceptions of the West held across the entire Arab world. Because of Western support, Israel has acquired the mightiest military power in the region, including nuclear capabilities, from technology that was transferred to it in the first place by France and Britain, then by the United States. With Western backing and a population of less than 10 million, Israel has also enjoyed a vibrant economy, with a GDP of US$530 billion according to IMF figures in 2024. That comes not too far from the total of US$580 billion for the neighbouring Arab countries including Egypt, Syria and Jordan together, whose total population is more than 140 million. Israel had a GDP per capita exceeding US$55,000, compared with a mere US$491 in the Palestinian case.

Other wars in the area were seen to have been encouraged or led by the West to further weaken the Arabs in the region and maintain a superior position for Israel. The two Gulf wars against Iraq in 1990 and in 2003 reinforced the thinking of Hamas, and many Palestinians and Arabs, that the West is and has been stridently against any Arab military power that could ever potentially counter Israel's military arsenal. Hamas has also repeatedly pointed out the influence that Jewish lobbies have had on the policies of Western governments, particularly in the United States. One manifestation of the supportive policies of Israel is the American Qualitative Military Edge (QME) congressional consensus, which ensures Israel's acquisition of the best American military technology that keeps a substantial gap over all other countries in the Middle East.

On the Palestinian issue specifically, Hamas sees the Western countries as never having exerted any serious pressure on Israel to comply even with the long list of UN resolutions on Palestine drafted carefully by the West itself. This list starts with Resolution 191 of 1949, giving Palestinian refugees the right to return to their lands and compensation for losing their homes and properties, and for being forced out of Palestine by the creation of the State of Israel in 1948. In the aftermath of the 1967 war and Israel's occupation of the West Bank (including East Jerusalem) and the Gaza Strip, the United Nations issued Resolutions 242 and 338 calling upon Israel to 'withdraw from lands that it occupied' and rejecting the Israeli annexation of East Jerusalem.

The Palestinians and Arabs in general have felt dismayed by almost every single UN resolution on Palestine. These resolutions have been drawn up, as Hamas has often reiterated, by the

Western powers in ways that have always ultimately secured the interests of Israel in the first place. However, Arabs and Palestinians eventually accepted all these resolutions. The irony is that Western countries have shown a complete lack of commitment to the UN resolutions that they themselves have brokered, and have had no interest whatsoever in pressurizing their prodigy Israel to implement these resolutions. In the successive Israeli wars against the Gaza Strip since 2008 and up until the genocidal war in 2023–2024, American and Western support of Israel has never yielded, creating a deeper sense of hatred and antagonism.

Ultimately, what shapes Hamas's negative perception of the West is not only the legacy of past biased Western policies concerning the Palestine–Israel question, but also the current persistence in not changing these policies and doing nothing when agreed-upon solutions are not upheld. Even despite this, Hamas does not consider the West to be its enemy. In its literature and declarations, Hamas keeps confirming that its sole enemy is Israel, and its battlefield is clearly limited to the boundaries of the historic land of Palestine. This has been a pragmatic position by which Hamas has avoided expanding the line of combat with its foes. Over years of acquired experience and maturation, Hamas's view of the West has become more sophisticated, and it is able to differentiate between various players and their different policies. Equally important has been Hamas's repeated distinction between the 'official West', that is governments and politicians, and the ordinary peoples in the West, many of whom have been supportive of Palestine.

Has Hamas targeted Westerners inside or outside of Palestine?

Hamas has never targeted Westerners either inside or outside Palestine. It has never considered individual Westerners, or even Western military and economic entities, as enemies or legitimate targets. The documented literature of Hamas as well as the record of events since its foundation attest not only to this strict policy but also to the ability of Hamas to uphold it. This policy is grounded firmly on two premises. The first premise relates to the above idea that Hamas does not consider the West either officially or practically to be an enemy. Therefore, Westerners and Western institutions and interests in Israel or in the West Bank and the Gaza Strip have scrupulously never been targeted.

The second premise is that Hamas distinguishes clearly between Western policies and Western publics and individuals. It publicly and disparagingly criticises the West's biased policies over the conflict with Israel. Yet, it has developed amicable contacts with many Western organizations, experts, supporters and ordinary people. Hamas's leaders talk about people in the West as being kept in the dark over what their governments truly do against the people of the Middle East. They say that open-minded Westerners who are keen to know about the situation in Palestine without prejudice easily understand the justness and fairness of the Palestinians' complaints.

Hamas's ascent to power in 2006 has only enhanced its pragmatic policies towards the West and Westerners. Senior officials, leaders of the movement and ministers of Hamas's government have all shown eagerness to open channels with the West. Despite the initial US-EU embargo against Hamas, its government has managed to defiantly survive that and to increasingly broaden its network of contacts with Western officials and institutions.

What are Hamas's perceptions of Western civilization and ideals?

Hamas's views and perceptions on Western culture and values have basically been drawn from the school of thought of its mother movement, the Muslim Brotherhood. A formative thought of the Islamists' and Hamas's view of the West is the distinctions between the scientific, technological and administrative aspects of Western civilization, and its underlying philosophies and values. Hamas, as well as other mainstream Islamist movements, accepts what it sees to be the 'neutral scientific' advancements of the West, and faces no principled trouble in borrowing and using them. It refuses to countenance, however, what it considers to be the 'materialistic morality' of Western modernity, and the lack of spirituality: the marginalization of the divine, and the secularization of humanity.

In practice, Hamas's dealing with, and de facto adoption of, 'imports' of Western political modernity expose the relative infirmity of the theoretical distinction between these technological and non-technological aspects of the West. In the absence of sufficient Hamas literature on these issues specifically, Hamas's political practice shows that the movement is actually absorbing more 'Western' values than it would like to acknowledge. Aspects of Western-sourced political modernity have been consciously or subconsciously internalized by Hamas and manifested in its political, organizational and societal interactions. For example, the very nature of Hamas's liberation struggle has evolved on the nation-state concept (not the borderless Islamic *Ummah* notion), its party-based hierarchy follows the formation of political parties in the West, its internal affairs are run on Western democratic practices, and its political rhetoric encompasses such Western notions as human rights and citizenship, in addition to the rule of the majority and the rule of law.

Many of Hamas's senior figures, and since 2006 Hamas's cabinet ministers, were trained in the West, or at universities that teach according to Western methods. Hamas's experts in various fields such as science, agriculture, administration, accounting, urban and rural planning, education, medicine and engineering perform their expertise in ways that were originally Western-fashioned. As can be seen with many other blue-collar Islamists, underneath the religious wrappings and appearances lies a technocrat essence that is driven by the pursuit of perfection and self-interest.

HAMAS AND THE UNITED STATES

What perceptions do the United States and Hamas have of each other?

The US perception of Hamas almost reproduces the Israeli one. When Hamas first emerged in the late 1980s and early 1990s, there were signs of tentative, pragmatic soundings. Indirect contacts and messages were delivered to Hamas via US ambassadors in the region or people around them. The stated aim was to closely 'explore' the positions and attitudes of the rising movement. In late 1992 and early 1993, the Americans had official contact and meetings with senior Hamas members in Amman, through the US embassy there. In those years, Israel itself was still hoping that the growing power of Hamas would eventually undermine the PLO and its main Fatah movement, and thus serving Israeli ends. Therefore, the low-key US exploring course of action was indirectly approved of by Israel, insomuch as Israel hoped that the United States would influence Hamas to change its views and strategies.

But as the US/Hamas contacts themselves caught public attention, Israel protested and the US side abruptly ended them. Hamas denounced the US decision to cut off contact, saying that it clearly proved the deep-rooted influence of the Jewish lobby on Washington. Thereafter, the official US position hardened quickly against Hamas. Weeks after ending contact with Hamas, Washington labelled the movement a 'terrorist organization' in its April 1993 report on global terrorism. Initial discussions on whether Hamas was a liberation movement or a terrorist organization were prematurely suppressed within circles of policymakers in Washington.

Later on and following Hamas's embracing of the strategy of suicide bombings on a large scale in 1995 and 1996, the official US position grew more hostile. Washington exerted enormous pressure on the Fatah-led PA during that time to suppress Hamas and dismantle its armed wing – a demand that always fell beyond the PA's capacity. Back home, US authorities banned the work of several Islamic and Palestinian associations and charities in the United States because they were accused of sponsoring Hamas. Politically, the Americans threw their weight with the PA, and saw no role for Hamas unless it would disarm itself completely, denounce 'terrorism' and recognize Israel. Hamas was not interested.

Over the next few years, in addition to their direct and bilateral assault, the United States and Israel continued to lobby the European Union to also proscribe Hamas. The European Union partly yielded and officially decided to consider the military wing of Hamas as a terrorist organization (see more below). The United States declared its 'war on terror' in the aftermath of the 9/11 al-Qaeda attacks in New York and Washington in 2001, and Hamas was further targeted. Pro-Israel neoconservatives in Washington lumped Hamas in with organizations such as al-Qaeda and its likes. In doing so they fulfilled Israeli demands to neutralize the 'national liberation dimension' of Hamas and relegate it to simply being part of 'global terror', although the differences between Hamas and these groups are many and unmistakable (see Chapter 7).

Washington faced the most difficult test concerning Hamas when the movement emerged victorious in the Palestinian Legislative Council (PLC) elections in January 2006. Hamas legitimately formed a government which was promptly attacked by the United States for neither recognizing Israel nor abandoning 'violence'. Ironically, these Palestinian elections themselves had been part of overdue democratic reforms that the PA had been pressured by the Americans and Europeans to undertake. The democracy that the United States had advocated in Palestine as well as in other Arab countries in the period preceding the elections had indeed brought Hamas to power. However, when it came down to it, the United States rejected the outcome of Palestinian democracy and mobilized an international political and financial embargo against the newly formed government. Succeeding in persuading the European Union to join forces with it, it stopped all financial aid to the Palestinians, bringing millions of Palestinians who mostly rely on the salaries paid by the PA to the verge of starvation.

On the other hand, the Hamas perception of the United States has also developed radically in response to the US 'unilateral war' on Hamas. It has just managed to stop one step short from considering the United States an enemy. The theoretical underpinnings upon which Hamas forms its relations with the world, and with Western countries in particular, have remained intact, however. These stress, as articulated in its Introductory Memorandum, that: 'Hamas's dealings with foreign states and international organizations, regardless of any pre-existing political and ideological baggage, will serve the interests of the Palestinian people, their cause, and their rights.' The movement has managed to hold its official line on not attacking other states: 'Hamas has no dispute with any foreign state or international organization, and the movement's policy is not to attack the interests or possessions of foreign states.'

Hamas's government, in 2006–2007, has followed the same line of policy and kept all channels and possibilities open for a new chapter, as a democratically elected Palestinian government dealing with the United States. The latter has shown no interest.

HAMAS AND EUROPE

What perceptions do Europe and Hamas have of each other?

In common with other Palestinian and Arab views, Hamas has nurtured a slightly friendlier attitude to contemporary Europe than to the United States. Europe also used to adopt its own line of policies about the Arab–Israeli conflict in general and the legitimacy of Palestinian rights, though not greatly different from that of the United States.

Hamas looks at Europe as a diverse pool of powers. What separates individual European countries on major foreign issues, demonstrated in the lack of an effective common EU foreign policy, transcends what unites them. Thus, for example, British, French and German positions on Palestine and Hamas vary from Spanish, Irish and Italian positions. These policies even differ further from, for example, one Scandinavian country to another, such as Norway and Sweden. Given this, Hamas has kept channels open and always pursued new ones with Europe. Both on the collective EU level and on the individual state level, Hamas has managed to have its voice heard in a reasonable way. Through European embassies in the Middle East, or through diplomats in the West Bank and the Gaza Strip, Hamas has maintained quiet European contacts, despite official declared proscription of the movement.

In September 2003, the European Union decided to denounce Hamas, while joining the US 'war on terror'. This decision implied that Hamas members, leaders or affiliated organizations would be banned from operating in any EU countries – something that never actually took place anyway. But to the dismay of Hamas and many European experts and diplomats, this pronouncement on the part of the EU could only be viewed as European collusion with hostile US foreign policy as pursued by the neo-conservatives. With that decision, the EU has effectively crippled itself from playing an effective role in Hamas-related Palestinian affairs. In particular, the EU has jeopardized its pivotal role in brokering temporary 'truces' with Hamas – a role which it played several times during the second Intifada of 2000.

The EU has also been perplexed on other issues concerning Hamas. A major one is how to deal with the effective and widespread grassroots Hamas-affiliated organizations. On the ground, and apart from the aid directed to the PA government, multi millions of annual EU funds have to be channelled to NGOs for community projects, where the social-charitable bedrock of Hamas has been very efficient. It would be strongly questionable to fund only ineffectual and often corrupt non-Hamas-run organizations, while dismissing effective and transparent Hamas ones. This dilemma multiplied even more when Hamas won the majority of local municipality elections in 2005 in the West Bank and Gaza Strip. Municipalities are the main providers of basic living services, and have always been thought of as apolitical bodies that the EU could deal with financially without sensitivities. When the social-charitable wing of Hamas took control of most of them, and in a short period of time showed considerable achievements, the EU was further embarrassed by not cooperating with them.

Since Hamas formed its government as a result of winning the 2006 PLC elections, the EU has faced the same dilemma but on an unprecedented scale. Hamas is now the official democratically elected government of the Palestinians, with which the EU should be dealing. Unlike the United States, the EU is looked on by the majority of Palestinians as more even-handed, humane and sensitive towards the suffering of the Palestinians, and less under the yoke of Jewish-Israeli lobbying. Thus, Europe has been shouldering a moral burden that materializes in the form of humanitarian assistance to the Palestinians, a burden which, it has to be said, has also been approved and acknowledged by other players, including the United States itself.

The European dilemma over Hamas was compounded exponentially in the April 2006 decision to suspend all forms of official aid to the Palestinians, pending Hamas's recognition of Israel and denunciation of violence. EU foreign ministers have approved a temporary suspension of US$600 million in annual aid to the Palestinians. Ben Bot, the Dutch foreign minister, voiced the justification of this move when he said: 'The Palestinian people have opted for this government, so they will have to bear the consequences.'*

---

*   Al Jazeera, 'EU Halts Palestinian Aid', 10 April 2006, www.aljazeera. com/news/2006/4/10/eu-halts-palestinian-aid.

For its part, Hamas's government has resolutely refused conditional aid but has tried to tone down its militant discourse. It has strongly condemned the European decision, which it considers to be a collective punishment against the Palestinian people. The entire reaction against the Palestinian elections has been viewed by Hamas, and many others, as a scandalous exemplification of hypocritical Western politics. An outcome of free and fair democratic elections has been shamefully rejected because the winners are not pro-West, or willing to accept or implement what has been imposed on them by their enemy, Israel. Hamas, however, has been able to do something of what it does best – exploiting the cracks and differences, in this case between European countries – to make some leaps over and around some of the obstacles of the EU decision. Again, quietly several European countries have acted outside the 'official EU policy' and are maintaining their channels and cooperation with the Hamas government.

Are we going to see Hamas members as Palestinian ambassadors in London, Paris, Brussels and Washington, among other capitals?

It is not a remote possibility that senior Hamas members will be acting as Palestinian ambassadors in Western and European cities. A far more highly unlikely idea – that of Hamas having become the Palestinian government in the first place – has already materialized. If Hamas survives the enormous pressures inside Palestine and the international blockade imposed on its government, all possibilities are open. In principle, the Hamas-run Palestinian foreign ministry has the discretion of appointing Palestinian ambassadors around the world. Judging from Hamas's past eagerness to cultivate its image and public relations, it should be expected that Hamas will reshuffle the current Palestinian diplomatic structure. Perhaps there are two reasons that would induce Hamas to do so. First would be the urgent need to reform Palestinian foreign affairs, in terms of both organization and message. Many of the present long-serving Palestinian ambassadors have run out of ideas and enthusiasm, especially those who have spent long head-banging years in their current posts – up to 20 years in certain cases. Equally important to Hamas will be the need to dispatch envoys abroad who are organizationally closer to the movement, or loyal to its political line. But once again, all depends on how successful Hamas's government will be in enduring the initial siege that it is facing in these early days. As events have proven later on, those predictions had no chance in reality as Hamas was removed from governance and, as of 2007, locked in the Gaza Strip with no single state officially acknowledging it as a ruling party there.

9

Hamas's Leadership and Structure

LEADERSHIP

What does the leadership hierarchy of Hamas look like?

The leadership structure of Hamas is divided into two somewhat parallel but slightly dissimilar parts: one inside Palestine and one outside Palestine. The 'inside' leadership has always been promoted from the rank and file of the movement via internal elections, a practice that is well established within Islamist movements that have a Muslim Brotherhood background and traditions. The 'outside' leadership evolved differently because Hamas understandably does not have the same sort of membership organization outside Palestine that it has in the West Bank and the Gaza Strip. This outside-Palestine leadership was originally formed in coordination with the 'inside' Hamas, primarily as a back-up mechanism at the time when the movement was formed in the late 1980s. It was plausibly thought that Hamas would need external support, financially and politically, and this was to be the job of the outside leadership in exile.

The strictly disciplined membership of Hamas is drawn from across poor and middle-class Palestinians, with a strong presence in refugee camps and in the most deprived areas. Many better-off Palestinians also give their loyalty to Hamas, in cities that are well known to be traditionally conservative such as Hebron and Nablus. Members of Hamas in local areas elect their representatives to the leading party body, *Majlis ash-Shoura* (the Consultative Council), which is charged with outlining the overall strategy of the Hamas movement. This council in turn chooses members of the smaller 'Political Bureau' of between 10 and 20 people, who deal with daily affairs.

The Consultative Council and the Political Bureau establish specialized committees that look after various aspects of Hamas's activities: charitable and social, educational, membership, military, financial, media and public relations; religious, women's affairs and so on. There is considerable, if deliberate, vagueness on the exact chain of command and control between the top political leadership and the Al-Qassam military wing. For security reasons, Hamas keeps ample distance between the functioning of each of its branches, and distances all of them from the military wing in particular.

Hamas's leadership is effectively divided between three geographical areas: the West Bank, the Gaza Strip (both inside Palestine) and exile communities, largely in Jordan, Lebanon and Syria (constituting 'outside' Palestine). Over the first 15 years or so of the movement's political life, power was more or less evenly distributed among these three parts. As from 2005 onwards, after the Israeli withdrawal from the Gaza Strip and until the 2023–2024 Israeli war, one could contend that the Hamas branch and leadership in the Gaza Strip has been the most powerful, effectively in the driving seat. In general, the balance of power has always favoured the inside leadership. After Hamas came to power in 2006, the inside leadership was strengthened even further. But while it is safe to say that the two-branched inside leadership (in the West Bank and the Gaza Strip) controls the muscles of the movement, the outside leadership controls financial resources and external contacts.

Over the years, this three-branched leadership has managed to exhibit an efficient 'decision-making management'. The challenge Hamas has faced in this regard has included not only sharing decision-making, but also day-to-day procedural management and coordination between the three branches. Hamas's spokespeople keep emphasizing the 'collective leadership' nature of their movement over personalities, and in practice they have shown a significant amount of adherence to this principle. For almost three decades since 1987, there had been no authoritarian personalities or ultra-charismatic leaders who have used their influence to impose any individual vision on the entire movement, as was the case with the PLO, Fatah and Yasser Arafat, for example. Sheikh Ahmad Yasin, the founder of Hamas and its charismatic leader until his assassination by the Israelis in 2004, was part of a collective leadership and did not consolidate the power in his own hands. Things took a different turn with the rise of Yahya Sinwar, Hamas's leader in the Gaza Strip since 2017. Sinwar's legitimacy and popularity comes from a long track-record in resistance, Israeli prison and co-foundation of Hamas's military wing. Determined, fearless and admired by Hamas's rank and file, he speedily out passed other leaders in Hamas, inside and outside Palestine. As proven in the 2023–2024 war, his unique position of straddling both military and political leadership in the Gaza Strip enabled him to amass authority and power never before enjoyed by any previous individual leader in the movement.

How cohesive and united is Hamas, and are there radicals and moderates inside it?

Hamas is a highly sophisticated organization, with a diverse membership yet with a coherent structure and strong culture that ensures internal harmony. One could argue that between the River Jordan and the Mediterranean Sea and since 1948, this is the only political/military organization (be they Palestinians or Israelis) that has preserved its unity over the long decades of struggle against colonial Zionism. Since its formation in the late 1980s, there have been no splits or even small splinter groups breaking away. This is partly due to the religious values that encourage cohesion and disparage rifts, and partly due to its organizational discipline and background, rooted in the Muslim Brotherhood culture. Central to this discipline is the prioritization of unity over temporal strategic gains that could create deep and risky differences. Also, the challenges that have faced Hamas have fed into its united stand. Confronted by extreme Israeli measures since coming into being, and then by a series of crackdowns by the Fatah-led PA since 1994, a deep sense of solidarity and purpose has only been consolidated further by all these security limitations and even arrests in neighbouring Arab countries.

Although Hamas has remained cohesive, the movement has witnessed the emergence of various and different views on some of the major issues. Moderate and radical voices have been markedly present at certain conjunctures, especially regarding the continuation of the strategy of suicide attacks. Some senior figures would project staunch positions on one issue, where others would use milder tones, leaving the door ajar for options and interpretations. The most important observation, however, is that there has been no development of any discrete group within Hamas that is geographically based, or politically or ideologically cohesive, that could be labelled as a 'radical' or 'moderate' faction. It is particularly inaccurate to issue a general description of the outside or inside leadership of Hamas as either moderate or radical, or to say that Hamas in general or in its leadership in the Gaza Strip is more radical or moderate than Hamas's leadership outside Palestine or vice versa. Actually, moderate and radical voices do exist within all three branches of the movement.

Therefore, the dichotomy of radicals–moderates that some tend to apply to the outside–inside leaderships of Hamas, or to the Gaza Strip–West Bank Hamas, is inaccurate. One of the reasons that Hamas has remained united is the inapplicability of that dichotomy to any geographical–ideological separation between its three branches. Had the moderate voices, or the radicals for that matter, overwhelmingly existed in any one of those areas, Hamas would have faced serious trouble and could have split up.

The cohesion and unity of Hamas, however, has faced a most serious challenge since its foundation after it assumed power in the elections of January 2006. Hamas has had to harmonize its organizational responsibilities with governmental ones under tremendous Israeli and Western pressure, without losing the confidence of the people and with close coordination between its three branches. The challenge is extremely complex: top Hamas leaders inside or outside Palestine versus the Hamas prime minister, Hamas government ministers versus Hamas movement leaders, Hamas's external relationships versus the foreign affairs of the Hamas government, and so on. Power and responsibility will inevitably be fragmented, disputed and fought over, and keeping all that under control has required and will require extraordinary skills. Hamas passed the test of managing governance and resistance without any division, and continued to show unity up until now, 2024.

What is the relationship between the political and military wings of Hamas?

The political leadership is the ultimate authority in Hamas. In theory, all other wings and branches are subject to the strategy and guidelines that are drawn by Hamas's Consultative Council and Political Bureau. As already explained, Hamas is multifunctional and has separate 'agencies' to deliver its overall services and strategy. In relation to Hamas's military action, it is the political leadership that decides whether at a certain period of time the military wing should carry on, halt military operations, increase or reduce them. Thus, the giving of a general green or red light is calculated politically and channelled through to the military.

At the same time, however, members of the political leadership repeatedly, and in all likelihood truthfully, claim that they know nothing about the specific operational technicalities of the military wing. For security reasons, Hamas's political leadership is kept almost in complete darkness about any detailed timing and places of attacks beforehand. So, while the military wing functions virtually independently, with regards to execution, it is governed by a political strategy that is drawn and exercised by the political leadership.

A central question in this context is the following: if a mutual ceasefire is agreed on, would its military wing be disciplined enough to implement it? Drawing on past experience, the answer is yes. Matters, however, have become more complicated since Hamas has won the 2006 PLC elections, and even more so after controlling power in the Gaza Strip in 2007. The stakes became higher, expectations weightier, and any miscalculation in military decision and action could bring costly consequences. As consolidating control over the Strip was a pressing issue, the need for the military in internal security and control multiplied, thus their role and leverage within the movement increased. More room has opened up for dissatisfaction and friction between the political and military wings. Previously, the military wing of Hamas has shown a great deal of discipline. On several occasions when Hamas's political leadership decided to stop military attacks for either political, security or strategic considerations, the military wing acted accordingly. During the lifetime of the organization, there has been no rift visible between the two Hamas wings.

For at least a year prior to its assumption of power, Hamas committed itself to 'a period of calm' brokered by Egypt, according to which Israel would stop targeting Hamas leaders and Hamas would stop its attacks. After Hamas's victory, it extended (unilaterally) that period of calm. Hamas acknowledged the pressure of other priorities which needed to be addressed urgently by the now Hamas government, and set aside the headache of military attacks, at least until matters became clearer.

As Hamas halted its attacks against Israel during its self-proclaimed period of calm, Fatah and other Palestinian factions started their own series of attacks – partly to embarrass Hamas and partly in response to the unstoppable Israeli attacks which were also aimed at provoking Hamas. While neither retaliating against the Israeli provocations, nor matching the attacks of rival factions, Hamas's military wing started showing signs of dissatisfaction and unrest. In the end, and as Hamas managed to spread its tight control over the Gaza Strip, all other factions were effectively subdued and further power gained by Hamas's military internally and externally.

Generally, one of Hamas's worst-case scenarios lies in the possibility of its political leadership losing control over the military, or part of it. It is indeed a far possibility given all the wars and events that the movement have experienced. However, the 2023–2024 war came at massive and unprecedented scale of brutality and death on the Palestinian side and many questions are being raised by Palestinians that Hamas's military needs to tackle. It is still too early to anticipate the course of events within and around Hamas after the war.

Who was Sheikh Ahmad Yasin, the founder of Hamas, and what is his significance?

Sheikh Ahmad Yasin is considered to be the founder, the spiritual figurehead and the most historic figure of Hamas. Fully paralyzed in a wheelchair since he was eleven years old, the calm and charismatic leader was until his death the most popular personality in the Gaza Strip. At the age of 66, he was killed by an Israeli helicopter, along with nine other Palestinians, just after finishing dawn prayers on 22 March 2004 at one of the Gaza City mosques.

When Yasin was aged ten, in 1948, his family and tens of thousands of Palestinians were forced out of their homes and villages and driven to areas outside the 'redistributed' territory that would ever since be known as Israel. He and his family became refugees in the Gaza Strip, where he lived a miserable and illness-plagued life. Despite his bad health, he became very active politically and religiously. Sheikh Yasin was one of the founders of the Muslim Brotherhood in the Gaza Strip, as well as the founder of the 'Islamic Complex', an Islamic educational and charitable institution that was for many years the centre of Islamic activism in the area.

A schoolteacher by profession, Sheikh Yasin ('sheikh', in addition to being a formal title of address for a hereditary chieftain or village leader, is often and in this case used by the community simply as a mark of deep affection and respect) was sentenced to prison twice by the Israeli military courts, first for 13 years in 1985, then for life in 1991 on charges of directing military cells against Israeli soldiers. On both occasions, he was eventually freed through deals. In 1985, Israel was compelled to free him with other Palestinian prisoners in return for releasing Israeli soldiers captured by Palestinian factions in South Lebanon. In 1997, he was freed after pressure by the late King Hussein of Jordan, who became infuriated with Israel for sending spies to Jordan to try to assassinate another Hamas leader, Khaled Mish'al, who was in the country at that time.

Sheikh Yasin was Hamas's main ideologue, mobilizer, pragmatist and populist. Projecting the typical model of a restless Islamist leader whose pragmatism never eclipsed his dreams of a principled utopia, Yasin's views and perceptions have formed to a large extent the political orientation of the movement. It was he who suggested the idea of a *hudna* (truce), with which Hamas could reach a mutual ceasefire with Israel, without breaking from its religious or nationalist principles. It was he who declared that 'civil war' between Palestinians was a 'no go' area. Even if Hamas was continuously attacked by the PA and its main Fatah faction, Hamas should never retaliate, Yasin insisted, because that could lead to an internecine Palestinian war. At the social and religious level, Yasin accumulated rare authority in the Gaza Strip. He was a respected arbitrator and judge to whom families and parties in dispute could go and settle their differences.

Yasin's influence preserved a great sense of unity inside Hamas, for he functioned above the level of competition among the second-ranking leaders. But that very same unassailable position of respect indirectly crippled the emergence of innovative ideas and initiatives that could have been suggested by others. Other figures felt the need to stay close to Yasin's ideas so that they were not alienated by the wider membership because of their views. Even after his death, Yasin's legacy and statements are repeatedly referred to by current leaders and senior figures of Hamas.

Another aspect that deserves attention in this context is the simplicity and modesty of Hamas's leaders and its senior personalities. These virtues have always amassed great popularity for Hamas. The highest-ranking Hamas leaders still live side by side with poor and ordinary people in the Gaza Strip (unlike Hamas's leaders outside Palestine, who live a more comfortable life). Sheikh Ahmad Yasin lived, and eventually was killed, in the very same refugee camp to which his family had been forcibly resettled when he was a child in 1948.

When Hamas won the PLC elections in 2006, Hamas's appointed head of government, Ismail Haniya, refused to leave his modest lower-class house and move to the comfortable residence of the former prime minister. In the first cabinet meeting of Hamas's government, which lasted for six hours on 5 April 2006, Haniya and his ministers had very simple humous and falafel sandwiches bought from the local shop for their lunch.

The Hamas cabinet declared that it would reduce by half all the salaries of the ministers and members of parliament, and would never pay them until all other Palestinians had received their salaries. The speaker of the parliament, Aziz Duwaik, another Hamas personality, refused to be allocated a special car with security and protection. He said that he will never cost the government budget an extra penny. Likewise, members of Hamas's leadership outside Palestine project a modest style of life and conduct. For example, Khaled Mish'al, head of Hamas's Political Bureau, surprised other passengers in economy class during his trip from Riyadh to Damascus in March 2006. The Palestinian people compare this simple and close-to-the-people behaviour with the lavish lifestyle and arrogance of top leaders of the defeated Fatah movement and previous senior members of the PA.

During Hamas's rule over the Gaza Strip from 2007 to 2023, the movement conduct and reputation among Gazans was mixed. The puritan image of the short-lived government in 2006 faded away and was replaced by a more realistic one, where good and bad cases in governance could be found. However, compared to the conduct of the PA in the West Bank during the same period of time, the effectiveness of Hamas's rule was much higher according to surveys and studies and its level of corruption were far lower.

Who were the founding and early leaders of Hamas?

Throughout Hamas's lifetime a number of names and faces have become familiar to the outside world as the main figures and spokespeople for the movement. In addition to Sheikh Ahmad Yasin, mentioned above, below is a list of people whose influence and roles are central in the formation of Hamas and its current politics. Yet, before discussing these individuals, it is helpful to say that Hamas leaders (especially those who are inside Palestine) project an almost common profile. The vast majority have: come from poor refugee camps or the lower-middle class; gained university education; belonged in their early youth to the Muslim Brotherhood organization either in the West Bank or the Gaza Strip (or abroad in the case of the outside leadership); spent a number of years in Israeli prisons; and either have been killed or have been targeted to be killed by the Israeli army. In terms of religious adherence, all of Hamas's leaders are deeply religious and conservative by the standards of ordinary Muslims. Their observance of Islamic teachings at the individual, family and societal level is visible, and it is a fundamental aspect of their personalities. The selective list below includes leaders from all three geographical branches where Hamas leadership operates: the West Bank, the Gaza Strip and in exile.

Abdul 'Aziz al-Rantisi
(Gaza Branch, assassinated by Israel in 2004)

For many years, al-Rantisi was considered to be the second in the leadership ranking after Sheikh Ahmad Yasin, the movement's long-time and spiritual leader. Al-Rantisi assumed leadership of Hamas in the Gaza Strip, in spring 2004, after the Israelis assassinated Sheikh Yasin. Less than a month after that, however, al-Rantisi himself was assassinated. He was one of the founders of Hamas and a lifelong comrade of Sheikh Yasin. Charismatic and articulate by nature, he combined modesty towards his 'brothers' in the movement and toughness towards his enemies, which made him widely popular within Hamas and with Palestinians at large. He held hardline views but never contradicted Yasin's more moderate outlook. Secular Palestinian politicians and intellectuals were never impressed by his politics or discourse, however. He was perceived by them to be a master at packaging unrealistic demands in very powerful religious rhetoric.

Al-Rantisi was born in 1947 in a village near Jaffa. A year after that, in the wake of the British pull-out from Palestine, war broke out between Zionist and Arab factions, and with the imposition of the new State of Israel, hundreds of thousands of Palestinians were driven from their villages and cities, including al-Rantisi's family, who ended up in the Khan Yunis refugee camp in the Gaza area. He went up through high school there, travelled to Egypt to study medicine, then returned to Khan Yunis as a paediatric practitioner. In later stages, he became a lecturer at the Islamic University of Gaza.

From his early youth, he was politically active with a clear-cut Islamic leaning, and was a member of the Palestinian Muslim Brotherhood organization. After the founding of Hamas, he was arrested several times, then in 1992 he was deported to South Lebanon for one year with more than 400 Palestinians. He was immediately jailed upon his return, in 1993, and remained in jail until 1997. A year after his release, he was jailed again but this time by the Palestinian Authority (yielding to Israeli pressure) because of his Hamas activities. When the jail itself was targeted by Israeli shelling, the Palestinian Authority released him and other Palestinians. In June 2003, he narrowly escaped an Israeli attempt to assassinate him, during which his bodyguard and a child passer-by were killed. His successful assassination a year later gave way to the rise of Mahmoud al-Zahar.

Mahmoud al-Zahar
(Gaza Branch, foreign minister in the Hamas government in
2006–2007)

Born in 1945, al-Zahar is a veteran Hamas figure, who became
the foreign minister in Hamas's elected government in early
2006. He studied medicine in Cairo, where he obtained a master's
degree, then practised as a doctor in the Gaza Strip. During his
early youth, first in Gaza then in Egypt, al-Zahar became an
active member of the Muslim Brotherhood. He was the founder
of several medical societies and cofounder of the Islamic University in Gaza.

He has been known for a long time as one of Hamas's relatively moderate voices. At one point, in 1996, he issued a rare
independent public appeal through the media to Hamas's Al-
Qassam military wing, asking them to halt their suicide attacks.
Immediately, he was harshly criticized by members of Hamas and
temporarily marginalized.

After the assassination of Sheikh Yasin and al-Rantisi, he was
elected as Hamas's leader in the Gaza Strip. He himself was the
target of several assassination attempts by the Israelis. In September 2003, an Israeli F16 bombed his house in Gaza, wounding
him and his daughter and killing his 29-year-old son Khaled.
The house was destroyed and many other people were killed or
wounded. The impact of that attack and the great loss of his son,
combined with an increasing drive on his part to compensate for
his lack of the charisma that his two predecessors enjoyed, led to
Al-Zahar's stance and discourse becoming noticeably radicalized
compared with his initial leanings. Yet, when he became foreign
minister, he issued mixed messages of moderation and radicalism, and the more moderate al-Zahar started to take over once
again.

Early on, al-Zahar was perhaps the first of Hamas's figures to
talk about a 'pragmatic' interim solution to the conflict with Israel.
In March 1988, four months after the foundation of Hamas, he

presented a four-point proposal to Shimon Peres, then the Israeli foreign minister, which included the following:

1. Israel would declare its willingness to withdraw from the territories it occupied in 1967, including Jerusalem in particular.
2. The Occupied Territories would be placed in the custody of the United Nations.
3. The Palestinian people inside and outside Palestine would name their representatives to the peace talks in whatever manner they chose. Israel could not object to the choice unless the Palestinians also had the right to object to the representatives of Israel.
4. At a time agreed by both sides, negotiations would begin among the representatives concerning all issues relating to all rights.*

Ismael Haniya
(Gaza Branch, prime minister in the Hamas government in 2006–2007, and Head of Hamas during 2023–2024 war on Gaza)

Born in the Shati refugee camp in Gaza in 1962, Haniya grew up completely immersed in the misery of the Palestinians who lost their land and ended up in impoverished refugee camps. His family was displaced from Asqalan near Jaffa during the 1948 war. Haniya finished his university degree in Arabic language studies from the Islamic University in Gaza, where his leadership fortunes were shaped as a prominent figure among the Islamist students in the early 1980s.

With the formation of Hamas, Haniya was at the forefront as one of the youngest founding members. After the first Intifada in 1987, he was arrested several times and, in 1992, he was deported to South Lebanon with more than 400 Islamist activists.

---

* Khaled Hroub, *Hamas: Political Thought and Practice* (Washington, DC: Institute of Palestine Studies, 2000), 74.

Although Haniya was less visible to the outside world than the two above-mentioned senior members, he was no less significant. A well-known moderate voice within Hamas, Haniya amassed deep respect with the membership and great popularity within the broader Palestinian constituency. Sheikh Yasin, the spiritual leader of Hamas, appointed him as his first confidant and aide, and he remained close to Yasin until the latter's death.

Haniya was one of the most acknowledged moderate senior figures in Hamas. He was always the man who sought settlements between his group and its foes. During periods of friction between Hamas and other Palestinian factions, Haniya was always seen as a moderator who was trusted by all parties and able to pacify volatile situations. His calmness and popularity, modesty and moderation led Hamas to charge him with the responsibility of leading its 2006 election campaign, which it won roundly. Since then, Haniya continued to be part of Hamas's politburo, until 2017 when he was elected as the head of Head of Hamas inside and outside Palestine – a position that he held until his assassination by Israel on 31 July 2024 in Tehran.

Haniya's moderate approach goes back to the mid-1990s. Hamas decided to boycott the 1996 elections for the first Palestinian Legislative Council – which was set up according to the Oslo Accords signed two years earlier between Israel and the PLO – because 'they were an outcome of the capitulating Oslo deal'. Haniya and three other Hamas figures decided to run for the elections, in opposition to the movement's stand. Under mounting pressure, Haniya and his colleagues backed down and adhered to the Hamas official line. At the time, Haniya explained his pro-participation position to this author, which gives great glimpses into his political thinking. He outlined eight carefully written points that show the advantages of taking part in the elections, as follows:

1. Participation in the elections will not amount to a surrender of Hamas's political position as long as the movement

contests the elections under the banner of all the principles with which it is identified.

2. Participation would guarantee a legitimate political presence for the movement after the elections, and Hamas would have secured a guarantee against decrees that could outlaw the movement.

3. Hamas would be kept informed of, and be in a position to participate in, the formulation of legislation governing civil society that will emanate from the elected Council, thus securing a guarantee against exclusion.

4. Hamas would be in a position to introduce significant and badly needed reforms in domestic institutions and could combat the spread of corruption.

5. Hamas could participate in the creation of official institutions, something for which it always has asked, in keeping with its emphatic desire to participate in civil society and to promote internal development.

6. Hamas would be well informed of developments in the final status negotiations and what is to come after that.

7. Hamas would secure protection for itself and the institutions it has sponsored over the years, and its political leaders and prominent figures would enjoy parliamentary immunity.

8. Participation in the elections would be a response to the demand of a significant number of our people who are looking for honest alternative and God-fearing candidates so that they can rest at ease about action in various areas of life.

Aziz Duwaik
(West Bank Branch, speaker of the Palestinian Legislative Council 2006–2007)

Born in 1948 in Hebron in the West Bank, into a middle-class family, Duwaik completed his high school in the city, and then obtained three master's degrees in education and urban planning before finishing his PhD in urban planning at the University of Pennsylvania. In his early years, he joined the Muslim Brotherhood and then Hamas, and became a prominent personality in the city of Hebron. He was deported to South Lebanon in 1992 with other Hamas members for one year, where he became very well known as the English-speaking spokesman for the 415 deportees. After his return to Hebron, he distanced himself from political activities, immersing himself in his academic professorship at al-Najah University in Nablus, where he established the Department of Geography.

His almost sudden reappearance on the public scene after the election, when he was chosen by Hamas as the speaker of the Parliament, was surprising. Because little is known about his political qualities, some question whether he is really fit for the post. Others see his appointment as a smart move on the part of Hamas, who are bringing to such a high-ranking position a man with no enemies and who is a very well-known moderate and professional. Also, his appointment as effectively the third most powerful person in the Palestinian Authority hierarchy (after the president and the prime minister) has reflected Hamas's determination to maintain tight control on power. According to the Palestinian constitution, Duwaik would replace the president Abu Mazen should the latter become incapable of undertaking his responsibilities. After the Palestinian split in 2007 and the dismissal of Hamas's government, Israel arrested Duwaik along with dozens of Hamas's figures including ministers and 16 members of the PLC. Duwaik himself was arrested five times by Israeli security and, in total, has served more than five years in jail.

Naser al-Sha'er
(West Bank Branch, deputy prime minister and minister of education and higher education minister in 2006–2007)

Born in 1961 in Nablus in the West Bank, al-Sha'er is one of the new faces of Hamas who came to public notice at the formation of Hamas's government in 2006. He was an active member and leader of the Islamic bloc at al-Najah University in Nablus, before he left to study in the United Kingdom, where he finished his PhD in Middle East studies at Manchester University. Al-Sha'er has accumulated experience not only in political activism but also in the academic field and research. In the late 1990s, he embarked on a course on religion and democracy at New York University as a research scholar. Before joining the Hamas government, he served as the dean of Islamic Studies and Law at al-Najah University for five years.

Al-Sha'er is considered to be one of the moderate voices within Hamas. His training and travel in the West exposed him to the complexities of world politics and left a visible realist stamp on his thinking. From the Islamic perspective, he has written and published on various subjects such as human rights, the religious curriculum in Palestine, globalization, gender and familial violence. Unless he is sidelined by hardliners in the movement, al-Sha'er will be pivotal in shaping part of Hamas's thinking in the near future. By virtue of his strong background in Islamic studies combined with his modern understanding and sophistication, he could be in the position of theorizing new paths for Hamas in the short term.

Khaled Mish'al
(Exile Branch [mostly in Qatar], head of Hamas outside Palestine during 2023–2024 war on Gaza)

Born in 1956 in the village of Silwad near Ramallah in the West Bank, Mish'al was displaced with his family to Kuwait after the war of 1967. He finished his studies in physics at the University of Kuwait, where he was an active leader of the Islamic bloc, which was the local manifestation of the Palestinian Muslim Brotherhood. In the late 1980s, he became involved in the external leadership circles of the newly established Hamas.

Following the Iraqi invasion of Kuwait, he and his family, along with thousands of previously displaced Palestinians, moved to Jordan where he started to become more known as a Hamas member and continued his Hamas external support. In 1996, Mish'al replaced Mousa Abu Marzouq as the top leader of Hamas outside Palestine, after the arrest of Abu Marzouq in the United States. In Amman, where Hamas's exile leadership was operating (only in the political and media areas as agreed with the Jordanian authorities), Mossad agents attempted to assassinate Mish'al in September 1997 but he survived.

In 1999, the relationship between Hamas and the Jordanian authorities soured greatly after the United States and Israel put pressure on the King of Jordan to expel Hamas's leadership, which he did in November of that year. Since then, the official address of Mish'al has been in Damascus, although he moves constantly between more than one country in the region including Lebanon, Qatar and Iran.

Mish'al is the face of Hamas outside Palestine, charged with strengthening the movement's relationship with governments and outside organizations. In rallying support for Hamas among states and individuals both inside and outside Arab and Islamic circles, there are times when some stand at odds with the other; Mish'al conveys moderate and radical views concurrently, appeasing different audiences. Although articulate and popular among Hamas supporters and within Islamic circles, he is seen by others as lacking charisma and leadership sophistication.

Mousa Abu Marzouq
(Exile Branch, deputy chief of Hamas's Political Bureau)

Born in 1951 in the Rafah refugee camp in Gaza, his family was originally displaced from Yebna village near Majdal during the 1948 war. After finishing his high school in the Gaza Strip, Mousa Abu Marzouq travelled to Cairo, where, in 1976, he obtained a university degree in mechanical engineering, and then moved to the United Arab Emirates for work. In 1981, he moved to the United States to continue postgraduate studies and remained there until he finished his PhD in 1992.

Starting his Islamist political activism in high school and then continuing in Egypt and the United Arab Emirates, his actual rise in prominence came among the Islamic societies in the United States where he headed several associations. By the time of the eruption of the first Intifada in 1987, Abu Marzouq had become very active in supporting and speaking for Hamas. Early on he helped in the establishment of the Islamic University in Gaza, and occupied a seat on its board of governors. Working behind the scenes, he was free to travel between the Gaza Strip, Egypt, the Gulf and the United States, organizing the well-being of the newly established movement. In 1989, he reorganized the structure of Hamas after it had been badly affected by continuous Israeli crackdowns and arrests.

Abu Marzouq moved from the United States to Jordan in 1992, when he was chosen as the head of Hamas's Political Bureau. His new position, however, did not deter him from visiting the United States several times for private business and political activism within Islamic organizations there, who were supportive of Hamas. But he was arrested in 1995 at a New York airport, after Jordan's decision to expel him, and Abu Marzouq remained in a US jail until May 1997, when he was deported to Jordan. Hamas installed Khaled Mish'al in his place as head of the Political Bureau while Abu Marzouq was in prison, and since his release he has been acting as Mish'al's deputy. In 1999, the Jordanian authorities decided to close down Hamas's offices there, forcing him and other leaders to move to Syria, where officially he has remained up to the present.

Abu Marzouq is considered to be a pragmatist. Operational and a good organizer, he is reckless as well. His repeated visits to the United States exhibited carelessness and cost him dearly. He was also criticized in 1994 for what was known then as the 'Political Bureau (PB) Initiative', which was believed to have been his brainchild, offering Israel a solution that was based on the two-state concept, similar to what the PLO was calling for. Abu Marzouq's main points in the PB Initiative were:

1. The unconditional withdrawal of Zionist occupation forces from the West Bank and Gaza Strip, including Jerusalem.
2. The dismantling and removal of the settlements and the evacuation of settlers from the West Bank, Gaza Strip and Jerusalem.
3. The holding of free general elections for a legislative body among the Palestinian people inside and outside [Palestine] so that they can those their own leaders and their real representatives. This legitimately elected leadership alone shall have the right to speak for our people's will and aspirations. It alone shall decide on all the subsequent steps in our struggle with the occupiers.

Where does Hamas get its money from?

There is of course very little public information about the finances or annual budget of Hamas. Before its PLC election victory in 2006, estimates have ranged from as modest a sum as US$10 million for the functioning of all aspects and branches of the organization, to as wild a projection as US$150 million. Prior to 2007, when Hamas controlled the Gaza Strip, and perhaps contrary to the received wisdom created by the press, the smallest fraction of Hamas's budget was allocated to the military aspect. The lion's share actually goes to the social and welfare programmes that the movement provides to the Palestinians, especially the poor. These programmes, along with clean-handed administration and moral discipline, feed Hamas with sustained support and popularity among the Palestinians. Matters changed dramatically over the years from 2007 to 2023, when Hamas had grown into a deeply sophisticated structure in particular in the Gaza Strip, and consolidated external relations with states and non-state actors in the region. It has become difficult for an outside observer to predict Hamas's financial sources or their size, or to differentiate between Hamas's money as an organization and Hamas's government's money, let alone the money that goes to its military wing.

According to Hamas itself, the sources of its funding have been mostly donations coming from individual Palestinian, Arab and Muslim supporters of the movement. It is plausible to believe this claim, given that neither Israel nor the United States has ever accused any state of funding Hamas, apart from Iran. Arab and Muslim countries, however, have been facing domestic pressure to support Hamas and the Palestinians, or at least to leave open the channels for popular support on a non-state basis. Before Hamas's rise to power in 2006 that ended up in it controlling the Gaza Strip, countries in which potential individual or organizational donors were being targeted by Hamas for fundraising tended to turn a blind eye. In so doing, the governments of these countries tried to stand on a middle ground between strong local desires to donate money to Hamas and US pressure prohibiting direct state funding to Hamas. Things have changed radically, however, and governments in the Gulf in particular shut down any funding to Hamas, direct or indirect.

Drying up Hamas's sources of money has always been a high priority of Israeli and US policies. Even funds that were clearly allocated for social services were targeted. The standard Israeli and US claim is that the Islamic social welfare organizations that are controlled by Hamas in the West Bank and Gaza Strip have been channelling funds to support the movement's military activities. In fact, the real purpose behind these Israeli/US accusations is to close down these organizations altogether, to deny Hamas the immense credibility, political currency and the appreciation it draws from them. Thousands of Palestinian families have been living for years on the monthly support given by Hamas's social organizations. By the end of the year 2003, and according to field data, these charities were providing monthly financial assistance to 120,000 Palestinians, with an additional 30,000 receiving help on an annual basis.*

---

* For more details, see Sara Roy, *Hamas and Civil Society in Gaza: Engaging the Islamist Social Sector* (Princeton, NJ: Princeton University Press, 2014).

Hamas has also been successful in soliciting funds from wealthy and middle-class Palestinians in the West Bank and the Gaza Strip. Challenging harsh Israeli obstacles and the American and Western international surveillance of any money that could go to Hamas, the movement has prudently maintained local sources of funding. In hundreds of mosques across Palestinian cities, Hamas supporters donate money that ends up directly in the coffers of Hamas, funding its activities.

When Hamas came to power early in 2006, it faced the new dilemma of securing enormous funds not for its own functioning, but to feed the entire Palestinian population, who were stricken by increased rates of poverty and unemployment. A concerted Israeli–US–European effort succeeded in cutting off the supply of the annual Palestinian Authority operating funds that the previous Fatah administration had received. Their goal has been to bring Hamas's government to a complete collapse, and to teach the Palestinian people a lesson for electing Hamas in the first place. In the eyes of most Palestinians, this international blocking of funds is a punishment against Palestinians for having exercised their free will in the democratic elections that were urged upon them. Ben Bot, the Dutch foreign minister, said on the eve of declaring the EU decision to halt European funds, 'The Palestinian people have opted for this government, so they will have to bear the consequences'.*

---

* Al Jazeera, 'EU Halts Palestinian Aid', 10 April 2006, www.aljazeera. com/news/2006/4/10/eu-halts-palestinian-aid.

10

A 2006 'New Hamas'

HAMAS AND THE 2006 ELECTIONS

In the first 20 years of its existence, the undoubted turning point in Hamas's political life was its unexpected victory in the January 2006 Palestinian Legislative Council elections in the West Bank and the Gaza Strip. Bringing about new realities and challenges, the significance of these elections is tantamount to a paradigm shift not only in the thinking and practice of the movement itself but also across the whole Palestinian political scene (see Chapter 5). A 'new discourse' had indeed been showing up in Hamas's thinking during the campaign for these elections and was consolidated after their win. In fact, Hamas was already readjusting itself to this course of political action a few years earlier.

Why did Hamas as a resistance movement decide to compete for 'governmental power' in the West Bank and the Gaza Strip in 2006 under Israeli ultimate control?

Understanding Hamas's road to the 2006 elections and subsequent power can be furthered by highlighting the meeting of two major developments – one external and the other internal. The external development deals with the international and regional atmosphere created by the American 'war on terror' unleashed in the aftermath of 11 September 2001 attacks. As discussed in the introduction of this Third Edition, Hamas felt the brunt of this 'war' that targeted countries (Iraq, Afghanistan, Syria and Iran, among others) and groups such as al-Qaeda and other Jihadist organisations. Hamas was included in the latter list, and wanted

174

to re-present itself as a political and democratic movement not a 'terrorist' one. This intended shift was made possible as it coincided with the other internal changes, ideological and intellectual, that Hamas had been undergoing in the years before the elections.

On the internal evolution, Hamas has striven hard since its inception in late 1987 to harmonize two impetuses within the movement: the nationalist liberationist drive and the religious Islamist one (see Chapter 2). These two intellectual and mobilizational agendas were neither necessarily contradictory nor fully harmonious. They strode hand in hand at certain periods, clashed with each other at other times, or simply moved at different paces. Which one took the lead and when has depended on the conjunctural political conditions at any given time. Hamas is thus simultaneously a 'nationalist' and 'religious' movement, moulded in the broader Palestinian context whose compass is to liberate the Palestinians from the Israeli occupation. The 'nationalist' and 'religious' have largely overlapped, but sometimes could be seen as a continuum.

Similar to other Palestinian movements, such as Fatah, Hamas's ultimate nationalist aim is to 'liberate Palestine'. Unlike other movements, however, Hamas adopted an Islamist, rather than a secular, ideology in order to achieve this aim. Initially espousing the ideological objective of other classical movements of political Islam, namely, the establishment of an Islamic state, Hamas's early rhetoric emphasized that once the 'liberation' of Palestine was achieved, the resulting Palestinian state would be an Islamic one. In later stages, as explained earlier, this rhetoric about the 'Islamic state' was toned down.

The tension between the 'nationalist' and the 'religious' tendencies within Hamas culminated in the idea of participation in the 2006 elections, and resulted from surrounding pressing conditions, which is the second introductory point to be made. The decision to run for the elections came about only after a traumatic birth in March 2005, impacted by the external factors mentioned above. In the minds of many Hamas supporters (and foes), the decision contrasted severely with Hamas's earlier rejection of any participation in similar elections in 1996. That rejection was based on the insistence that those elections were part and parcel of the Oslo Accords of 1993–1994 between the Palestine Liberation Organization (PLO) and Israel, which Hamas strongly opposed. The 2006 elections, practically speaking, were however organized within the political framework resulting from those Accords, hence the controversy within Hamas prior to its reaching the final decision to participate. In fact, the March 2005 decision was coupled with two equally significant decisions: the suspension of Hamas's suicide attacks against Israel and the agreement in principle to join the PLO. Hamas was thus making important leaps in the direction of playing a more political role and reducing its military activities.

The military factor itself was indeed significant behind Hamas's decision to participate in an electoral process, which would in fact legitimize the very same authority that Hamas has strongly opposed. In the years following the 2000 Intifada, Hamas accumulated considerable military power; at the heart of it was the strong, well-organized and armed military wing, Al-Qassam. In the very same years, however, the Palestinians became exhausted, harvesting no concrete achievements from either the peace talks track of Fatah and the PA or the resistance track of Hamas. Facing a visible impasse and bearing the weight of its ever-growing mini army of more than 10,000 strong men at the time, Hamas felt a pressing need to protect its military force by attaining further forms of legitimacy, within the system and not outside of it. Becoming part of the Palestinian Legislative Council would enable Hamas to maintain its military wing, vetoing any potential measures to crack down on the resistance factions in general, unlike the paralysis that Hamas had suffered in the past when the PA took free rein in imposing crippling measures against any military activity. Thus, the engagement in the political process (through entering the Legislative Council) was envisaged by

Hamas as a way of protecting its military capabilities, whether they are active or idle. A new Hamas had come into the making.

The decision to run for the elections was promptly translated into action. 'On the day following that decision,' as one of Hamas' leaders told me after the announcement of the results of the elections, 'we immediately started practical preparation, wasting no time'. Hamas's campaign for the 2006 elections was organized under the heading of 'Change and Reform'. It issued a significant 'Electoral Platform' of 14 pages covering all political, social, educational, legal and environmental aspects. The most interesting dimension of this electoral platform was the deliberate minimization of the religiosity of Hamas, allowing for more political and nationalist discourse. Most of Hamas's pronouncements in its electoral agenda came to fit neatly within the thinking of any other secular Palestinian faction.

What was the content and significance of Hamas's 'Electoral Platform' for the 2006 elections?

Demarcating the lines of 'newness' in Hamas's thinking, two significant election-born documents were issued by the movement: the 'Electoral Platform for Change and Reform' upon which Hamas ran in the elections, and the 'Government Platform', in which a victorious post-election Hamas suggested a basis for a national unity cabinet to other Palestinian factions in March 2006 (discussed below).

In the 'Electoral Platform', Hamas incorporated the changes and experiences that had evolved in its organization over the past years, and showed how it had developed its perceptions, discourse and priorities. Measured against its original bold positions expressed in the early years of its inception, both in the Charter (discussed in Chapter 2) and elsewhere, the 'Electoral Platform for Change and Reform' promoted an almost new Hamas. Yet, drawing any conclusions about political parties based only on their electoral platforms can be misleading. Parties naturally try to draft their finest political statements at election time in order to attract as many voters as they can, and this electioneering rhetoric does not always reflect their real convictions and politics. Scepticism as a first impression is thus understandable when reading Hamas's carefully written electoral document, where the movement clearly was striving to tone down its controversial views, broaden its national appeal and reposition itself at the heart of mainstream Palestinian politics. This rhetoric will be examined against what Hamas was ready to offer in its cabinet programme, which is dealt with in Chapter 11.

The significance of the 'Electoral Platform' stems from several aspects. First, it provided the political justification for Hamas's own change in position regarding the very idea of participating in any electoral process that was initially a product of the Oslo Accords. Hamas opposed those Accords and never acknowledged the legitimacy of any measures or structures resulting from them, including the PLC and its elections. On the basis of this, Hamas refused to participate in the first round of elections for the Council in 1996.

The Electoral Platform explains that Hamas's participation in the elections 'takes place within a comprehensive programme for the liberation of Palestine and the return of the Palestinian people to their lands, and the establishment of an independent Palestinian state with Jerusalem as its capital'. It reiterates that 'this participation will support resistance as a strategic choice accepted by the Palestinian people to end the (Israeli) occupation'. In confirming these principles in the preamble of its electoral statement, Hamas was anxious to make a clear distinction between its participation and its rejection of the Oslo Accords. Knowing this distinction would not be fully convincing for many Palestinians because the PLC itself is indivisible from the framework of Oslo Agreements, Hamas raised the tone of its rhetoric and asserted that its participation 'constituted a form of its wider resistance programme'. At the end of the long 14-page statement, Hamas made the even bolder statement that 'realities on the ground have made Oslo all but in the past ... all parties including the Zionist occupier speak about the demise of Oslo'.

Second, although the Electoral Platform reiterated the conventional canons of Hamas thinking and outlook regarding the struggle against the Israeli occupation, it did so in more nuanced language than previously. For example, there was neither talk about the 'destruction of Israel' – an eye-catching phrase that has been used repeatedly by the press to describe Hamas's ultimate goal – nor any mention of establishing an Islamic state in Palestine. Instead, the discourse of the Platform focused on 'ending the occupation', a term that cut consistently throughout the length of the document. On two occasions this document borrowed the language of previous literature of Hamas. The first came in the preamble, which stated that Hamas's participation in the elections was an integral part of 'the wider programme for the liberation of Palestine', and the second was mentioned in the first article, which confirmed that 'historic Palestine is part of Arab and Muslim lands, and irrefutably belongs to the Palestinian people'. One could safely argue that these declarations were meant to sustain continuity with the previous discourse of the movement, and represent more rhetoric than politics. This is fairly demonstrated in that the rest of the document offered no mechanisms to implement these goals, as was the case with other detailed and pragmatic declarations in the statement.

Third, in the Electoral Platform document, Hamas gave considerable focus to the themes of 'change and reform', reflected as they are in the very name of its platform of issues for the elections. In fact, it was rather surprising that Hamas, as a self-defined resistance movement with a military/jihadist outlook, chose such a mild theme and name for its election campaign. However, there was no lack of cleverness in concentrating on 'change and reform' against a backdrop of its corrupt and failed Fatah rival, and Hamas's electoral platform effectively relegated 'military resistance' to the back seat. There is simply no comparison between the more weight and detail given to civilian aspects of governance promised by Hamas in this document, and the lesser weight and detail given to military resistance. Attempting to link the urgency of internal reform with the wider cause of the struggle against the Israeli occupation, Hamas stated that:

> Change and reform will endeavour to build an advanced Palestinian civil society based on political pluralism and the rotation of power. The political system of this society and its reformist and political agenda will be oriented toward achieving Palestinian national rights.*

Fourth, the Electoral Platform document significantly provided the broadest vision that Hamas had ever presented concerning all aspects of Palestinian life. Throughout the detailed 18 articles, Hamas covered virtually every aspect of the societal and political setting of the Palestinians. It outlined what it would do if it won the elections in areas including resistance to the occupation, internal affairs, foreign affairs, administration reform and fighting corruption, judicial reform and policies, public liberties and individual rights, educational policy, religious guidance, social policy, cultural and media policy, youth issues, housing policy, health and environmental policy, agricultural policy, economic, financial and fiscal policies, labour issues, and issues over transportation and passage between Gaza and the West Bank.

Hamas had never before tackled such a wide-ranging spectrum of issues. Typically, Hamas (as well as other Islamist movements) has been accused of lack of pragmatic political vision: its rhetoric and mobilization override practical programmes and detailed perceptions. It is clear that this accusation was in the mind of the Hamas members who drafted its Electoral Platform. Compared with previous pivotal documents issued since its inception (such as the Charter in 1988 and the Introductory Memorandum in

---

* For extended analysis of Hamas's Electoral Platform, see Khaled Hroub, 'A "New Hamas" through its New Documents', *Journal of Palestine Studies* 4 (Summer 2006): 6–28.

1993), this document moved Hamas further into the realm of realistic politics, yet without diminishing the visible dose of religious and cultural mobilization that had been injected into it.

Fifth, Hamas's Electoral Platform also implied elements of what could be interpreted as its tacit desire, combined with quiet effort, to achieve the Islamization of society. These elements were received negatively by many secular Palestinians and others. Hamas persistently justifies this stance by arguing that these aspects reflect the true aspirations of society. Many people vote for Hamas at least partly because of these aspects, and the sector of Hamas's electorate who do not are fully aware of the presence of these aspects in the movement's programme, to varying degrees of controversy. Among these aspects is the confirmation that 'Islam is our frame of reference and the system of all political, economic, social and legal aspects of life'.

Other articles stipulate that 'Islamic sharia law should be the principal source of legislation in Palestine', which is a somewhat standard, if ambiguous, statement existing in the constitutions of all Arab and Muslim countries. In this clause and similar ones, the point of controversy is over whether sharia law should be the 'sole and ultimate source', or 'one of the' sources of legislation.

In the articles that dealt with education and social aspects, Hamas's Electoral Platform emphasized that the values of Islam should be respected and included because they provide strength and wholesomeness to society. For secular Palestinians, an even more worrying statement occurred in the context of tackling cultural and media provision, stressing the need for 'fortifying citizens, especially the youth, from corruption, westernization and intellectual penetration.'*

THE SIGNIFICANCE OF HAMAS'S VICTORY IN THE LEGISLATIVE COUNCIL ELECTIONS OF 2006

On 25 January 2006, Hamas, which is still officially branded as a terrorist organization by the United States and the European

---

* See Hroub, 'A "New Hamas" through its New Documents'.

Union, won the Palestinian Legislative Council elections in the West Bank, the Gaza Strip and East Jerusalem and became in charge of the Palestinian Authority. Hamas won 74 seats out of 132 while Fatah, the largest party of the PLO that had controlled the PA until then gained only 45 seats. This stunning triumph ran against the wishes (and efforts) of many parties: its main rival Fatah, Israel, the United States, the European Union, the United Nations and a number of Arab countries. Harvesting an unexpected victory in the elections, Hamas faced a situation for which it had never been prepared: forming a Palestinian government under the framework of Oslo Accords. The movement had long trained its candidates for the Legislative Council to function as an opposition – not a ruling party. After its unexpected victory, Hamas immediately chose to call upon all other Palestinian factions to join it in a coalition government. Leaders of the movement spent almost two months trying to convince other parties to join them. As had been expected, Fatah refused the offer, hoping that an inexperienced Hamas at the top of the Palestinian Authority would quickly fail, which would bring Fatah back to power. Leftist Palestinian factions and other independent personalities equally rejected Hamas's offer, protesting against its government political programme. Their position was hardened by Hamas's refusal to declare bluntly in the government programme that the PLO was the sole and legitimate representative of the Palestinian people. In the end, on 29 March 2006, Hamas formed an exclusive government of its own members and close supporters.

In response to the formation of Hamas's government, the Quartet states (the United States, the European Union, Russia and the United Nations) imposed three conditions before they would establish normal relations with (and provide aid to) the government: recognition of Israel, acknowledgement of all previous agreements between the PLO and Israel, and a complete stop to 'terrorism'. The three conditions were rejected by Hamas. Western and non-Western diplomatic relations with the Hamas government were either immediately severed or not established. In the following months, and apart from a very few countries, Hamas ministers were unwelcome almost everywhere. Many Arab and Muslim countries had carefully synchronized their moves towards the Hamas government with Western policies. The immediate and disastrous outcome of the resulting embargo placed on the government was felt most catastrophically at the level of ordinary Palestinians. European and other international funding to the Palestinian Authority, which is one of the two main sources of income for Palestinian public life, was stopped. The second main source of income, the monthly Palestinian tax revenues controlled and collected by Israel, in accordance with the Oslo Accords, were also frozen.* Caught between the hammer of rising internal dissatisfaction and the anvil of external embargo, Hamas's policies started to grow nervous. Yet the movement and its government has also demonstrated a great level of steadfastness and remained intact and coherent.

In addition to facing the cutting-off of all funds, the Hamas-led government had to endure continuous Israeli military pressure and incursions into areas of the West Bank and the Gaza Strip. At the risk of erosion of its own 'resistance legitimacy', Hamas leaders pressured its military wing to exercise restraint and to maintain the shaky truce (*hudna*) that had been in place since months prior to the elections. But, at the same time, they allowed other factions, such as Islamic Jihad, to resume launching rockets and conducting other military activities in response to the relentless Israeli raids against the Gaza Strip.

At a factional level, Fatah, which had been defeated in the elections, decided to make Hamas's time in government as difficult

---

* In the year 2005, according to the World Bank statistics, the PA expenditure was a US$1.92 billion, of which international aid provided $349 million whereas the tax and customs transfers controlled by Israel accounted for $814 million. See World Bank, 'Coping with Crisis: Palestinian Authority Institutional Performance', Jerusalem, November 2006, https://documents1.worldbank.org/curated/zh/102561468139178380/pdf/430620WP01NO0P1lPerformanceNov07006.pdf.

as possible. The goal, whether overtly stated or covertly planned, was to foil Hamas in power and force it to step down, resulting in a need for early new elections. Because of Fatah's domination over the Palestinian civil service by virtue of its control of the PA during the previous 12 years, tensions between the new Hamas ministers and their Fatah staff paralysed the work of many ministries and the public sector in general. On the security front, and particularly in the Gaza Strip, several Fatah-controlled security organizations remained outside the control of the Hamas interior ministry, making the government appear to be toothless. To compensate for this awkward situation of having the security forces out of governmental control, the interior ministry established its own 'official' security apparatus, the 'Executive Force'. Predictably, a growing friction between this new force (most of whose members were drawn from Hamas) and the old Fatah-controlled forces continued to increase, leading to military clashes between the two parties during January and February and then again in May and June 2007, pushing the situation in the Gaza Strip to the brink of an all-out civil war. This was only briefly averted in early 2007 by the sudden heavyweight intervention of the Saudis, culminating in the Mecca Agreement between Fatah and Hamas in February 2007. Based on this agreement, a 'national unity government' was formed. However, it failed after only three months, when Hamas took over all the security strongholds of Fatah in June 2007. This is further discussed below.

What were the implications of Hamas's victory for the Palestinian polity and legitimacy?

At the level of Hamas as a movement and in the eyes of Palestinians at large, Hamas's victory in the elections and the subsequent formation of its government brought about new realities. For the first time in the history of the Palestinian national movement, a party that subscribed to Islamist/religious ideology had managed to eclipse all other secular factions, leftists and nationalists allied together, and advanced to the forefront. This dramatic change challenged the traditional leadership of the Palestinian 'nationalist liberationist project', which had been controlled almost entirely by secular forces since the days of the British Mandate in the 1920s.

Furthermore, Hamas's 2006 victory meant that the legitimacy of the historical Palestinian leadership of the PLO was contested on all fronts: in terms of armed resistance, popular representation, and trust and credibility. If embracing and practising resistance against the Israeli occupation was the source of popular legitimacy for any Palestinian faction, Hamas not only achieved that but also garnered a democratic victory that bestowed on it unprecedented moral and political leverage.

Hamas's triumph also accentuated the dichotomy in Palestinian politics between itself and Fatah. The weakness of other factions with either leftist or liberal orientations was further exposed. In many ways, this was an unfortunate development that can be attributed in large measure to the disorientation that many Palestinian elites had and have suffered before, during and after the Oslo Accords. Suffice to say that in light of the sharp Fatah–Hamas polarity, the chances of the emergence of a popular and powerful 'third way' in Palestinian politics have grown slimmer for the foreseeable future. After one year of Hamas rule, the formation of the short-lived national unity government in March 2007 could have represented a historic milestone in Palestinian politics. In fact, the agreement could have helped create a political consensus upon which the Palestinians could deal with Israel, thus bridging the destructive gulf that had so far crippled Palestinian political thinking and strategy.

Over 15 years or so prior to the formation of the national unity government, Palestinian forces had been divided between two strategies for achieving Palestinian rights and self-determination: peace talks with Israel (the stance of the PLO and the PA) or military resistance against the Israeli occupation (Hamas and other factions). Both strategies worked against Israel but also against each other, yielding little for the Palestinians. Because they worked in opposing directions, these two strategies have effectively frustrated one another: what might have been achieved by one of them would be wasted by the opposite party. The lack of a unified leadership (and vision) that could harmonize the duality of 'resistance and negotiation' resulted in the dynamism of mutual destruction between the two opposing strategies. Sustaining a united platform as embodied in the national unity government could be seen therefore as a necessity for internal coherence of the Palestinian national movement and the resolution of the conflict with Israel. External actors certainly have helped in the early collapse of the national unity government and the potential of long-term consensus-building among the Palestinians. The continuation of economic and financial embargos on the national unity government and the explicit policy of sustaining Mahmoud Abbas against Hamas caused the resumption of clashes between Hamas and Fatah and the collapse of the national unity government by June 2007. Not only did Western and Israeli policies provoke the return of a destructive polarity in the Palestinian national movement, but they also encouraged the formation and reformation of smaller militant groups which listen neither to Fatah nor to Hamas.

What were the implications for Israel and for the future of a peace settlement?

Hamas's electoral victory had posed two main questions regarding the conflict, peace talks and the future of Palestine. First, would Hamas in power help or hinder the achievement of a peace settlement? And two, would Hamas in power pose more or less of a threat to Israel and the Israelis? Concerning the first question, it is necessary to clarify some assumptions. Before and during Hamas's taking power, there had been no genuine peace talks in motion to be helped or hindered by Hamas. The peace track had gone astray well before Hamas's rise to power. Since the second

Intifada in 2000, which erupted in response to Oslo's failure to bring about any tangible gains for the Palestinians, the peace process had effectively been idle. Although Mahmoud Abbas had been the leader of the Palestinians for more than a year before the 2006 elections and is still at the top of the Palestinian polity hierarchy, Israel has not engaged with him in serious negotiations. Abbas is seen as the most moderate Palestinian leader with whom Israel could (or should) make peace. Yet, he was considered to be incompetent as a 'peace partner' by Israel, and his political capital in the eyes of the Palestinians has gradually been eroded as he failed to change their dire status quo.

Furthermore and regardless of the internal make-up of the Palestinian government, there have been strong doubts whether the Israeli side is ready to make any serious moves towards concluding a peace agreement. The current Israeli leadership was somewhat damaged politically and humiliated militarily after the Lebanon war in summer 2006, and in addition a number of top Israeli figures have faced prosecution for financial or sexual corruption. If the labour party Israeli government were forced to resign, any potential alternative – either another Kadima-led government, potentially as weak as the current one, or a Netanyahu/Lieberman-led government, representing the far right – would not be expected to gear up the agenda for any peace process with the Palestinians. It is worth noting that after the Annapolis Conference (held in November 2007 in the United States, which relaunched negotiations between the Israelis and the Palestinians), talks between the Israelis and the Palestinians in December 2007 faced intractable difficulties, not because of Hamas, but because of Israel's insistence on building new settlement units in East Jerusalem.

In terms of military threat or security for Israel, there is an apparent irony: the period in which Hamas was either in full control of the PA or engaged in power-sharing with Fatah (March 2006–June 2007) was almost the most peaceful and calm period that Israeli cities had enjoyed over the past few years. The year running up to the elections and the year of Hamas in power witnessed almost zero suicide attacks conducted by Hamas in Israel. Here, Hamas's pragmatism again was in the lead, and realistic cost–benefit calculations overrode religious or jihad calls for unguided resistance.

Another security scenario that was contemplated, largely related to changes within and surrounding Hamas, is the possibility of the emergence of al-Qaeda cells within the Palestinian territories. This could have been the result of a combination of several factors. Among these was, the possibility that angry and frustrated Palestinian factions could see an appeal in the uncompromising al-Qaeda model which has been embraced in Iraq and elsewhere in the world. This might also be true for the many disenfranchised ultra-religious zealots within Hamas, who have become disillusioned by the 'futile political line adopted by their leadership'. These factors were exacerbated by the chaotic situation in the Gaza Strip in particular and the free market of arms. Nonetheless, and perhaps against all favourable conditions, al-Qaeda, and ISIS later on, failed to establish their own cells in Palestine. Effectively, Hamas has functioned as a bulwark blocking any newly emerging extreme groups. However, things could start to change. The erroneous external policies by Israel and the West in general that have placed the Gaza Strip under blockade, starving people and humiliating them, will naturally provoke more radical tendencies than the already existing ones.

11
Hamas in Power

THE MIXED FORTUNES OF HAMAS IN POWER

Following its electoral victory and the formation of an exclusive Hamas-led government in March 2006, then a short-lived national unity government (from March to June 2007), the pressures were mounting on Hamas leading to an implosion within the Palestinian political scene that ended up in the movement's military takeover of the Gaza Strip in mid-June 2007. Consequently, the Palestinian president dissolved the government and banned Hamas in the West Bank. Israel tightened its blockade on the Gaza Strip and Hamas was basically besieged in the narrow Strip that it would govern over the coming years. Hamas legitimized its rule over the Gaza Strip as being the party that was elected by the people and ultimately deprived from assuming full power. Either as a government, fully controlled or shared in 2006–2007 in both the West Bank and the Gaza Strip, or throughout the subsequent years of its exclusive control over the Gaza Strip, the balance sheet of Hamas's performance in power is mixed. Notwithstanding the fact that central to the tremendous difficulties that Hamas has faced is the international and regional blockade imposed on its government and the cutting-off of aid and diplomatic relations with the Palestinians, Hamas in power, as opposed to Hamas in opposition, has structurally changed the rules of the game in the Palestinian struggle against the Israeli occupation. Hamas, acknowledged as a major party on the Palestinian political scene, has now become an integral part of the Palestinian leadership. Without its participation, or tacit approval at the very least, any lasting peace agreement between the two sides seems to be inconceivable. Hamas's experience in power moved from forming an exclusive government, to participating in a national unity government, to military control of the Gaza Strip. Each of these episodes deserves a closer look.

What is the content and significance of the Hamas 'Government Platform'?

Perhaps more important than Hamas's 'Electoral Platform', discussed in Chapter 10, is the 'Government Platform' delivered by Hamas's Prime Minister Ismail Haniya on 27 March 2006 before the newly elected parliament, his speech seeking a vote of confidence. In this highly significant statement, Hamas was addressing the entire world in new and carefully crafted language. Obviously, it was an audacious undertaking by Hamas to try to appeal to a host of completely different audiences. It had to live up to its promises and the expectations of its own membership, and to appease the wider Palestinian constituencies, in particular reassuring Fatah and other big losers in the elections. It also had to send the right and definitive message to Israel and beyond, that Hamas is a liberationist movement, not a war-loving or aimless group. The statement thus projected a moderate discourse with the hope of having an impact on international (mainly American and European) audiences, who were shocked and displeased by Hamas's victory. Concurrently, the statement had to appease and assure other Islamist movements and exponents of political Islam in the Middle East and beyond that the Hamas in power was and would continue to be the same Hamas that they had always known. At the same time, it was essential that Hamas portray itself as a responsible moderate government, trustworthy to its neighbouring sceptical Arab regimes, which feared the ramifications of Hamas's victory on their domestic affairs.

As tedious a statement as it might seem to be, the Government Platform was indeed an exercise in reconciling somewhat irreconcilable concerns and parties. Nonetheless, it has represented a true turning point in Hamas's political thinking. In it, Hamas tackled the conflict with Israel in a language that was borrowed from international law and conventions. It focused on the fact that the Palestinian people suffer from the Israeli military occupation, and thus they have a legitimate right to resist it by all means. The entire thrust of the statement was confined directly and indirectly to the parameters of the concept of a two-state solution. There was no mention or even the slightest of a hint of the 'destruction of Israel' or the establishment of an 'Islamic state in Palestine'. It reflected very little inclination to radical positions and religious overtones. Reading this statement without knowing it had been produced by Hamas could justifiably give the impression that it had been written by any secular Palestinian organization.

At the beginning of his speech, Haniya made a clear reference to the fact that his government would operate 'according to the articles of the (Palestinian) basic law modified in 2003'. Referring to the Palestinian Basic Law was clearly extremely significant because this law was developed on the basis of, and because of, the Oslo Accords. Legally and literally speaking, Hamas was functioning within the parameters created by the peace talks between Israel and the PLO, which it vehemently opposed.

The Government Platform stipulated seven major challenges that would make up the government's agenda:

First, resisting the occupation and its oppressive undertakings against the [Palestinian] land, its people, resources and holy places. Second, securing the safety of the Palestinians and ending the security chaos. Third, relieving the economic hardships facing the Palestinian people. Fourth, undertaking reform and fighting financial and administrative corruption. Five, reordering internal Palestinian affairs by reorganizing Palestinian institutions on a democratic basis that would guarantee political participation for all. Sixth, strengthening the status of the Palestinian question in Arabic and Muslim circles. Seventh, developing Palestinian relationships at regional and international levels to further serve the ultimate interests of our people.*

The statement called upon the international community to respect the choice of the Palestinians in electing Hamas, and to reconsider the initial negative responses to the Hamas victory. It also assured international donors who had been complaining about the corrupt management of the PA that any new aid would be spent through the right channels, and invited donors to establish whatever monitoring mechanisms they considered necessary to guarantee the proper expenditure of their money in Palestine.

On the United States and its position on Hamas's government, the document stated that:

> the American administration which has been preaching democracy and the respect of people's choices across the world is required before anyone else to support the will and choice of the Palestinian people. Instead of threatening the Palestinians with boycotts and cutting aid it should fulfil the pledges that it made to help the establishment of an independent Palestinian state with Jerusalem as its capital.**

Pertaining to the major rights of Palestinians, the statement stressed 'upholding the rights of Palestinian refugees to return to their homeland and for compensation, for this right is indelible and uncompromisable at the individual and collective level'.*** It also declared the government's commitment to work to free (about 8,000–9,000) Palestinian prisoners from Israeli jails, defend Jerusalem against Judaization and challenge all manner of collective punishments against the Palestinians.

---

* From Hamas's 'Government Platform' delivered by Prime Minister Ismail Haniya on 27 March 2006.
** Ibid.
*** Ibid.

On the peace agreements signed by the PLO or the former Fatah-led government and Israel, the statement assured other parties' that the government would treat those agreements:

> with high national responsibility, and in ways that assist the interest of our people and their unchangeable prerogatives. It will also deal with the UN resolutions [on Palestine/Israel] with a high sense of national responsibility and in ways that protect the rights of our people.*

The statement addressed at length, and with pride, the Palestinian exercise of democracy, and confirmed the government's adherence to that concept. It stated that:

> as this government is a result of fair and free elections, it would adhere to the democratic choice, protecting Palestinian democracy and the peaceful rotation of power. It would also broaden the platform of political participation and pluralism because these are the guarantors of the sound functioning and stability of our political system.

It is noteworthy that this document, which was produced by a religiously oriented movement whose popularity was cultivated on what was seen as primordial allegiances, is critical of all sorts of non-citizenship affiliation. It declared that the government would work to get rid of tribal and provincial loyalties and instead 'would encourage the concepts of citizenship and equality of rights and duties'. The notion of citizenship was emphasized as being the overriding one over other local, tribal or religious affiliations:

> we will protect the rights of citizens and strengthen the concept of citizenship without any discrimination based on creed or political association, and will fight together against the practice

---

* Ibid.

193

of political or professional exclusion, and will struggle against [any] injustices inflicted on people.*

References to 'good governance' were plentiful, covering a wide range of issues:

the government will fight corruption and the misuse of public money and confirm transparency and fairness ... [and will adopt] new strategies to develop a public administration based on modern concepts of management.**

On the economic side of Hamas's Government Platform, free-market thinking was visibly expressed, but with a close eye to social justice and care for the poor. But it started by emphasizing self-reliance within the constraints imposed by the Israeli occupation:

our economic program strives to achieve sustainable development through the release of our own [national] resources and by making the best use of our fortunes. We are aware, however, of the political restrictions and the effects of occupation that besiege our people and which have caused drastic damage to our infrastructure.***

The statement then moved on to encourage Arab, Muslim and other business groups to come to Palestine and explore investment opportunities, promising that 'we will make available to them all help possible toward creating the appropriate investment climate including safety, economic protection and the issuing of necessary regulations'. It also stressed the role of such foreign investment as opposed to external donations, stating that:

---

*   From Hamas's 'Government Platform' delivered by Prime Minister Ismail Haniya on 27 March 2006.
**   Ibid.
***   Ibid.

investment is one of the underpinnings of sustainable development, where aid should not be relied on entirely, although this aid is necessary at this period of time. One of the utmost priorities of our economic program is to encourage investment in Palestine, and our government will be actively ready to negotiate all the details that are required by foreign investment.*

How was the performance of the year-long Hamas government in 2006–2007?

The balance sheet of Hamas's one year in power offers a melange of success and failure. It is important to point out from the beginning, however, that a considerable part of Hamas's failure can be attributed to the blockade and aid suspension imposed on the government by Israel and the international community. In the eyes of many Palestinians, Hamas was partly, if not largely, absolved of much responsibility for failing to deliver public services, which were largely crippled by its failure to pay the salaries of more than 160,000 civil servants. This failure was blamed on Western and Israeli policies, which were seen as a punishment against all Palestinians because of their democratic choice of Hamas.** But at the level of Hamas as a political movement, the experience was painfully diverse. A frequent sentiment heard from Hamas's leaders about their time in power revolves around what Ahmad Yousef, the then political advisor to the Hamas-appointed prime minister Ismail Haniya, told me in March 2007, that 'it was a tough year but a great one as well; like an intensive course on politics where

---

* Ibid.
** Commenting on the formation of Hamas-led government after the elections, the German foreign minister at the time, Frank-Walter Steinmeier said that 'Unfortunately we [the EU] can't see any clear signal that would make it possible for us to continue financing (of the Palestinians) in the same way as we did in the past'; *Associated Press* quoted in 'Chronological Review of Events/April 2006 – DPR Review', United Nations: The Question of Palestine, April 2006, www.un.org/unispal/document/auto-insert-198923/.

we had to learn in one year what would otherwise take us 10 or 15 years to learn'.

During Hamas's year in power, one of the several remarkable and speedy transformations that took place within the movement's discourse was the shift in its justification of its 'hardline' positions. Religious justifications and rhetoric increasingly gave way to political justifications and discourse. The increasing exposure to politics and the outside world engendered a discourse that was formulated more in accordance with external conditions rather than being shaped by unfettered internal ideological thinking. This further confirms the predominance of the nationalist pragmatic line in Hamas over the religious one in recent years. Hamas in power felt the burning need to repackage its positions in a more political format. While this could appear to have been a surface change, it nonetheless permeated deeper into the layers of the political and ideological thinking of Hamas. The impact of such a discourse of justification would prove to be most considerable among the lower ranks of the movement, where the religiosity was stronger and rigidity of thinking more apparent. External factors would play a significant role in this context, in transforming what could have been a mere passing momentary shift into deeply rooted change. It was thus the set of surrounding political and social conditions with their pressures and diktats that would ultimately determine Hamas's responses and shift.

Examples of this shift were many, yet it is sufficient to highlight three major ones that have immediate relevance to the debates on Hamas and its changing fortunes. The first example is the question of recognizing Israel. Hamas's 'starting position' on this question was purely religious. Recognizing Israel was perceived to be tantamount to an infringement of Islam, and thus was considered to lie beyond the practice of politics. Hamas's initial Charter was blunt in denouncing any party, Palestinian, Arab or Muslim that would undertake such an anti-religious stance. Palestine was declared to be a *waqf* or an endowment for Muslim generations with which no one has the right to compromise.

The justification Hamas-in-power started to offer on the same position, however, was political and not religious. Hamas argued that Israel is a 'borderless' state and that it has never identified clear borders. So, what is the geography of Israel, Hamas's leaders wondered, that the movement and the Palestinians at large were asked to recognize? Hamas's spokesmen also contended that the PLO has recognized Israel since 1988 yet this has never brought any tangible benefits for the Palestinians. Hamas leaders pointed to the Arab Summit Peace Initiative adopted in Beirut in 2002, which offered Israel full and collective Arab recognition and normalization of relations in return for accepting the two-state solution according to UN resolutions. Their point is that when Israel refuses such a collective Arab recognition, how and why would Hamas's recognition of Israel change Israel's attitudes and positions?*

The second example of the change in the justification used by Hamas regarding its position relates to the movement's policy of suspending military attacks in Israeli cities, before and after the elections. This policy, rigidly and religiously speaking, is akin to stopping the jihad, the *raison d'être* of Hamas. Perhaps no other notion was more repeatedly confirmed in Hamas's early litera-ture in the late 1980s and early 1990s than that of jihad. Yet, when Hamas is now asked why it has frozen its jihad against Israel, it resorts to political and not to religious justifications. Its leaders link this decision to the delicate calculations that account for the unfavourable political conditions of Hamas's position as a gov-

* These positions have been repeatedly expressed by Hamas leaders' statements and written articles. For example, see Ismail Haniyeh, 'A Just Peace or No Peace', *Guardian*, 31 March 2006, www.theguardian. com/commentisfree/2006/mar/31/israel; Mousa Abu Marzook, 'What Hamas is Seeking', *Washington Post*, 30 January 2006, www.washington-post.com/archive/opinions/2006/01/31/what-hamas-is-seeking/293f-ce5e-00b0-4f4d-a271-e8c635c53061/; and statements made by Khaled Mish'al, Hamas's political bureau chief, to *Al-Quds al-Arabi*, 28 February 2007. By contrast, statements that would refer to religious qualification of this position have dramatically diminished.

ernment. The significance of such thinking denotes the extent to which Hamas is willing to subjugate its ideological, and seemingly inflexible, convictions to its political pragmatism and goals. Hamas's rhetoric still stresses resistance as the core of its thinking and action, even when this resistance is effectively idle. More significant is the new confirmation that resistance is a political means and not an objective in itself – in the words of Khaled Mish'al, the head of Hamas's Political Bureau, 'resistance is not an end in itself, but a means to an end'.*

A third example that underlines the shift in Hamas's political thinking in terms of offering political rather than religious qualification of its practices is the movement's stance towards the PLO and the question of joining this organization. The PLO has been the embodiment of Palestinian legitimacy and representation for many decades, recognized as the sole and legitimate representative of the Palestinians. Established in 1964, and controlled by Fatah, the main Palestinian nationalist movement, all Palestinian factions – nationalist, Marxist and pan-Arabist – joined the organization at different points in time, seeing it as the umbrella for Palestinian nationalist resistance against Zionist aggression in Palestine.

Hamas, relatively a latecomer to the resistance scene in 1987, neither joined the PLO nor acknowledged it as 'the sole' representative of the Palestinian people. It considered the PLO only as 'a' representative of the Palestinians. One of Hamas's main objections to the PLO was its 'secular nature'. It was indeed seen as

---

* This position has been articulated by Mish'al and other leaders of Hamas repeatedly since then, see Al Jazeera, ' مشعل يدعو العرب للتوحد ضد إسرائيل' ['Mish'al calls on Arabs to Unite against Israel'], 25 June 2009, www.aljazeera.net/news/2009/6/25/مشعل-يدعو-العرب-للتوحد-ضد-إسرائيل ; and until one year after the 2003–2004 genocide war on Gaza, see Ultrapal, ' خالد مشعل للتلفزيون العربي: نعمل على وقف العدوان ونتنياهو يعطل المفاوضات ', ['Khaled Mish'al to Al-Arabiya TV: We are Working to Stop the Aggression, and Netanyahu is Obstructing the Negotiations'], 10 October 2024, https://ultrapal.ultrasawt.com/-خالد-مشعل-للتلفزيون-العربي-نعمل-على-وقف-العدوان-ونتنياهو-يعطل-المفاوضات/التراث-فلسطين/أخبار.

the antithesis of Hamas, the latter being a religious organization. Other main objections presented by Hamas included the PLO's tacit recognition of Israel by endorsing the principle of the two-state solution. Yet the position of Hamas as from 2005 onwards concerning the PLO and the justification of that position have become significantly different. Further, Hamas has engaged in dialogue with Fatah and other Palestinian factions to reform the PLO and include Hamas in it. In all the discussions and debates about a 'new' PLO, which would include Hamas, there has not been a single statement or condition pronounced by any Hamas leader about the 'secular nature' of the PLO or its 'un-Islamic essence'. All the talk is political. Even the recognition of Israel by the PLO has been downplayed as Hamas's positions since 2006 have also been converging on the idea of a Palestinian state in 1967 borders.

THE MIXED FORTUNES OF HAMAS IN POWER SHARING AND CONTROL

What was the national unity government (and the agreement with Fatah) of March 2007 and why did it fail?

The rivalry between Fatah and Hamas since the PLC January 2006 election results has pushed the internal Palestinian situation from bad to worse. By January 2007, marking exactly one full year since Hamas's victory, the spectre of civil war had become a serious potentiality as it never had been before in recent Palestinian history. Egyptian, Syrian, Qatari and Jordanian attempts to mediate between the two fighting factions had failed one after the other. In early February 2007, the Saudi King Abdallah took the initiative and called the leaders of both movements to convene in Mecca.

The Saudi initiative was successful at first and, from 6–8 February 2007, Fatah and Hamas concluded what would be known as the Mecca Agreement. Putting an immediate end to

Palestinian in-fighting in the Gaza Strip, the agreement paved the way for the formation of a Palestinian national unity government, which took place in March 2007. The political programme of the would-be government confirmed the pragmatic line of Hamas, in which it agreed to 'respect' previous agreements signed between the PLO and Israel. It also stipulated the establishment of a Palestinian state using the 1967 borders as the national aim of the government, yet without conceding a blunt recognition of Israel. The Mecca Agreement was a breakthrough, offering a potential Palestinian consensus, however shaky, on a unified political programme (on the implications of Hamas's victory for the Palestinian polity and legitimacy, see also Chapter 10).

The national unity government did not change the Quartet and Israeli policies of isolating and boycotting Hamas. The new government did not succeed on two fronts: breaking the international boycott; and unifying the internal security forces under the control of the interior ministry. The skirmishes between Fatah-affiliated groups and security forces and Hamas's Executive Force and Al-Qassam Brigades intensified. A new round of violent internal fighting in May and early June culminated in mid-June with Hamas's taking control of the security forces in the Gaza Strip. Dozens of Palestinians from both sides were killed and hundreds wounded. The Gaza Strip fell entirely under Hamas control. Immediately after that, Abbas nominated a non-Hamas government in the West Bank, which was quickly recognized and supported by the Quartet and by Israel. Since then, the Palestinian polity and society and geography have come to an unprecedented divide, where the West Bank is under the control of Fatah and the Gaza Strip under the control of Hamas, and each claims to be the legitimate government. The 'international community' sided with the government in the West Bank and tightened the blockade on Hamas and the over 1.5 million Palestinians living in the Gaza Strip.

Why did Hamas take over the Gaza Strip by force in June 2007?

The military takeover of the Gaza Strip can only be understood from the perspective of 'rational-players' power politics. Hamas and Fatah were stubbornly engaged in a rivalry over power, where the surrounding conditions would allow for the use of force more than reconciliation. On Fatah's side, and even though this occurred a year and a half into Hamas's electoral mandate, Fatah still considered it to be merely a short interruption to the 'natural' course of Palestinian leadership, with Fatah always at the helm. Fatah and the Palestinian president have spared no tactic to bring about the failure of the Hamas government. In the two weeks following the results of the elections, several presidential decrees were quickly issued, aimed at stripping basic powers from Hamas's government-in-waiting. Abbas brought back to the 'presidency' all the powers that he himself had struggled hard to wrest from the former president Yasser Arafat when he was prime minister in 2003. The 'presidency' started to accumulate excessive power, which, had Hamas not been in government, would have been criticized worldwide. Hamas's incoming government and its ministries were stripped of real authority, especially in the areas of finance and security, even before they assumed any responsibilities.

All security forces would, by virtue of the new decrees, be the responsibility of the president himself, and would be run by the National Security Council, which had played only a consultative role until it was reactivated after Hamas's victory. Official media, mainly Palestinian television, radio and the Palestinian news agency, were moved from under the jurisdiction of the Ministry of Information and became the responsibility of the presidency. All border points, especially the Rafah border (with Egypt), which had been under the control of the national security forces, belonging to the Interior Ministry, were brought under the authority of the presidency through its 'presidential guards'. The latter had rapidly been beefed up to become a most important military force, assuming far more responsibilities than safeguarding the president. Several presidential decisions were also taken in which Fatah officials were appointed or promoted to occupy key security posts, so that it would be almost impossible for the incoming movement to take control over security. Even since the formation of the national unity government in March 2007, the failure to resolve the thorniest of issues, the control over security forces, has only confirmed the coming prospect of use of force by Hamas.

On Hamas's side, the mounting pressures were also eliminating any alternatives but the resort to force to restructure the status quo. Because of its lack of control over security forces, Hamas's government failed in maintaining security for ordinary Palestinians, leaving the streets of the Gaza Strip to fall into the hands of various groups of thugs and militant gangs. The chaotic situation was partly provoked by militant elements affiliated either to Fatah or to the 'official' apparatus of the Preventative Security. Their aim was to prove that Hamas was incapable of delivering security, discrediting it in the eyes of the Palestinians. Muhammad Dahlan, Fatah's strongest man in the Gaza Strip, was reported as stating on the record that he would 'drive Hamas's government nuts'.

Israel was closely watching and facilitating the Palestinian incoming fight and split. Intelligence reports, published by Wikileaks in December 2010, reports messages between then Israeli Director of Military Intelligence, Major General Amos Yadlin, and US Ambassador to Israel Richard Jones on the eve of Hamas' military takeover of Gaza in June 2007. According to Wikileaks cable, 'Yadlin told the US Ambassador that he would be "very happy" if Hamas formed a government in Gaza "as long as they have no (air or sea) port"'. He added that Israel would then work with the rival Palestinian political party, Fateh, 'to form a government in the West Bank and work to undermine the Hamas government in Gaza'.

To make things worse, and as a result of cutting off external aid, Hamas had failed to provide salaries to tens of thousands of

public sector employees. Exploiting the situation, Fatah mobilized widespread strikes among civil servants, especially teachers,
which have truly harmed Hamas's image. The compounded pressures on Hamas created panic and unrest among the rank and
file of the movement. The wisdom of engaging in such a political
process, as opposed to remaining on the 'resistance' and opposition side, came into deep question.

Internally, anger and impatience were increasingly dominating
Hamas's ever-growing military wing, which until then had been
kept under the full control of the political leadership. In the days
preceding the military takeover, Hamas's military had been caught
in a feeling of compounded humiliation. On the one hand, and to
avoid harming the political agenda of Hamas's government, they
had ceased their attacks against Israeli targets which had fallen
easily within their reach and capacity. This had invoked criticism and mockery of their 'resistance project'; Fatah was prompt
in pointing at Hamas's relinquishing of resistance for the sake of
governmental posts. On the other hand, the chaotic security situation spreading across the Gaza Strip was seen to be mobilized by
their rival groups, from or close to Fatah, which Hamas's military
wing felt they could have ended if they were only given the green
light. Hamas's Al-Qassam Brigades were not allowed to inter-
fere in the daily business of the government, although Hamas
oversaw and trained the Executive Force, which the government
did establish to function as a police force. Hamas's military wing
by then had started to see itself as an impotent or put-to-pasture
army, losing its respect and aura.

However, the most intolerable and decisive factor for Hamas's
military leadership was the continuous arming of Abbas's presidential guards and other security forces in the Gaza Strip.
Shipments of arms arrived in the Strip from Egypt, Jordan and
Israel. For Hamas's military, it looked as if they were merely
naively waiting for their rivals to reach their military threshold,
the point when it would be practically feasible for them to crush
Hamas. They argued that it was necessary to take preventive

action to save the movement from this almost inevitable scenario. For many of Hamas's military leadership, it was a life-or-death decision, defending their very existence. It was them and their soldiers who would be on the 'wanted list' or even killed, not their political leadership which could coexist with others and live with the new status quo.

In a nutshell, Hamas's government was put under enormous pressures externally, internally and organizationally. Cut off financially and diplomatically, 18 months after assuming power, Hamas lacked any political capital to present to its own members or the Palestinian people at large. It was made to look crippled in delivering even the most conventional responsibilities of any government. On top of that, its military leadership perceived a ticking clock that would lead to the eventual destruction of their power that they had spent years in building. All those pressures culminated in the political leadership giving way, perhaps for the first time in Hamas's political life, to its military wing, to decide how to deal with Fatah on the ground and implement these decisions. In November 2007, Hamas issued what it called the 'White Paper' (*Al-Kitab al-Abyad*), in which it explained its reasons behind the 'military takeover' of the Gaza Strip. The subtitle of this document is 'Out of Coercion not Choice', which reflects the hesitation and confusion that had engulfed Hamas's decision-making process prior to the takeover.

12
Hamas and the Arab (Spring) Revolutions (2010–2011)

What are the Arab revolutions of 2010–2011 (or the Arab Spring) and what are their implications for Palestine, the Palestinians and Hamas?

In the late 2010s and throughout the following years, the Arab region witnessed a wave of strong popular protests against authoritarian regimes and their policies. Starting in Tunisia and rapidly spreading to Egypt, these protests were remarkably successful in toppling both regimes within a span of a few weeks. Slogans of freedom and dignity swept through the cities of both countries, with millions chanting them in the streets. Libya, Yemen, and Syria followed, yet their outcomes were not as successful as the Tunisian and Egyptian cases. Even in monarchies such as Jordan, Morocco, Bahrain and Oman, regimes felt immense danger and declared radical reforms to contain widespread protests and people's demands. The root causes behind these revolutions varied, but they mostly centred on the failure of these corrupt governments in economic and political spheres. The accumulation of economic deprivation, unemployment and political repression culminated in the multiple uprisings that were termed the 'Arab Spring', or more accurately, the Arab revolutions. There were two phases to these revolutions: the first phase, comprising Tunisia and Egypt, was marked by peaceful demonstrations that ended in impressive success. The second phase was bloody and messy, ending in total failure or, at best, greater failure than success, as seen in Libya, Yemen and Syria.

The outcome of the Arab revolutions, particularly in Tunisia and Egypt, revealed a persistent resistance at regional, international and Israeli levels against Arab democratization, which could threaten the existing pro-Western authoritarian regimes. Regionally, an axis of 'counter-revolution' quickly formed, led by some Gulf states (the UAE, Saudi Arabia and Bahrain) and Egypt after the overthrow of Muslim Brotherhood President Mohamed Morsi in 2013. The central goal of this axis was, and still is, to thwart any movement towards democracy, from Egypt and Jordan in the Levant to Tunisia and Morocco in the Maghreb, fearing that the demand for democratization would spread contagiously in these countries.

It was difficult for this axis to explicitly declare war on democratic transformation, so they adopted the easiest and most marketable pretext by linking this transformation to Islamists, labelling them as 'terrorist groups', including those who won elections in their countries. According to this approach, Islamists in their entirety, whether moderate or radical, were considered terrorist outlaws. Ironically, various forms of Islamism and Islamists were, until recently, traditional allies of many Gulf regimes in their ideological wars against Arab nationalism, leftist and Marxist ideas, or even against extremist jihadist groups. In this context, the 'counter-revolution' axis supported the 'deep state' forces in Egypt, Libya and Tunisia with money and diplomacy, and Bahrain militarily, and stood on the lookout for any success, even relative, of any potential democratization path produced by the Arab revolutions.

On an international level, despite public and media sympathy in the West for the Arab revolutions, official positions in Washington and in European capitals (as well as in Beijing and Moscow) remained cautious, fearful of any alternative to the regimes that the West was accustomed to dealing with easily and knew closely. The West's positions were characterized by reluctance and pragmatic hesitation. These fluctuated and cautiously checked the possibility of tilting the balance of power in favour of pro-Western factions, without being principally of the people's democratic choice regardless of the winner. In the most significant country of the Arab revolutions, Egypt, Western positions manifest the highest degree of hypocrisy. They supported the military coup of Abdel Fattah el-Sisi against the elected Muslim Brotherhood-elect government in June 2014.

For its part, Israel closely and tensely watched the first successes of the Arab revolutions in overthrowing the Hosni Mubarak regime, which Israelis used to describe as a 'strategic treasure', and the regime of Zine El Abidine Ben Ali in 2010–2011, and feared for the other 'moderate' authoritarian regimes that it was good at dealing with and relying on. In several ways, Arab tyranny plays the role of a solid ally in protecting Israel. Israeli views have been explicit that 'Tacit understandings and written agreements with Arab autocrats ... were long a foundation of Israel's national security mindset', and this also applies to some regimes that loudly condemn Israel and use Palestine as justification to maintain their internal political legitimacy, such as Syria. 'As for the Assad regime, Israel deemed it preferable to stick with the devil it knew – the phrase prime minister Ariel Sharon used in 2005 to convince George W. Bush not to push for regime change in Syria.'*

Tyranny's mechanism and structure is what prevents the translation of popular will in Arab countries into foreign policy, including towards Israel. Conversely, democracy opens the channels for such a public will to become represented and carried out by states. And this is why Israel had always been fearful of genuine Arab democratization. Ehud Barak, a former Israeli prime and defence minister, 'warned' in March 2011 of 'irresponsible popular opinion' in Arab countries. Thus, any real democratic process in any Arab country that leads to the embodiment of the will of the people in decision-making is a potential danger.

---

* 'How Israel Kept the Arab Spring from Becoming the Winter of its Discontent', *The Times of Israel*, https://2u.pw/fVq8Qhr.

Against this background, most Palestinians including Hamas expressed warm support to the revolutions that removed Arab dictators. The anticipation was to finally see governments that express people's demands and positions including their support of Palestine. Immediately in Tunisia, for example, the post-revolution government in 2011 stipulated a constitutional article that criminalizes any normalization with Israel – reflecting the public mood. In Egypt, toppling Mubarak had removed one of the most powerful regimes that was known for its anti-Hamas policies. The Islamist parties across many other Arab countries made successes that had created a euphoric atmosphere for Hamas. A large-scale shift seemed to be underway in the region in the direction of democratization that was benefiting the Islamists as being the best organized force. Hamas' fortunes seemed very promising, albeit temporarily, as the following events had had a sharp and costly turn for the movement.

What were Hamas' gains during and after the Arab (Spring) revolutions?

The achievements of almost all Islamist parties that used peaceful means in the Arab revolutions had been welcomed by Hamas wholeheartedly. These Islamists were the closest in ideology and sentiment to Hamas. Beyond the Islamists, other nationalist and anti-colonial forces which were also identified as pro-Palestine and pro-resistance occupied a significant part in the new revolutionary or post-revolution public space. Encouraged by the fall of rulers in Tunisia and Egypt, Hamas thought that a near future of Arab politics would be marked by forces that would be democratically elected and not obedient to the West. A few months after the fall of the Tunisian dictator in January 2011, and for the first time since Hamas' inception, prominent leaders of the movement arrived in Tunisia to receive an official and public warm welcome. Side by side with their Tunisian Islamist brethren, they spoke to the masses in the street as well as meeting with leaders of all political forces in the country.

The zenith of Hamas' jubilant feelings of the Arab revolution, however, came along in February 2011 when the Egyptian president officially stepped down. At the time, his removal never occurred in Hamas' wildest dreams, given his power and control over the state. What then mattered for Hamas was to end the Mubarak regime's role in the blockade on the Gaza Strip and Hamas. As discussed in Chapters 10 and 11, Hamas was besieged by Israel, by land, air and sea, since the movement's control of the Gaza Strip in 2007. Part of the blockade was along the Egyptian–Palestinian borders where Egypt's military did its best to comply with Israeli and American pressures in tightening the movement of the Palestinians across the borders. Many of Hamas' political leaders, let alone its military leaders, were unable to leave Gaza because of the security monitoring on the borders. Smuggling weapons was of course the most policed activity overground or via the tunnels.

During the almost two years between the fall of Mubarak and mid-2013, Hamas enjoyed the best times perhaps in its entire history. The tight measures on the borders with Gaza were loosened, either consequentially because of the chaotic situation that followed Mubarak's fall, or officially after the election of Mohammed Morsi, the Muslim Brotherhood candidate, as Egyptian president in June 2012. Morsi's government, busy at home with a mounting pressing agenda, turned a blind eye towards Hamas' activities across the borders as well as in the tunnels. Also, dozens of Hamas' prisoners in Egypt were released. Having an Islamist Egyptian president next door to Gaza was a real, if short-lived, dream for Hamas. The real test came in November 2012 when Israel launched its second war on the Hamas-controlled Gaza Strip, with the first being in 2008–2009. In firm and hostile statements, Morsi announced that Egypt stands with Gaza and warned Israel. Hamas, along with many observers then, considered the Egyptian warning the main reason behind the quick end of that war, lasting only eight days compared to longer ones before and after. Morsi's regime became the 'strategic treasure' for Hamas. Yet, blinded by this gain, it sacrificed other strategic assets as explained below.

What were Hamas' losses during and after the Arab (Spring) revolutions?

Losing Syria: For more than two decades before the Arab revolutions (2010–2011), Hamas allied itself with what is known in the region as the 'resistance axis', comprising Iran, Syria and Hizbullah, and enjoyed financial and military aid from Iran and Hizbullah. From the Syrian regime, it was offered political and diplomatic coverage, along with proximity to refugee camps in Syria and next-door Lebanon. Hamas's leadership and headquarters were based in Damascus, a pivotal place for the movement. Placed in Syria, Hamas was right in the middle of the Levant, ideal geography symbolically and materially.

The Syrians, influenced by their Arab brethren, went into the streets in March 2011. The protests, featuring chanted demands of freedom, dignity and political reform as in neighbouring countries, spread across the country and remained peaceful for the following few months. As in the cases of other revolutions, the Syrian one enjoyed wide-ranging support within Arab publics and beyond. That it dragged on longer than the successful Tunisian and Egyptian revolutions put Hamas in a precarious position. For long months, Hamas attempted a delicate balancing act to maintain a neutral position regarding an internal Syrian affair. At one point, it tried to offer mediation between the regime and revolutionaries – a move that antagonised the regime. However, the regime started to deploy brutal force against civilian protests, pushing groups of them to use arms thus justifying more use of force by the regime. The mounting repression and continuous killing of thousands of protesters had morally cornered Hamas. Eventually, in February 2012, the movement was seen as taking the side of the Syrian people and was asked by the regime to leave the country. The decision to sever its ties with the Bashar al-Assad regime was one of the most difficult and costly decisions taken by the movement as it came with huge losses – abandoning a vital political base in the region, adjacent to Palestine. That said, Hamas's bold move also had a fallback safety net. While the movement was losing a very important base in Syria, things were moving greatly in Hamas's direction in Egypt with the continuous rise of the Muslim Brotherhood in the post-revolution political scene. The loss of Syria was compensated for by the win of Egypt.

Almost losing Iran and Hizbullah: The repercussions of Hamas's position towards the Syrian revolution went far beyond cutting off relations with the Assad regime. Iran and Hizbullah, the main regional backers of Assad, became equally antagonized. Both considered Assad's regime the vital link in the arc of Iranian influence that stretches from Baghdad to Beirut passing through Damascus. Thus, defending the regime against all its enemies, even if these include the Syrian people, is a matter of life or death to the Iranian and Hizbullah alliance. At that time, ditching Syria by Hamas was seen by the regime, Iran and Hizbullah as no less than a betrayal and a stab in the back. Relations between Hamas and these three parties deteriorated to an unprecedented point. Again, to compensate for what seemed to be the loss of Iran, Hamas strengthened relations with Turkey under Erdoğan, who came to power in 2003. However, the support that Iran used to provide to Hamas could not be matched by Turkey, particularly in military and intelligence.

Losing Egypt again: The brief period of relief that Hamas enjoyed during the Muslim Brotherhood's Morsi rule in 2012 was followed by near complete suffocation with Sisi's military regime, which removed Morsi in July 2013. The new army man in Cairo considered the Muslim Brotherhood and all its affiliated groups, including Hamas, as the overarching enemy of the state. Soon this materialized when Egypt accused Hamas of collaboration with militant Islamist groups in Sinai that targeted and killed dozens of Egyptian army soldiers. The trade-off, or wager, that Hamas made by severing ties with Syria and weakening its relationship with Iran in exchange for gaining Egypt had now failed.

Losing the Gulf, except Qatar: The Egyptian coup in 2013 that brought the army back to power marked a turning point. Supported by the UAE and Saudi Arabia, the coup had effectively reversed the Arab revolutionary tide against the authoritarian regimes of the region. A post-revolution regional landscape and alliances became clear. The counter-revolutionary axis led, unofficially, by the UAE that included Egypt, Saudi Arabia, Bahrain and to lesser degree Jordan had by then gained the upper hand. The main target of this axis was democratization under the disguise of fighting the Islamists, including Hamas. On the other side, the axis of resistance was fragmented and weakened. Syria was devasted over the long years of what became a chaotic civil war with many militant groups like ISIS and al-Qaeda hijacking the peaceful revolution. Mending broken fences between Iran and Hamas consumed a few subsequent years. Eventually, Hamas returned to Syria but without enjoying its previous privileges. Hamas was once again besieged in the Gaza Strip, yet focusing on building up its military capabilities and tightening its grip on power. On the eve of 7 October 2023, Hamas's relationships with Iran and Hizbullah had returned to their strongest levels.

13

Hamas and the Wars on Gaza (before 2023)

A year into Hamas' control over the Gaza Strip, Israel launched its first war against the movement and the Strip in 2008–2009. This was followed by a series of wars or large-scale strikes in 2012, 2014, 2018, 2020, 2021 and 2022, culminating in the genocidal war of 2023. The intervals between these wars never witnessed total quiet from the Israeli side. Assassinations of leaders, selective short strikes and keeping Hamas and the entire Strip on edge were integral parts of Israel's strategy of exerting continuous pressure. Within the broader blockade imposed on the Gaza Strip, the military aspect of this pressuring strategy, known as 'mowing the grass' and/or 'low boiling', directed against Hamas, complemented the non-military aspect, known as 'putting the Gazans on a diet', which targeted the entire population in the Strip. The objective was to provoke the Palestinians to revolt against Hamas's rule. Hamas and other resistance groups' tactic of launching rockets against Israel over the years had been the repeated pretext for Israeli wars. Hamas's use of these rockets, as well as other military tactics, had one overarching and immediate goal: to end the land, sea and air blockade on the Gaza Strip and its Palestinians.

The discussion below gives more attention to the 2008–2009 war, as it was the first against the Gaza Strip under Hamas rule and served as a 'textbook' for later wars. The justification for all the wars was similar: crushing Hamas or weakening it to maintain Israel's safety and keeping the Palestinians divided. The last part of the chapter will briefly cover other wars in 2012, 2014, 2018, 2021 and 2022. The scale of each confrontation differed, the casualty figures varied and Hamas's military performance fluctuated, yet the West's support of Israel remained unwavering, and Israel's disregard for international public condemnation persisted.

Was it not Hamas's insistence on firing rockets into Israeli cities and kibbutzim across the border that triggered the first Israeli war on Hamas-controlled Gaza in December 2008–January 2009, and all the consequences it brought upon the Palestinians?

Before Hamas won the elections in January 2006, a truce (or *tahdiyeh* in Arabic) was brokered by the Egyptians between the resistance factions, including Hamas and Israel. According to the truce, Hamas and other Palestinian groups would refrain from firing rockets in return for reciprocal restraint by Israel, which would refrain from launching any military strikes against Gaza and its resistance. At the time, and according to Israeli intelligence and military leaders, Hamas showed an impressive record in adhering to the terms of the truce and even discouraging other Palestinian factions from undertaking rocket attacks. Israel, however, did the opposite and exploited any chance that arose to assassinate Hamas members. The truce helped both parties and kept the violence to a minimum for a while.

In June 2008, the truce ended without Israeli renewal, despite Hamas's repeated declarations of its willingness to extend it. Hamas was keen to maintain calm as it had many other major agendas to tackle: strengthening its control over the Gaza Strip after seizing power and defeating Fatah forces in July 2007; giving Gazans a sense of normal life; proving itself as a functioning government in Gaza; and prioritizing the dismantling of the extremely harmful and inhumane blockade imposed on the Gaza Strip after its election victory.

In contrast, Israel had no appetite to renew the truce and escalated its incursions into various areas of the Gaza Strip, increasing its assassination strikes on Hamas members and the movement's governmental facilities. Intensifying military pressure on Hamas was a complementary part of Israel's strategy of blockading the Gaza Strip, making life unbearable for the people and compelling them to rise against Hamas. Hamas began to retaliate by firing rockets, carefully linking any firing to specific Israeli attacks to avoid bearing the blame for the growing hostilities.

Hamas felt burdened by various political, ideological, economic and resistance-related challenges. Politically, its participation in the elections and becoming part of the Palestinian political process was not yielding concrete results for its Gazan constituencies and members. Ideologically, the significant transformations it made by limiting its struggle to the West Bank and the Gaza Strip were not welcomed or rewarded internationally. Economically, it found itself responsible for the deteriorating lives and conditions of 2 million Palestinians in the Strip. In terms of resistance, it abided by a truce that effectively froze its actions, contradicting its rhetoric about resistance. Refraining from reacting to continuous Israeli military provocations would further expose Hamas.

However, the prevailing thinking in Israel was to maintain those provocations and refuse the renewal of the truce. Israel's plan to attack Gaza was in place well before the war in December 2008, and it needed Hamas's rockets as a convenient pretext.

Israel could have spared its southern towns Hamas's rockets if it had agreed to renew the truce on mutually acceptable terms. Some Israeli military leaders have made this point clear. Brigadier General (Retd.) Shmuel Zakai, the former commander of the Israel's Gaza Division, told the Israeli daily *Haaretz* on 22 December 2008 that:

We could have eased the siege over the Gaza Strip, in such a way that Palestinians, Hamas, would understand that holding their fire served their interests. But when you create a *tahdiyeh* [truce], and the economic pressure on the Strip continues, it's obvious that Hamas will try to reach an improved *tahadiyeh*, and that their way to achieve this is resumed Qassam fire.

Has Hamas been weakened by the 2008–2009 war militarily and politically?

Wars and armed conflicts do in many cases have unexpected consequences and create new realities quite different from what they intended to achieve. This applies squarely in the case of the Israeli war against Hamas in the Gaza Strip. The outcome of the war has left Hamas stronger and with an enhanced legitimacy among the Palestinians and within the region. Israel has pursued its official goal of achieving a new security situation in southern Israeli areas with ferocity: its use of massive military force killed over 1,400 Palestinians in three weeks, most of them women and children. Yet, it has failed either to silence Hamas's primitive rockets or to destroy its ability to function as a coherent entity.

In operational terms, Hamas's capability has been reduced (if only temporarily). Out of Hamas's strong fighters, estimated then by Israeli intelligence at around 15,000, Israel killed no more than 400 in the operation. The movement's leadership remained intact, and its popular support and regional standing had risen. In the aftermath of the war, Hamas proved to be an indispensable player in Palestine and in its future.

The last point was seen as sufficient evidence of Israel's failure in the war. But furthermore, the reduction in Israel's capacity to subdue its enemies was exposed. The army that in the Six-Day War in 1967 defeated the militaries of four Arab states and seized massive territories of Egypt, Syria and Jordan which far exceeded Israel's then area has followed the embarrassment of the war against Hizbullah in 2006 with another inconclusive campaign against a non-state militia. This had significant political and military consequences. As discussed above, the core of Israel's strategy since Hamas's electoral victory in 2006 has been the imposition of economic blockade against Gaza, which would create such misery as to press people to turn against the Hamas's rule. What Israel ended with was a worldwide condemnation and a UN report accusing it of perpetrating war crimes (Goldstone Report, September 2009).*

There may be another twist of history at work here. Lack of concrete military achievements would not block political accumulative gains. Steadfastness on its own against the enemy, in the case of liberation movements, seems good enough at certain junctures. Hamas's advancement to the fore of the Palestinian national movement since 2006–2007 has been a gradual process of displacement of the previously dominant Fatah movement. Fatah's own early history after its foundation in the early 1960s was also a two-track one: military (where it marched from one impasse to another: patchy operations against Israel in the second half of the 1960s, a defeat by the Jordanian army in 1970, then expulsion from Lebanon in 1982 after being defeated by Israel); and political (where it kept moving ahead, consolidating its legitimacy and political leadership of the Palestinians). Broadly speaking, Hamas's military performance, even if modest and unimpressive in some confrontations, paved the way for more political legitimacy and national support.

Fatah's rise halted with the (in the end) futile peace process that started in 1991 with the Madrid Conference after the war with Iraq over Kuwait. By the mid-2000s, it was evident that Fatah had indeed failed to end Israel's post-1967 occupation via an endless series of negotiations that came to erode its political and national capital. To put the same point in another way, the route to Palestinian legitimacy and leadership has always hinged upon offering a plausible strategy to resist and reverse the Israeli occupation. If this criterion fails to be met – as became the case for Fatah and the Ramallah-based Palestinian Authority led by the president, Mahmoud Abbas – the Palestinians will look in other direc-

---

* United Nations, The Goldstone Report, Report of the United Nations Fact-Finding Mission on the Gaza Conflict, 25 September 2009, https://digitallibrary.un.org/record/666096?ln=en&v=pdf.

tions. This suggests that long-term trends as well as short-term events worked against Fatah and for Hamas. The indications are that Palestinian opinion in the West Bank increasingly regards Mahmoud Abbas as incapable of fulfilling the core responsibility of Palestinian leadership, and irrelevant at a time when they see their compatriots facing daily war crimes by Israel. As shown in Chapter 6, since 2005–2006 and up until and during the 2023–2024 genocide war, a decline in Abbas' image and standing has continued to parallel Hamas' growth in popularity with Palestinians almost everywhere.

The pressures of war and suffering surely create exceptional circumstances, and responses that can prove fleeting. It is also certain that some Palestinians in the Gaza Strip then and now directed their anger and frustration onto Hamas, on the grounds that the movement has brought down a terrible assault upon them. Apart from the outcomes of the last war of 2023–2024, a grounded judgement can be made where the evidence is clear. The larger and longer-term political picture is of a movement that has gained additional domestic support from the war, to become regarded as a symbol of defiance and courage for millions in the Arab and Muslim worlds, and become an unavoidable reality at future diplomatic negotiations.

Has the Gaza war strengthened or weakened Hamas's regional standing and allies?

The 2008–2009 Gaza war not only affected Hamas and the Palestinian balance of power, but also impacted regional dynamics. In his first term of office (2001–2005), George W. Bush wanted to create a 'new Middle East' – 'terrorism'-free and democratically reformed. By the end of his second term (2005–2009), Bush had indeed created a 'new Middle East', but one that was almost the opposite of what he rhetorically and initially advocated. Bush's post 9/11 Middle Eastern agenda marginalized Palestine, while prioritized fighting 'terrorism' that ironically included crushing

Saddam Hussein's regime. At the same time, Israel was granted an effective carte blanche to enhance its occupation of the West Bank and the Gaza Strip which started in 1967, despite all the peace talks and proposals. All this has backfired, not only killing any idea of a peaceful 'new Middle East', but also giving birth to a more resisting Middle East, where the so-called moderates have been knocked out, the resistance forces have become stronger, anti-Americanism is deeper, and Palestine as the core issue in the region is as persistent as ever.

The 2008–2009 Gaza War was in certain ways, a result of Bush's short-sighted Middle Eastern policy: that is, to leave things to shape up in Israel/Palestine without external intervention. The same 'templated' American policies surrounded the following series of wars on Gaza. Things have indeed shaped up, yielding new realities where moderate Arab countries (mainly Egypt, Saudi Arabia and Jordan) had felt the brunt of their moderation, and temporarily adopted harder stances. During the war, Jordan distanced itself visibly by using strong language condemning Israel. During and because of this war, Qatar and Turkey, both moderate allies of the United States, had become closer to the Syrian/Iranian 'axis of resistance', side by side with Hamas and Hizbullah. This new ad hoc regional formation materialized at the Doha summit on 16 January 2009, which was organized quickly by Qatar to orchestrate a collective Arab position against the war. The war indicated a shift in the atmosphere in the region, more towards a resisting Middle East. The rise of the 'new resisting Middle East' is in fact grounded in two great failures over the past decades. The first is the Israeli failure to end its occupation of the West Bank and the Gaza Strip, especially after the historic Palestinian compromise accepting the two-state solution in 1988 and in the Oslo peace process. The second is the American failure to adopt an even-handed policy towards Palestine/Israel, fuelling further radicalization among Palestinians, Arabs and Muslims, which has helped strengthen the 'resistance' camp.

The traditional 'Arab system' hinged upon the League of Arab States, that comprises all Arab countries. Although weak, fragile and fractured, the League has managed to sustain itself over decades. It allowed Arab countries to pretend that they were exercising politics via summit meetings and collective declarations. In so doing, this system served to absorb public anger, and channel it through a new 'strategic' orientation, mostly taking its cue from Washington. On a number of occasions, the 'Arab system' cracked completely, mainly over its position on the first and second American wars against Iraq, in 1991 and 2003, respectively. On the Arab–Israeli conflict, it broke down after the visit of the former Egyptian President Sadat to Jerusalem in 1977 and his subsequent peace treaty with Israel. However, after this, the 'Arab system' used the Palestine issue as a unifying one, until the Gaza war. On this occasion, Egypt and Saudi Arabia have taken positions that have been seen by many Arabs as tacitly approving of Israel's attempt to crush, or at least weaken, Hamas. On the other side, Syria, Qatar, Iran and, not unsurprisingly, Turkey have taken strong positions against the Israeli war.

In dealing with large-scale crises in the region, the 'Arab system' has always offered the least effective of actions packaged with the greatest degree of rhetoric. Alas, it has maintained a sustained fragility, a status quo that allows for a minimum unified appearance although it is hollow in action. This has worked, not particularly well, but at least to the degree needed to enable it to survive. The reaction of this system to the Gaza war fell within the same maximum rhetoric–minimum action parameters. This time, however, it did not work and the system collapsed. It did indeed fracture under the scale and magnitude of the Israeli military brutality and the enormous Palestinian death toll and destruction. What makes this collapse unlike previous breakdowns of the same system is the new political environment in the region, where Iran and Turkey have grown eager to play a central role in regional politics. Thus, the political and leadership vacuum created by Arab inaction has prompted the two 'non-Arab countries' to step in and fill the void. Both were welcomed by most Arab public opinion, as reflected in the press, on television screens and in angry demonstrations. For some commentators, the Turkish Prime Minister Recep Tayyip Erdoğan was seen as a defiant Ottoman sultan who would never accept the humiliation of fellow Muslims, coming to the rescue with an echo of those glorious centuries. Never would either Turkey or Iran enjoy such a warm welcome by the Arab publics for any issue other than Palestine. In the following year, and although the picture became further mixed, the general political landscape remained more or less the same.

The Gaza summit in Doha represented the inauguration of the 'new resisting Middle East'. Seen by Egypt and Saudi Arabia as an overt attempt by Qatar to play a bigger regional role than its size merits – and one they considered intolerable – they pressured other Arab countries not to attend the summit. Angry and frustrated, the Qataris went ahead and convened the informal summit, hosting 13 Arab countries in addition to Turkey, Iran and Senegal. More daring, though, was the presence of Khaled Mish'al, Hamas's leader, Abdullah Shalla, the leader of the Islamic Jihad in Palestine, and Ahmad Jibril, the leader of a smaller leftist/pan-Arab nationalist Palestinian faction, who occupied front seats at the meeting. The strong presence of these non-state actors at a heads-of-state summit was a significant feature of the new emerging regional system.

For the Arab publics, the Doha summit proved that their governments could do much if they wanted to. The proof was that Qatar, a tiny and marginal state, was able to play a much bigger role than its size and leverage should have allowed. Nobody expected that Qatar and the 'Doha group' would declare war against Israel – but they did take a firm stance. The maximum realistic action was the freezing of Qatari and Mauritanian, which were already nominal, diplomatic relations with Israel, and threatening the withdrawal of the Arab Peace Initiative. This initiative was made by the Beirut Arab Summit in 2002 offering Israel full normalization of relations with all Arab countries, in return for accepting the two-state solution based on 1967 borders. Israel (and Bush's administration) ignored it.

Clearly, any further enhancing of the 'resistance camp' by extension or deepening is chilling news to the Egyptians and Saudis, and of course to their Western backers. The immediate Saudi response, at a previously scheduled Arab summit in Kuwait on 19 January 2009, convened just three days after the Doha summit, was a package of tougher language against Israel and a series of actions. It too threatened to withdraw the Arab Peace Initiative, pledged to give US$1 billion to reconstruct the Gaza Strip, reconciled with members of the 'resistance camp', Syria and Qatar, and boldly called for Palestinian unity. After the Gaza war, the Arab moderate camp was on the defensive. Barack Obama's coming to office in 2010 was their last hope, that his administration might undertake a more even-handed policy which at least embraces the Arab Peace Initiative, end the Israeli occupation and make the creation of an independent Palestinian state a reality. The hope faded away too, allowing for the continuous rise of the 'new resisting Middle East', with Hamas as part of it, all coupled with another wave of radicalization.

What about the other wars on Gaza Strip in 2012, 2014, 2018, 2021 and 2022?

Two main strategic views were advanced within Israeli leadership circles on what to do about Hamas-controlled Gaza since 2007. One advocated a military re-occupation of the Gaza Strip entirely to finish Hamas and remove it from rule. Another argued that invading Gaza is costly, unjustified internationally, and burdens Israel with the responsibility of governing the 2 million Palestinians. Instead, a containment strategy that keeps high pressure on Hamas and Gaza is more effective, aiming at keeping Hamas weak enough not to pose any threat to Israel, but strong enough to keep stability over Gaza – the 'mowing the lawn' strategy. The latter approach led Israeli politics and military action concerning Gaza until 2023. Judging whether it was successful or otherwise over the years is an open question. But what has become clear is the explosion of 7 October 2023 was the direct outcome of the years-long strategy of pressuring, mowing and involuntary 'dieting'. The series of wars on the Gaza Strip are best understood and placed within the perspective of this approach.

Each war on Gaza has had its immediate spark, yet such a spark is just an excuse to activate the cyclical strategy of continuous pressure. Sometimes Israel initiates a war, even if there was no pretext. In 2012 and after three years of a relatively 'quiet' period, Israel assassinated Ahmad Jabari, a military leader, and who was the principal negotiator with Egyptian mediators in releasing the Israeli soldier Gilad Shalit in return for freeing 1,000 Palestinian prisoners. In 2014, a two-month war that killed more than 2,100 Palestinians and 73 Israelis was launched on the pretext of the killings of three Israelis in the West Bank at the hands of Hamas. The horrors of this war, the killing of civilians on a large scale and destroying infrastructure provoked international condemnation. In hindsight, the 2014 war can be seen as a small-scale rehearsal for the massive and genocidal war of 2023.

In March 2018, various Palestinian forces including Hamas in the Gaza Strip organized the peaceful 'Great March of Return', along the fences of the Strip, on the 70th anniversary of the *Nakba*, or Palestinian catastrophe in 1948. The main objective of the March was to break the siege and draw international attention to the miserable conditions that the Palestinians in the Gaza Strip have been enduring. The March lasted for about nine months but the cost in Palestinian deaths and injuries was very high. According to UN reports, 214 Palestinians were killed including 46 children and over 36,100 injured.* The outcome of the March of

---

* 'Two Years On: People Injured and Traumatized during the "Great March of Return" Are Still Struggling', United Nations: The Question of Palestine, 6 April 2020, www.un.org/unispal/document/two-years-on-people-injured-and-traumatized-during-the-great-march-of-return-are-still-struggling/.

Return was mixed, but it exacerbated the bitterness and frustration felt by the trapped Palestinians in the Gaza Strip. Non-violent and violent means to end the blockade have both failed.

The next bloody round came in May 2021 and lasted for about two weeks. It was triggered by Israel's incursions into Al-Aqsa Mosque in the holy month of Ramadan, along with the Israeli court's eviction rulings aimed at dozens of Palestinian families in the Sheikh Jarrah neighbourhood of Jerusalem. During the weeks preceding the war, Israeli forces injured more than 1,000 Palestinians in Jerusalem and allowed extremist religious Zionist groups to enter Al-Aqsa's surroundings. The boiling atmosphere exploded with Hamas's threat to Israel that unless it stops incursions and evictions, the movement would hit Israel with rockets. Israel rejected, Hamas fired rockets, and the outcome was eleven days of war that resulted in the killing of 253 Palestinians and injured more than 2,000. In the ceasefire agreement brokered by the Egyptians, Israel backtracked from evicting Palestinian families and de-escalated the tension. Hamas enjoyed some minor victory by broadening its demands beyond breaking the Gaza blockade and to include wider and crucial Palestinian issues such as Jerusalem. The name that Hamas gave to this confrontation, The Sword of Jerusalem, reflected that connection.

On 5 August 2022, Israel launched surprise strikes against targets and personnel of the Islamic Jihad Movement in Gaza. The strikes lasted three days and killed 49 Palestinians and injured many more. Hamas was neither targeted in these strikes nor did it respond. Hamas's refraining from engagement in this round prompted criticism within some Palestinian circles. The movement's justification was anchored in its attempt to maintain calm and save the Gaza Strip and the Gazans from more suffering. In hindsight and taking into account the October 7 attack in the following year, it seems clear that Hamas didn't want to engage in a premature operation triggered by the Islamic Jihad that could spoil or slow its preparation for the October strike. One major conclusion which is acknowledged by most observers after more than a decade of ongoing wars related to Hamas's political steadfastness, its strong rule over Gaza and its military power. In almost all these aspects, and certainly in the latter, Hamas has been amassing growing capabilities, skills and sophistication. The biggest test of all these came with the October 7 attacks and the ensuing war on Gaza.

What is the ratio of the Palestinians killed by Israel and Israelis killed by Palestinians in the Israeli wars on Gaza?

The figures provided by the UN, international groups and credible human rights organizations including Israeli B'Tselem, show that Israel has always been targeting and killing Palestinian civilians at an extraordinary rate. Staring at least from the late 1980s, the death toll of the first Palestinian Intifada, 1987–1993, was 1,376 Palestinians and 94 Israelis; at a ratio of 1:14. During the second Intifada, 2000–2005, the respective figures were 10,559 killed Palestinians and 881 killed Israelis; at a ratio of 1:12. Since the first Israeli war on the Gaza Strip in 2008 up until September 2023, the Palestinians killed by Israel, according to UN reporting, were 6,665 while Israeli fatalities were 314; a ratio of 1:21. The injured Palestinians in the same period were 156,803 while injured Israelis were 6,346; a ratio of 1:24. Removing Israeli soldiers and Palestinian fighters from these figures, wouldn't change these ratios and general trends. This ratio rises exponentially in the 2023–2024 genocide war. At the time of writing, November 2024, the figures of civilians killed were as follows (including Palestinians killed and injured in the West Bank):

Killed: 43,508 Palestinians and 1,139 Israelis at a ratio of 1:38.
Injured: 102,684 Palestinians and 8,730 Israelis, at a ratio 1:11.
Missing (most likely killed): over 10,000 Palestinians.

The 1:38 ratio of Palestinian versus Israeli killed is based on the most conservative figures. If the over than 10,000 missing Palestinians in the Gaza war, practically considered among the dead, are added to the death toll, the ratio jumps to 1:48. Further, the highly respected medical journal the *Lancet* published an estimate of direct and indirect deaths of the war on Gaza that could exceed 186,000.* If this figure is considered, the ratio rises astronomically showing that for each Israeli killed on 7 October and after, there was more than 163 Palestinians killed.

---

* Rasha Khatib, Martin McKee and Salim Yusuf, 'Counting the Dead in Gaza: Difficult but Essential', *The Lancet* 4040, no. 10449 (July 2024): 237–38, www.thelancet.com/journals/lancet/article/PIIS0140-6736(24)01169-3/fulltext.

14

Hamas and Trump's 'Deal of the Century'

WHAT IS THE 'DEAL OF THE CENTURY' AND WHY IS IT SIGNIFICANT?

In January 2020, the United States President Trump's Administration announced what was promoted as the 'Deal of the Century', officially titled as 'Peace to Prosperity: A Vision to Improve the Lives of the Palestinian and Israeli People'. The goal of the deal was to end the Arab–Israeli and Palestinian–Israeli conflicts. In 182 detailed pages, the Vision outlines what it calls a 'practical approach' to the conflict and its major issues that basically denies all Palestinian rights as stipulated by UN resolutions and international law conventions. The proposed solutions in areas of security, refugees, Jerusalem, settlements, natural resources and the form of the final political Palestinian entity are all formulated to reflect Israeli interests. Far from being neutral, in the view of most observers, or anything close to a 'peace plan', the Vision is in fact a repackaging of Israeli right-wing and Christian Zionists' positions on the conflict. Many non-Palestinian critics of the Vision saw it as a reproduction of the terms of South African apartheid, carrying the same hallmarks and characteristics, as 50 former foreign ministers and leaders across Europe expressed in an open letter condemning the Vision. In the words of Alon Leil, a former Israeli diplomat who was in charge of the Israeli foreign ministry's South Africa desk during the apartheid period and Israel's ambassador to South Africa from 1992 to 1994, 'Israel is seeking to introduce and develop the new millennium's version of the old South Africa's deplorable policy'.* Rejected by Palestinians across the political spectrum and by most of the Arab countries and the Arab League, the document completely legitimizes Israeli colonial policies including the annexation of East Jerusalem, the Golan Heights, parts of the West Bank and the Jordan Valley.

In the first place, the Vision introduces a narrative that breaks away from the universally agreed-upon and UN-based articulations that the root cause of the conflict is the Israeli military occupation of Palestinian and Arab lands. The term 'occupation' is completely absent from the text. Instead, the plan repeatedly cites 'Palestinian terrorism' as the main cause of the conflict, justifying its focus on Israeli security throughout its content. The Vision's presentation of the current reality is distorted, prioritizing Israel and its security, while marginalizing the Palestinians, their national rights and their security. There is no mention of the origins behind the rise of Palestinian resistance and armed struggle over more than a century. Nor is there any acknowledgement that Palestinians of various political and ideological leanings have been engaged in a struggle for national liberation and self-determination.

Instead, the Vision employs a 'new' language that equates the 'suffering of the two peoples', omitting any mention of Palestinian rights. For example, the Vision repeatedly uses terms like 'Jewish communities' or 'Jewish residents' when referring to Israeli settlements or religious extremist settlers on confiscated Palestinian lands in the West Bank and East Jerusalem. The Palestinian occupied territories are referred to only as 'contested territories', with no recognition of an occupier or the occupied. By framing the problem as a mere internal ethnic conflict, the Vision focuses on creating inventive ways to resolve 'tensions' between Jewish residents and Palestinian residents. In doing so, the plan effectively legitimizes the illegality of hundreds of settlements in the

---

*   Alon Liel, 'Trump's Plan for Palestine Looks a Lot Like Apartheid', *Foreign Policy*, 27 February 2020, https://foreignpolicy.com/2020/02/27/trumps-plan-for-palestine-looks-a-lot-like-apartheid/.

West Bank and East Jerusalem, in complete defiance of UN resolutions and international law.

The Vision disregards the continuous settlement building – even after the signing of the Oslo Accords in 1993 – that has blocked any possibility of creating a Palestinian state. This ongoing settlement activity has deepened Palestinian frustration, contributing significantly to the eruption of the second Intifada in 2000, which resulted in the deaths of *five times* as many Palestinians as Israelis and the destruction of many parts of the West Bank and Gaza Strip.

The Vision ignores the historic concessions already made by the Palestinians in recognizing the Jewish state created on 78 per cent of the historical Palestinian homeland. In contrast, it praises Israeli generosity in returning territories to Egypt that it 'captured' in 1967. Since the PLO's recognition of Israel in 1989 and its renunciation of armed resistance, there has been no real progress concerning Palestinian national rights, including self-determination, refugees, Jerusalem, borders and other issues. The elusive Palestinian state promised in many agreements has continued to fade away over time. Alongside these decades-long false promises and the resulting frustrations and failures on the Palestinian side, Israeli strategy has been to pursue a policy of 'creating facts on the ground' through the Judaization of territories, effectively killing any possibility for a future Palestinian state.

Bringing this context back into the picture is essential for any sensible discussion about Hamas, the Deal of the Century and the future of Palestine. Against this backdrop of political and physical disasters befalling the Palestinians since at least 1989, one can reasonably understand the shift in the Palestinian mood and the rise of Hamas's popularity, influence and power. Dismissing this recent history, as the Vision does, ends up projecting Hamas – and sometimes even the Palestinian Authority – as alien and rootless organizations that mysteriously landed in Palestine, rather than as natural, expected responses to a continuous military occupation.

How does the 'Deal of the Century' project Hamas and the Palestinian resistance?

The Vision's repeated emphasis on being 'security-focused' translates into the constant framing of Hamas as the main obstacle to achieving regional peace. Trump's Deal reveals a significant American-Israeli convergence in their view of Hamas. As the most notable move in American 'peace-making' efforts in the region since the Oslo Accords in 1993, it warrants deep analysis regarding its positioning of Hamas. The Vision reflects Israeli and American insistence on projecting Hamas as an unchangeable 'terrorist organization', sometimes lumped together with ISIS. This designation is seen by many Palestinians as a renewed practice of exploiting the pretext of 'terrorism' to expand, perpetuate and legitimize the occupational and colonial status quo.

Beyond this general inference, the Hamas-related allusions in the plan are intriguing. The Vision consistently expresses two major approaches towards Hamas: reducing it from a multifaceted political, social and governing party to a 'terrorist group', and imposing an impossible list of conditions on the Palestinians and Hamas that they must fulfil before Israel commits to any obligations outlined in the 'peace plan'. The Vision insists on labelling Hamas as a terrorist organization, without considering the movement's changes in political outlook, platform and practice over the years. It seems the drafters of the text were either ignorant of the extensive literature on Hamas's thinking, politics and functioning, or they deliberately ignored it, regurgitating standard perceptions and accusations against Hamas. The text obsessively includes 53 references to Hamas or terror/terrorism, clearly used as euphemisms for Hamas. Several times, the Vision stresses Hamas's commitment to the 'destruction of Israel', an objective not found in any official statement of Hamas, even in its early, rash and ill-written Charter of 1988. Hamas has since evolved in its political discourse and revamped its political thinking in many statements, with many advising Western governments to

open channels of communication with it, especially after the publication of its 2017 'Document of Principles and General Policies'.

Contrary to such advice, the Vision's pronounced message is
that Hamas is unwelcome in the realm of politics. Removing the
designation of Hamas as a 'terrorist organization' runs counter to
Israeli and American interests by undermining a major pretext
behind many of their policies. This refusal to view Hamas as
anything else was evident in Benjamin Netanyahu's response to
Hamas's 2017 document, when the Israeli prime minister the-
atrically tore it apart in front of the cameras. It is necessary for
Israel to keep Hamas pigeonholed as a terrorist group because
this serves Israeli interests regarding Hamas and Gaza.

The Vision refers to the conditions placed on Hamas after it
was elected in 2006 by the Quartet (the UN, the USA, the EU
and Russia) that would have to be met in order for the Hamas-
led government to be recognized internationally: to renounce
violence, recognize Israel and accept all agreements signed by
Israel and the PLO. A fair and pragmatic assessment after years
of practice might have concluded that Hamas did indeed move
halfway towards meeting these conditions: its armed struggle was
reduced to defence rather than initiating attacks, it accepted a
Palestinian state based on the 1967 borders, and its governance
operates within the Palestinian Basic Law and other legal principles established by the Palestinian Authority, itself a product of
the Oslo Accords. As the de facto government of more than 2
million Palestinians in the Gaza Strip, any pragmatic and serious
'peace plan' should have taken this reality – and Hamas's capacity
to 'change and be changed' – into account. The authors of the
Vision, however, were not interested in doing this.

The other approach the Vision adopts regarding Hamas (and
the Palestinians in general) is the imposition of lengthy and
impossible conditions that they must meet for Israel to commit to
its 'obligations' under the 'peace plan'. Most objective analyses of
the Vision concluded that the 'peace for prosperity' plan for Pal-
estine/Israel was less intended for implementation and more for

providing American approval and legitimacy for Israel's de facto occupation of Palestinian land and future annexation of more. This is even more obvious when considering the impossible obligations the Vision places on the Palestinians during a new trial period of four years, during which they would be subjected to a strict testing process.

If the Palestinians pass the test and are deemed worthy of political acknowledgement, the USA would recognize a fragmented Palestinian territorial entity resembling isolated Bantustan townships, with no sovereignty over its borders, natural resources, economy or ports, and entirely at the mercy of Israeli control. Palestinians would have the freedom to call this fractured entity a 'state'! In return for American and Israeli recognition of this 'state', I have counted 16 solid conditions that the Palestinians in general (and Hamas in particular) would have to meet:

1. recognize Israel as a Jewish state (which would mean the historical delegitimization of Palestinians in Israel and both the Palestinian past and present);
2. accept land annexation of parts of the West Bank and the Jordan Valley by Israel;
3. accept and protect the permanent presence of the settlers and settlements in the West Bank and East Jerusalem;
4. accept and surrender to Israeli sovereignty over Palestine's borders, air-space, water and natural resources;
5. renounce 'terrorism' (resistance) in all forms;
6. accept a demilitarized 'state' and demilitarized Gaza Strip and dismantle 'terror groups' such as Hamas and the Islamic Jihad;
7. accept all security arrangements made by Israel however often they change;
8. end all rights of Palestinian refugees;
9. accept the projected 'swap solution' for the 'Jewish refugees' from Arab countries which the Vision links to the solution for Palestinian refugees;

10. accept that Israel will continue to keep thousands of Palestinian prisoners in its jails and only release some as it wishes;

11. return of the paltry few Israeli prisoners or bodies retained to Israel prior to any release of any Palestinian prisoners who might have moderate sentences;

12. stop any payments to the families of activists who were killed in the cause of Palestine (martyrs);

13. end what Israel and the USA describe as 'incitement' content in schoolbooks and the media;

14. accept and facilitate normalization between Israel and other Arab countries;

15. commit to never resorting to the International Criminal Court or any other international law mechanism or organization to file cases against Israel;

16. to end all claims relating to all present and historical conflict and consider the case closed forever!

As they stand, these are surrender terms of the most humiliating nature. Ironically, there is not a single condition that the Vision places on Israel. Further, Israel is left with the ultimate power to approve or disapprove whether the Palestinians have met this or that condition. The Vision allocates two sections under the subtitles 'Gaza Criteria' and 'Security Criteria', where most of these conditions are reiterated and directed at Hamas. Both sections hold Hamas responsible for all the dire conditions facing the more than 2 million Palestinians living there, without mentioning the inhuman blockade that Israel has imposed on the Gaza Strip for the past 13 years (until the publication of the plan).

Hamas's position on the Deal of the Century was, expectedly, fierce rejection. This time its position was aligned with the positions of its main rival in the Palestinian scene, Fatah, the PLO and the PA, as well as that of all other Palestinian organizations. The movement did not vow to undertake any military action to foil the Deal. There was no need for that, as the general anticipation, be it within the Palestinians arena or regional and international circles, was pessimistic about its success. Without a Palestinian partner, the much-celebrated Deal would never fly – and such was the case.

15
October 7 and Hamas: Causes and Motives

October 7 is not an isolated event but a consequence. This reasoned and unavoidable reality has been brushed aside by American and Western politicians and the media, and of course by Israel. Immediately after the October 7 attacks, Western mass media exhibited a bewildering one-sided coverage, seen by many as spoon fed by Israeli perspectives, misinformation and *hasbara*, painting a universal criminal image of Hamas and the Palestinians at large. The views of the movement and its explanation of the events, and the broader and historical context of the conflict, were almost absent in this media. Against this tide, the following account attempts to offer space to Hamas' views, without agreeing or disagreeing with them. The chapter relies greatly on Hamas's statements, original documents and official positions made by its leaders. The discussion here complements the analysis presented in the introduction to this edition. The aim here is to provide as comprehensive a picture as possible of the events and the subsequent genocidal war on Gaza and leave it to the reader to draw their own conclusions. Next to leaders' statements and formal declarations made by Hamas, the discussion will use one of the main documents published by the movement during the war: 'Our Narrative ... Operation Al-Aqsa Flood', a 16-page document issued in January 2024 outlining Hamas' positions and explanation of the attacks, aimed 'to clarify to our people and the free peoples of the world the reality of what happened on Oct. 7, the motives behind, its general context related to the Palestinian cause, as well as a refutation of the Israeli allegations and to put the facts into perspective'.*

Before delving into the main specific issues and questions, a brief description of what happened on 7 October 2023 is in order. At around 6.30am that day, Hamas launched 5,000 rockets into southern Israel. Within the same hour, hundreds of Al-Qassam Brigades fighters broke through the heavily fortified security fences on the eastern border of the Gaza Strip, and stormed dozens of Israeli sites, military, kibbutzim and towns. The preparation and execution of the carefully planned operation went under Israeli security radar and intelligence along the borders. For a few hours, Al-Qassam Brigades seemed to have full control over dozens of Israeli sites.

Controversy over who killed whom and at what scale remains open. The initial figure that was disseminated by Israel, 1,400 people, of whom 1,200 were civilians, continued to decrease over time. Two months after the attacks, it dropped to 1,200, and in December 2023 a 'final' Israeli official figure put the death toll at 1,139, among them 695 civilians. The Israeli army admitted that they deployed Apache helicopters and tanks to the sites, and that these 'may' have killed 'some' Israeli civilians. This 'some' was investigated and questioned by Israeli and American media, including *Haaretz* and the *New York Times*. Hamas and the Islamic Jihad captured 248 hostages, military and civilians, and took them to the Gaza Strip.

Shocked and humiliated by the attacks, Israel vowed to take revenge by punishing Hamas and the Gaza Strip as a whole. The only comparably surprising attack in Israel's history was the 1973 war when Egypt and Syria coordinated a military campaign that aimed to liberate the Sinai desert of Egypt and the Golan

---

* 'Our Narrative ... Operation Al-Aqsa Flood' was published in Arabic and English. Quotes here are taken from the English version as published by Hamas; see Hamas Media Office, 'Hamas Document Reveals: Why We Carried Out Al-Aqsa Flood Operation – Summary and PDF', *The Palestine Chronicle*, 21 January 2024, https://shorturl.at/8X5lX.

Heights of Syria. This time round, however, the successful attack that evaded security and intelligence came from a group, not a state, and from a nearby area under Israel's full blockade. On the same day, Israel started its war against Hamas and the Gaza Strip, deploying its military might on land, by air and by sea. Over the year that followed, Israel dropped massive and unprecedented firepower on the Gaza Strip that amounted to four times what was dropped on Hiroshima. The unprecedented scale of destruction and killing of civilians, with evidence that such killing has been deliberate, placed Israel's war on Gaza within the category of genocide according to human rights and UN organizations. Cases have been filed and are still under examination, at the time of writing, at the International Court of Justice (ICJ) and the International Criminal Court (ICC) accusing Israel of committing genocide against the 2.3 million Palestinians in the Gaza Strip.

What were the causes and objectives of the October 7 attack?

Two main texts help us here to understand the causes behind the attacks and their objectives as seen by Hamas: a speech given by Mohammed al-Dhaif, the leader of Al-Qassam Brigades, Hamas's military wing, on the morning of the attacks,* and the 'Our Narrative' document.** Al-Dhaif's speech captured the intensity of the moment, while the explanation of the 'Our Narrative' document benefited from the advantage of hindsight.

In his audio-recorded speech, al-Dhaif outlined Hamas's objectives of the operation and the reasons behind it. He outlined the

---

*   Mohammad al-Deif, 'The Speech: Al Aqsa Flood', Institute for Palestine Studies, 7 October 2023, *Majallat al-Dirasat al-Filastiniyya* 137 (Winter 2024), www.palestine-studies.org/ar/node/1654998.
**   Israel claimed that it killed al-Dhaif on 13 July 2024 in a strike that targeted a crowded 'safe zone', in the Mawasi area close to Khan Yunis in the Gaza Strip. The strike resulted in the killing of more than 100 displaced Palestinians, mostly children and women. Up to the time of writing, Hamas has not confirmed the Israeli claims.

long list of immediate suffering the Palestinians endured under Israeli occupation as the main causes behind the attacks:

> The Zionist entity occupied our land, expelled our people, destroyed our cities, villages and towns, and committed hundreds of massacres against the innocents. It thrashed all world conventions, human rights, international law. We warned the [Israeli] occupation leaders about the continuation of their crimes, and called upon world leaders to act and stop the crimes of the occupation, yet they didn't move. Rather, the crimes of the occupation increased and crossed all limits, particularly in Jerusalem and against the Al-Aqsa Mosque. The incursions of the occupation troops into Al-Aqsa increased, and they desecrated the holiness of the Mosque, dragged praying women, the elderly, the children and the youth and prevented them from arriving to the mosque.

Al-Dhaif broadened his speech to include the wider historical context and the national goals of the Palestinians. The liberation of the Palestinian people was the ultimate goal, and the aspirations for an independent state lay at the top of the agenda, as pointed out in the speech. Noticeably, al-Dhaif referred to the backing of UN resolutions and international law to such aspirations. The immediate and *longue-durée* context are merged:

> ... every day they attack our people in Jerusalem, steal their houses and land. At the same time, the occupation authorities still imprison thousands of our heroes and practice against them the most brutal methods of humiliation and torture. There are hundreds of our prisoners who spent more than twenty years, and dozens of them, males and females, whose bodies were eaten by cancer and illnesses, and many of them died because of lack of medical treatment, and deliberate slow death. All our offers to undertake exchange of prisoners based on human reasons were rejected ...

... the occupation troops attack our cities, villages and towns in the West Bank and incurs damage. They attack houses of innocent people, killing and wounding and arresting. Hundreds of martyrs were killed, and more injured in this year only because of these crimes. At the same time, they confiscate thousands of donums of land, expel its owners and build in their place settlements and protect settlers letting them ransack, burn and steal ... [along with this] the crime of occupation continues in imposing the brutal blockade on our beloved [Gaza] Strip ...

The speech links all these detailed practices of the Israeli occupation to the attacks on 7 October 2023, stating that military action is the only option left after Israel's dismissal of international laws and resolutions:

... Considering these relentless crimes against our people ... and its rejection to international resolutions and laws, enjoying American and Western support and international silence, we have decided to put an end to all of that by the help of God, so that this enemy understands that the time where it continues roistering in our land without accountability has come to an end. We announce the beginning of the Al-Aqsa Flood operation, and we announce that by the help of God the first strike of Al-Aqsa Flood that targeted the enemy's positions, airports, and military fortresses included more than five thousand rockets and shells in twenty minutes only. Oh our people and the freemen of the world, today the anger of Al-Aqsa erupts, the anger of our people, of our nation, of the freemen of the world ... our fighters this is your day against the criminal enemy, its time is over, kill them as they kill you, and expel them as they expelled you, *don't kill the elderly and the children*, [emphasis added] and remove this enemy from your land ... today, yes today, our people restores its uprising, rectify its way forward, and embraces the project of return, liberation and the establishment of its state ...

For its part, the 'Our Narrative' document combines the historical context of the struggle of the Palestinians for liberation and the recent suffering of the Palestinians including the blockade on the Gaza Strip as the shaping motives behind the attacks. It starts by referring to the decades-long colonization of Palestine stressing that 'The battle of the Palestinian people against the occupation and colonialism of Palestine did not start on Oct. 7, but started 105 years ago, including 30 years of British colonialism and 75 years of Zionist occupation.'* Then, the document points out that: 'According to official figures, in the period between January 2000 and September 2023, the Israeli occupation killed 11,299 Palestinians and injured 156,768 others, the great majority of them were civilians.'** Despite all the suffering and catastrophes the Palestinians have faced, the world looked the other way. The USA in particular and Western countries in general maintained their support for Israel, and 'have always been treating Israel as a state above the law', shielding it even from any condemnation by the UN or international law. Even after the Palestinians' concessions of 78 per cent of the historic land of Palestine in the Oslo Accords in 1993, the document maintains, Israel never accepted the idea of a Palestinian state on the remaining part: the West Bank, the Gaza Strip and East Jerusalem. Frustration and impasse surrounded the Palestinians from all sides:

> The Israeli officials confirmed at [sic] several occasions their absolute rejection to the establishment of a Palestinian state. Just one month before Operation Al-Aqsa Flood, Israeli Prime Minister Benjamin Netanyahu presented a map of a so-called 'New Middle East', depicting 'Israel' stretching from the Jordan River to the Mediterranean Sea including the West Bank and

---

*   Hamas Media Office, 'Our Narrative', 3.
**   Hamas Media Office, 'Our Narrative', 4.

Gaza. The entire world at that – UN General Assembly's – podium were silent towards his speech full of arrogance and ignorance towards the rights of the Palestinian people.*

Did Hamas target civilians in its October 7 attacks and what was the rationale behind that if this was the case?

In its statements, Hamas denied targeting civilians and unequivocally rejected the accusations of committing rape or killing children. The movement acknowledged that civilians were killed but it said such killing was caused by Israel's military response against its fighters. Hamas also acknowledged that some mistakes took place during the operation. Here too there are two texts that help us understand Hamas's argument about the killing of civilians. The first one is a translated excerpt from a long interview on Al Jazeera with Saleh al-Arouri, a Hamas senior leader and deputy of the head of the politburo (until his assassination by Israel on 2 January 2024 in Lebanon), on 13 October 2023.** This specific interview is extremely important, for it came less than a week after the attacks and offered Hamas' early and fresh account. Al-Arouri elaborated on his fighters' conduct and other aspects of the operation including the killing of civilians:

> let me here present our official position ...: what happened is that when [Israeli] Gaza Division collapsed at a speed that was not expected and the entire military scattered, the ordinary people in Gaza realized that and crowds of them entered the open borders. This created chaos in clashes and other aspects that went against the initial plan. The access to the kibutzes and settlements became easy, and there were Israeli guards and

---

* Hamas Media Office, 'Our Narrative', 5.

** العاروري للجزيرة: لهذه الأسباب أطلقنا "طوفان الأقصى" وخطتنا الدفاعية أقوى، 'من الهجومية' ['Al-Arouri to Al Jazeera: The Reasons Why We Launched "Al-Aqsa Flood" and Our Defensive Plan is Stronger than the Offensive One'], *Al Jazeera*, 13 October 2023, https://shorturl.at/v22ls.

soldiers that engaged inside these places against Al-Qassam fighters resulting in the killing of civilians. Another important point that must be clear here is that the Israeli army adopts what it calls the Hannibal Directive according to which they would kill their own prisoners and those who captured them in the case of hostage taking. During the operation this doctrine was activated ... we are certain that some of our fighters were along with the Israeli prisoners they held. Al-Qassam fighters had a plan that was announced by the brother [Mohammed] al-Dhaif [Al-Qassam leader] in the first hour [of the operation]. He said we are going to fight the Israeli army, and gave official instructions to the fighters to avoid killing women, children and the elderly. The recording of his message is available publicly. These are the orders to our fighters. Also, there were many videos that showed Al-Qassam fighters accompanying women to their children and make them safe, and leave them ... our fighters don't target civilians, and it is impossible for them to commit the crimes that the occupation accused them of such as rape and killing children and civilians. The Israeli army collapsed and didn't do its duty in protecting itself and the civilians fell in the crossfire in open areas ... we don't say that no civilians were killed, but [I say] it is a hundred percent that hurting or killing civilians was not part of Al-Qassam plan.

We are a responsible party, and we act according to our religion that prohibits us from hurting civilians or civilian life, and we act in accordance with international laws of war. We practice our resistance against the [Israeli] occupation in line with international legitimacy that gives us the right to fight this enemy, until the world recognises our right in life and freedom as the rest of other peoples.

In the same line of argumentation, yet clearer than the content of a live, televised interview, the 'Our Narrative' document states the following:

In light of the Israeli fabricated accusations and allegations over Operation Al-Aqsa Flood on Oct. 7 and its repercussions, **we in the Islamic Resistance Movement – Hamas clarify the following** [emphasis in the original]:

1. Operation Al-Aqsa Flood on Oct. 7 targeted the Israeli military sites, and sought to arrest the enemy's soldiers to put pressure on the Israeli authorities to release the thousands of Palestinians held in Israeli jails through a prisoners exchange deal. Therefore, the operation focused on destroying the Israeli army's Gaza Division, the Israeli military sites stationed near the Israeli settlements around Gaza.

2. **Avoiding harm to civilians, especially children, women and elderly people is a religious and moral commitment by all the Al-Qassam Brigades' fighters. We reiterate that the Palestinian resistance was fully disciplined and committed to the Islamic values during the operation and that the Palestinian fighters only targeted the occupation soldiers and those who carried weapons against our people. In the meantime, the Palestinian fighters were keen to avoid harming civilians despite the fact that the resistance does not possess precise weapons. In addition, if there was any case of targeting civilians; it happened accidently and in the course of the confrontation with the occupation forces.** [emphasis in the original] …

3. Maybe some faults happened during Operation Al-Aqsa Flood's implementation due to the rapid collapse of the Israeli security and military system, and the chaos caused along the border areas with Gaza.

    As attested by many, the Hamas Movement dealt in a positive and kind manner with all civilians who have been held in Gaza, and sought from the earliest days of the aggression to release them, and that's what happened during the week-long humanitarian truce where those civilians were

released in exchange of releasing Palestinian women and
children from Israeli jails.

4. What the Israeli occupation promoted of allegations that
the Al-Qassam Brigades on Oct. 7 were targeting Israeli
civilians are nothing but complete lies and fabrications.
The source of these allegations is the Israeli official narrative and no independent source proved any of them. It is a
well-known fact that the Israeli official narrative had always
sought to demonize the Palestinian resistance, while also
legalizing its brutal aggression on Gaza.*

What did Hamas say about 'beheading babies', 'raping women' and burning civilians?

As from the very same day of 7 October 2023, the Israeli propaganda and *hasbara* machine succeeded in framing the event
and promoting a narrative that dominated Western and even
non-Western media. This narrative revolved around the deliberate killing of hundreds of civilians, beheading babies, mass rape
and burning people alive. Also, Israel announced on the first
couple of days that the figure of the people killed by Hamas was
1,400. The entire media world was simply fed information disseminated by one source, Israel. There was no other media or
political source that had access to the information or the scene to
verify what Israeli sources spread.

Later investigations by Israeli media and some other outlets
exposed fabricated elements in the Israeli narrative, lies and
exaggerations, including the number of victims and its break-
down into military recruits and civilians.** Despite the passage
of one year of the war, many details of what really happened on

---

* Hamas Media Office, 'Our Narrative', 7–8.
** Arun Gupta, 'American Media Keep Citing Zaka – Though its
October 7 Atrocity Stories Are Discredited in Israel', *The Intercept*, 27
February 2024, https://theintercept.com/2024/02/27/zaka-october-7-
israel-hamas-new-york-times/.

7 October 2023 are still not fully known. However, the dominance of the official Israeli account has remained just as powerful within Western circles of politics and media. Hamas failed to counter the international Israeli campaign that demonized the movement. The statements by its leaders and the documents it had issued came late and only after the media discourse had already been shaped. Hamas's main documents in explaining the events, outlining its objectives and responding to accusations, 'Our Narrative', was published four months after the events, and by that time the Israeli story dominated the mainstream media. The following long excerpts from 'Our Narrative' offer the movement's account and responses to accusations:

Here are some details that go against the Israeli allegations:

- Video clips taken on that day – Oct. 7 – along with the testimonies by Israelis themselves that were released later showed that the Al-Qassam Brigades' fighters didn't target civilians, and many Israelis were killed by the Israeli army and police due to their confusion.
- It has also been firmly refuted the lie of the '40 beheaded babies' by the Palestinian fighters, and even Israeli sources denied this lie. Many of the western media agencies unfortunately adopted this allegation and promoted it.
- The suggestion that the Palestinian fighters committed rape against Israeli women was fully denied including by the Hamas Movement. A report by the Mondoweiss news website on Dec. 1, 2023, among others, said there is lack of any evidence of 'mass rape' allegedly perpetrated by Hamas members on Oct. 7 and that Israel used such allegation 'to fuel the genocide in Gaza'.
- According to two reports by the Israeli Yedioth Ahronoth newspaper on Oct. 10 and the *Haaretz* newspaper on Nov. 18, many Israeli civilians were killed by an Israeli military helicopter especially those who were in the Nova music

festival near Gaza where 364 Israeli civilians were killed. The two reports said the Hamas fighters reached the area of the festival without any prior knowledge of the festival, where the Israeli helicopter opened fire on both the Hamas fighters and the participants in the festival. The *Yedioth Ahronoth* also said the Israeli army, to prevent further infiltrations from Gaza and to prevent any Israelis being arrested by the Palestinian fighters, struck over 300 targets in areas surrounding the Gaza Strip.

- Other Israeli testimonies confirmed that the Israeli army raids and soldiers' operations killed many Israeli captives and their captors. The Israeli occupation army bombed the houses in the Israeli settlements where Palestinian fighters and Israelis were inside in a clear application of the Israeli army notorious 'Hannibal Directive' which clearly says that 'better a dead civilian hostage or soldier than taken alive' to avoid engaging in a prisoners swap with the Palestinian resistance.

- Furthermore, the occupation authorities revised the number of their killed soldiers and civilians from 1,400 to 1,200, after finding that 200-burnt corpses had belonged to the Palestinian fighters who were killed and mixed with Israeli corpses. This means that the one who killed the fighters is the one who killed the Israelis, knowing that only the Israeli army possesses military planes that killed, burned and destroyed Israeli areas on Oct. 7.

- The Israeli heavy aerial raids across Gaza that led to the death of nearly 60 Israeli captives also prove that the Israeli occupation does not care about the life of their captives in Gaza.*

---

* Hamas Media Office, 'Our Narrative', 8–9.

16
What Comes Next for Hamas?

Did Hamas expect the scale of Israeli retaliation and its brutal war on Gaza, and did they admit committing mistakes?

Neither Hamas nor any other party involved in the conflict, nor even closely watching experts, could have anticipated the scale, magnitude and genocidal nature of Israel's response. Equally shocking was the de facto green light given to Israel by the West and the international community to carry out its war. Despite the horrific death toll and the destruction of Palestinian civilian life, Israel faced no serious consequences. Evidence showed that Israel intended to render the Gaza Strip uninhabitable, forcing many Palestinians to 'voluntarily' leave in search of better lives for their families, thereby fulfilling Israel's goal of expelling as many Palestinians as possible.

The immediate short-term Israeli retaliation and the deployment of long-term plans into action, including the expulsion of Palestinians and the possible re-occupation of Gaza, were beyond Hamas's calculations. Mousa Abu Marzouq, a member of the movement's politburo, reflected a significant deliberation within Hamas in March 2024, by saying that no one expected that Israel would 'wage such a barbaric war on us in violation of international law'. Though Hamas's spokespersons tried their best to avoid the hypothetical question of 'what if the movement had known the consequences …', several statements and media interviews reflected a sense of shock and disbelief at the scale of Israel's response.

Regarding the October 7 operation and its conduct, the movement did admit that mistakes were made throughout the execution. This was made clear in several statements by its leaders, including Saleh al-Arouri, another member of the movement's politburo, and Mousa Abu Marzouq, quoted above. Additionally, the 'Our Narrative' document referred to the fact that 'mistakes might have happened'. In all statements related to the attacks, Hamas strived to stress that the killing of civilians was neither a policy nor an approved tactic in the attacks, and its fighters were trained and disciplined to only fight combatants and pursue military targets.

How was Hamas's military and governance performance during the war?

Hamas's resistance during a year of the war has been unyielding. Facing the might and sophistication of the Israeli army, backed by the continuous military support and intelligence from the USA, the UK and France during the war, while cut off from the outside world with no material supply, the movement's steadfastness and resilience has been impressive. Hamas's military has been significantly weakened, but certainly not finished. Media and military reporting showed the movement resurfacing in various parts of the Gaza Strip where Israel thought it had destroyed its battalions. Entrenched in a complex network of tunnels across the Gaza Strip, Hamas succeeded in keeping most Israeli captives in its hands. More telling is that despite more than a year of security scanning of every corner of the Gaza Strip by Israeli and American drones and intelligence, Hamas retained a structure and chain of command in the Gaza Strip.

Hamas's control over civil administration and the running of ministries, municipalities and official services has been badly weakened. Government bodies and civilian infrastructure, including hospitals, schools, water reservoirs, electricity stations and sanitation plants, were all severely stricken by the Israeli carpet bombardment. While Israel aimed to dismantle the official network of government to the point of paralysis, it did not fully succeed. Many organs of Hamas's government remained functioning at a reasonable level against all odds. Months into the war, Israel attempted to organize alternative local entities, such as tribal chiefs and others opposing Hamas, to take over responsibilities. These attempts failed, and Hamas's supporters sustained their control, albeit with difficulty and more challenges.

To what degree has Hamas been weakened by the war on Gaza, militarily, politically and publicly?

As stated above, Hamas has been significantly weakened militarily and administratively after long months of a vicious and relentless war. The movement's military capabilities have been drastically compromised, with more than 17,000 fighters killed according to Israeli sources at the time of writing. Estimates of Hamas's original military force at the beginning of the war range from 30,000 to 35,000. Hamas's ability to launch rockets into Israel appears to have been almost destroyed, and several of its high-ranking military and political leaders were also killed. Additionally, its civilian apparatus was deliberately targeted, with Israel aiming to inflict total paralysis on Hamas's capacity to function as an authority during the war. Israeli attacks spared no governmental or semi-governmental body, including civil defence teams attempting to rescue the injured and retrieve bodies from the debris.

The real and elusive question is whether this weakening in military and administrative areas has rendered Hamas dysfunctional to the point of being unable to control the post-war Gaza Strip, or at least to remain as a force that any post-war arrangement must include or secure the approval of. Identifying such a point of dysfunctionality is difficult, particularly as events continue to unfold at the time of writing. A year into the war, one could tentatively say that matters for Hamas hang in the balance and could go either way. If a ceasefire is agreed upon (around a year into the war), Hamas seems to have spared enough military, organizational and governmental assets to play a central role in the Gaza Strip – not necessarily retaining power in its pre-October 7 form. However, if the war drags on for longer, as some Israeli generals suggest it might for another year, Hamas's power in all aspects will be further weakened to the point of crippling the movement so badly that it would not be capable of taking part in the post-war arrangement for the Gaza Strip.

As has been repeatedly stressed, even by Israeli and American officials, Hamas is more than just an organization – it is an idea. You can hit it, but you can't uproot it. For many Palestinians, this idea of Hamas is the present-day translation of their resistance against the Israeli occupation. As long as this occupation continues, the idea of resistance represented by Hamas, its predecessors or its successors will remain alive, continually producing new forms and movements. Thus, even if Hamas has been drastically weakened in material aspects, its presence will remain strong and rooted within the Palestinian people in the Gaza Strip, the rest of Palestine, and among Palestinians and their Arab and Muslim supporters around the world.

This brings us to the question of whether Hamas has been weakened publicly and in terms of the support it has enjoyed over time, both inside and outside Palestine. The easier part of this question concerns Hamas's standing among the Palestinian people in the diaspora, the West Bank and Jerusalem. Based on surveys and manifestations of support such as demonstrations and media portrayal, Hamas seems to have amassed stronger and broader support, being seen as the bearer of the resistance flag against Israel. The trickier part of the question concerns the Palestinians in the Gaza Strip. Here, there are mixed messages: some reports indicate a decline in the movement's support due to the severe price paid by civilians, while others show steady support. Israel's campaign to inflict maximum destruction and pain on the Palestinians of the Strip, pushing them to blame Hamas at least in part, has had some effect. Generally speaking, without risking specific figures and percentages, it is safe to suggest that while

Hamas's support has increased in the West Bank, East Jerusalem and outside Palestine, its support in the Gaza Strip has indeed decreased.

What are the future scenarios facing Hamas?

Perhaps this question is the most difficult of all, especially as developments are still unfolding at the time of writing. Exceptional and unprecedented conditions have evolved, including the possibility of a long-term Israeli military re-occupation of the Gaza Strip, or at least parts of it. Much of the 'day after' reality and arrangement depends on the outcome of the war, which remains unforeseen. Another key factor in assessing Hamas's future is the extent to which the movement is weakened and its capacity to function in various aspects. Additionally, the potential role of the Palestinian Authority or a new form of Palestinian consensual leadership is an important factor.

Other dynamics will also influence the outcome and the future of Hamas, including Israel's policies in the West Bank and the situation there, and whether it is becoming more volatile or stable. The positions of other key players, particularly the USA and Arab states such as Egypt, Qatar, Jordan and the UAE are crucial in shaping Hamas's fortunes. In such a complex matrix of factors, any consideration of possible trajectories for Hamas after the war must be approached with extreme caution. With this in mind, future scenarios for Hamas could follow one of the following paths or a combination of them. I start by suggesting the best and worst-case scenarios from the perspective of Hamas, followed by other possibilities that fall between these two extremes.

Hamas's best-case scenario: In this scenario and despite being weakened both militarily and administratively, Hamas joins forces with other Palestinian factions to form a post-war, unified Palestinian leadership responsible for administering the Gaza Strip as part of a broader, nationwide Palestinian structure that also governs the West Bank. In this arrangement, Hamas relinquishes the full military and political control it once exercised over Gaza prior to 7 October 2023. Statements from Hamas's leaders during the war indicated a lack of desire to govern Gaza exclusively after the war, even if such an option were available. Instead, they called for a collective Palestinian leadership that includes all factions.

In accordance with this optimistic scenario, Hamas's military activities would be largely muted, with the possibility of a long-term truce with Israel in exchange for an Israeli withdrawal from Gaza. Hamas, along with Fatah, the Palestinian Authority and other factions, insists that the administration of Gaza and the arrangements for the 'next day' – including reconstruction – should remain an exclusively Palestinian affair. However, Israel strongly rejects this scenario. Any direct or explicit inclusion of Hamas in the governance of post-war Gaza, let alone power-sharing in the West Bank, is not acceptable to Israel. Additionally, Israel rejects any arrangement that would create political, demographic or geographical contiguity between Gaza and the West Bank. One of Israel's key strategies is to maintain and deepen divisions within Palestinian territories.

Hamas's worst-case scenario: In this scenario, a post-war Gaza Strip would come under partial or full Israeli military reoccupation. Militarily, Israel would reimpose security control over Gaza, similar to how it was prior to its 2005 withdrawal. Administratively and politically, Israel might establish a form of 'civil administration' to manage the affairs of the Palestinian population, as it did before the Palestinian Authority was created in 1994. Israeli officials have floated various ideas within this scenario, including involving Arab states like Egypt, the UAE and Jordan in administrative matters, while keeping security strictly under Israeli control. A more popular idea within Israeli circles is the creation of a Palestinian collaborationist body in Gaza responsible for managing daily life but operating under full Israeli authority – a situation resembling the West Bank, where Israel retains ultimate security control. In such a scenario, Hamas's remaining military forces would be closely monitored by Israeli military and intelligence agencies. Hamas's fighters would likely continue finding new forms of resistance, engaging in attritional confrontations with Israeli forces. Administratively, Hamas would lose its authority and influence, being sidelined and forced underground.

Scenarios between these poles include the creation of a Palestinian local authority (separate from the Palestinian Authority in the West Bank) that would govern only the Gaza Strip with regional and international legitimacy and support. This backing might include security assistance and personnel, potentially with Israel having significant influence or even a veto over security arrangements in the Strip. These arrangements might be reached through mediated talks that could involve Hamas, at least indirectly. Proposals for such a local, Gaza-focused authority have been discussed, with some Palestinian figures, including former officials with international respect, being suggested as possible leaders. Hamas's position in this scenario remains unclear, largely depending on the movement's strength after the war, the leadership's political mandate and the nature of the security arrangements. Another scenario that surfaced during the war involves engaging Arab and Muslim states in the administration, control and reconstruction of the Gaza Strip. Hamas and most other Palestinian parties rejected such proposals, criticizing them as forms of regional tutelage that would further subjugate and humiliate Palestinians.

Postscript
What Did Sinwar Want?
– In His Own Words

In the first months of Israel's genocide on Gaza, its official *hasbara* produced the term 'The butcher of Khan Yunis' to describe Yahya Sinwar, Hamas's leader who was killed by Israel while fighting in Rafah on 17 October 2024. Western media promptly and blindly picked up the vilifying label. The haste and uncritical manner at which this media has used the term has been truly astounding. Cursory research shows that almost every mainstream Western media used the term (*New York Times, Washington Post, CNN, BBC, Le Monde, Le Figaro, Deutsche Welle, Der Spiegel*, among many others).* What is utterly shocking is the claim by Israeli propaganda and its Western allies that Sinwar was given that name by Gazans. For someone who spent around 30 years researching Hamas, its political thought, praxis and leaders, I was stunned by the term as well as by Western complicity in consuming it along with whatever lies Israel had thrown on them. I have asked dozens of Palestinians from the Gaza Strip, and mainly from Khan Yunis refugee camp, where Sinwar was born, and the city of Khan Yunis, about the alleged 'nickname' of Sinwar. Nobody had ever heard of it before it was fabricated

---

* Even some Arab writers fell into the *hasbara* trap, using the term in a remarkably lazy and uncritical way. Tarif Khalidi and Mayssoun Sukarieh, for example, write 'This ire seems to have increased in time and is what gave Sinwar the title "Butcher of Khan Yunis" for killing anyone who is proven to be a collaborator', in their otherwise meticulous review of Sinwar's novel *Thorns and the Carnations* (*Al-Shawk wa'l Qurunful*); see 'Leader of Underground Tells All', *Mondoweiss*, 4 February 2024, https://mondoweiss.net/2024/02/leader-of-the-underground-tells-all/.

by the Israeli propaganda machine and then exported to Western media. Even Sinwar's critics and opponents expressed revulsion over such a defaming title purportedly attributed to him by his fellow Palestinians.

For historians of Palestine and of the successive wars on the Palestinians, there is indeed a qualified candidate whose name comes first as the real 'butcher of Khan Yunis'. This was the late Moshe Dayan, Israel's chief of staff, whose troops massacred at least 275 civilian Palestinians in Khan Yunis on 3 November 1956.* Sinwar was born six years after that massacre, whose haunting and enduring memories had impacted the destinies of many young Palestinians in the Gaza Strip, leaving them, including Sinwar himself, angry and prepared for future resistance.

In 1988 and at the age of 26, Sinwar was arrested and given four life-term sentences, amounting to 426 years. In prison, where he spent 23 years, he gradually grew into the leader that many would come to know – educating himself, reading extensively, writing novels and learning Hebrew – all while serving as the prison leader of his group. As his leadership talents were further polished in jail, he built strong relations with other imprisoned Palestinian leaders of rivalling factions including Fatah. Those leaders, along with Sinwar, produced the 'Prisoners' Document of National Unity' in 2006, which has been since regarded as a major reference point for Palestinian national consensus, based on accepting a Palestinian state in 1967 borders.** Sinwar was freed from jail in 2011 in a prisoner exchange involving more than a thousand Palestinian prisoners in return for an Israeli soldier that was captured by Hamas in 2006. Upon his release, Sinwar wasted no time in resuming his path of resistance, showing little interest in embracing the newfound freedom for personal gains. Speedily,

---

*   Jean-Pierre Filiu, *Gaza: A History* (Oxford: Oxford University Press, 2014), 97.

**   See ' نص وثيقة الأسرى الفلسطينيين للوفاق الوطني ' ['The Text of the Palestinian Prisoners' Document of National Unity'], *Al-Jazeera*, 26 May 2006, https://bit.ly/48r3VxN.

he rose within Hamas's ranks and became a member its Political Bureau in 2014; then, in 2017, he was elected as the movement's leader in Gaza. On 6 August 2024, two months before his death, Hamas chose him to replace Ismail Haniya, Hamas's top leader who had been assassinated by Israel in Tehran a week earlier.

SINWAR'S STAGES OF RESISTANCE AND POLITICS

Beyond being a resolute military commander, Sinwar emerged as a shrewd political figure, skilfully blending ideology with pragmatism. In retrospect, we can trace the phase-based political and military action that he had envisioned and followed through from at least 2017. This approach began with efforts to end the Palestinian division, where Sinwar made the needed compromises to Fatah to achieve unity, offering readiness to give up Gaza's rule to a national unity government under the presidency of Mahmoud Abbas.* The proposed 'National Accord Government' would need comprehensive support from all parties to guarantee its success, including freezing Hamas's military resistance and adhering only to non-violent resistance. Although the unity government never materialized, Sinwar's next phase was to embrace non-violent resistance that started in March 2018 in the form of the Great March of Return and lasted until December 2019. Hopes that this effort would garner the worlds' attention proved unfulfilled. Consequently, Hamas resorted to military resistance as exemplified in the May 2021 Sword of Jerusalem confrontation against Israel, intervening in support of the Palestinians in Jerusalem and the Sheikh Jarrah neighbourhood. Again, the world betrayed the Palestinians and Gaza was left suffocating by the

---

* Sinwar agreed to dissolve Hamas's government in Gaza and join a 'National Accord Government'. The Palestinian Authority, accordingly, would send 3,000 security officers to Gaza in the first phase of transferring power. Mahmoud Abbas, however, had no appetite for the agreement and eventually scrapped it; see 'هل يستطيع السنوار تحقيق :ميدل إيست آي ['Middle East Eye: Can Sinwar Achieve Palestinian Unity?'], *Al-Jazeera*, 12 August 2024, bit.ly/4f5wHGL.

Israeli blockade. Misery, impasse and anger led to the next phase: 7 October 2023, which Sinwar had not so vaguely warned about for many years. All was laid out publicly at a press conference that Sinwar convened on 26 May 2021 following the Sword of Jerusalem confrontation.* In what follows and in Sinwar's own words, the warnings and 'suggested' phases of forms resistance were identified as if Sinwar was outlining his plans on air.

FIRST: THE NON-VIOLENT RESISTANCE OF THE MARCH OF RETURN

Clearly and straightforwardly, Sinwar stated that his and Hamas's approach prioritizes non-violent resistance considering it the movement's number one option.

> ... to spare our people the horrors of war, we truly believe – as we have always believed – that our people must combine different means of resistance: peaceful or popular resistance, ... along with armed resistance in its various forms, in addition to political and diplomatic efforts. Everyone knows and acknowledges that we, and the other Palestinian resistance factions, from March 2018 to March 2020, participated in those wonderful peaceful popular resistance demonstrations – the Great March of Return. By the grace of Allah, we portrayed an incredibly beautiful image through these marches, of a civilized people engaging in such peaceful, popular resistance, which sometimes involved some rougher methods.

In fact, these words echo much of Sinwar's talk in a long interview conducted by an Italian journalist and published in the

---

* See the televised press conference on *Al-Jazeera*, 'قرار السنوار للاحتلال: زوال دولتكم مرهون بتنفيذكم مخططاتكم في القدس' ['Al-Sinwar to the Occupation: The Decision to Eliminate your State Depends on your Implementation of your Plans in Jerusalem'], *Aljazeera Mubasher*, 26 May 2021, YouTube, www.youtube.com/watch?v=hL0pusi6Rlw.

Israeli press in May 2018, where he said, 'who would like to face a nuclear power with slingshots?'*

The goal of return marches, according to Sinwar, was to draw world's attention to what is happening in Gaza and Palestine, and create political action:

We hoped that the free and civilized world and international organizations would respond [to our non-violent March of Return] on two fronts: First, to appreciate this peaceful movement and curb the enemy's use of excessive force and deadly violence against our people. Second, we hoped they would pressure the enemy and the occupation to fulfil our people's demands and rights. But unfortunately, over two years, the Zionist war machine continued to target our sons and daughters, with snipers from the occupation army killing them. They started to amuse themselves by targeting our sons and daughters, sniping them in their foreheads, hearts, and eyes or severing their limbs – legs and arms.** We now have a significant number of these wounded and martyred, while the world just watches. [Meanwhile], the conscience of the free world didn't wake up, and it didn't move. *We say once again that we prefer to confront this occupation through peaceful means, through popular resistance.* We prefer that to be the way. But if this enemy continues to commit crimes and crosses red lines, we must resort to armed resistance. Our first option to achieve our people's goals and demands through peaceful means. However, if the world does not respond, and if this occupation does not respond or commits serious crimes, then our resistance must act to deter them. (emphasis added).

---

* Francesca Borri, an interview with Yahya Sinwar, 'Sinwar: "It's Time for a Change, End the Siege', *Ynet Magazine*, 10 May 2018, www.ynetnews.com/articles/0,7340,L-5364286,00.html.
** See this long report in *Haaretz* by Hilo Glazer, '"42 Knees in One Day": Israeli Snipers Open Up About Shooting Gaza Protesters', 6 March 2020, https://bit.ly/3UuCTzI.

SECOND: THE MILITARY RESISTANCE
AND THE SWORD OF JERUSALEM

Sinwar spoke passionately and in high, threatening tone about Jerusalem and Al-Aqsa as being intolerable red lines by Hamas. At the press conference, he sequenced the engagement of Hamas in the Sword of Jerusalem confrontation as necessary move by his movement after the inaction showed by the whole world regarding Hamas's non-violent resistance in the March of Return. He said that the Sword of Jerusalem was only a message of warning:

> We ... had no choice but to say our word with iron and fire and with missiles on Jerusalem first, so that the entire world and the leaders of the occupation would know that Al-Aqsa has men who protect it and that we are prepared to sacrifice the most precious and valuable things for the sake of Al-Aqsa Mosque, for the sake of Sheikh Jarrah, for the sake of Al-Bustan neighbourhood, and for all the issues of our homeland, especially in the holy city.
>
> ... we have risen up. For the sake of our sanctities, for our rights, and we wanted to send a message: believe me, we only wanted to send a message to the enemy and to the entire world that enough playing with fire, and that when we say enough playing with fire, we mean enough playing with fire. We do not issue threats or warnings in vain, let someone come with a one statement or a threat that we once issued and did not implement it on the ground ... *the world should know that this* [the Sword of Jerusalem] *was just a rehearsal. Just a small manoeuvre for what could happen if* [Israel] *touches Al-Aqsa Mosque again* (emphasis added).

THIRD (OR THE IN-BETWEEN PHASE):
PRESSURE AND POLITICAL SOLUTIONS

As in the case with the March of Return, Sinwar hoped that after the Sword of Jerusalem that drew the world's attention to Palestine, a political momentum would be created and cracks on the deadlock faced the Palestinians would appear. At the press conference he explained how the Palestinians have made themselves ready, including Hamas, to function in line with international law and resolutions:

Regarding the international diplomacy that took place during this round of conflict with the Zionist occupation and aggression against us in Gaza, there has certainly been significant action. The whole world, including major powers, even the new American administration in the United States, as well as major European powers, moved towards the idea that there must be a comprehensive solution to the Palestinian situation. It has become very clear that the triggers for explosion are still present, and things could erupt again at any moment. We say, therefore, that today there is an opportunity for the world to seize this moment and pressure the occupation to comply with international law and international resolutions. Earlier, I was in a meeting with various foreign agencies and television channels from around the world. One of the reporters from an American television asked me, 'What is your message to President Biden?' I replied with one sentence: Compel the occupation to adhere to international law and international resolutions. If the occupation complies, there is the possibility for a long-term truce, whether for four years, five years, or more.* If the world can pressure the occupation to withdraw from the West Bank, dismantle the settlements in the West Bank, and withdraw from East Jerusalem, then there is a possibility for this long-term ceasefire.

---

* 'The long-term truce' (*hudna* in Arabic) with Israel is a frequent idea that Hamas has offered since early 1990s. According to Sheikh Ahmad Yasin, Hamas's founder, and some of its other leaders, the suggested truce could be for 10 or 20 years, during which a new climate could be created. On this, see Khaled Hroub, *Hamas: Political Thought and Practice* (Washington, DC: Institute of Palestine Studies, 2000), 81–2.

... [And] the release of the prisoners, lifting the blockade on Gaza, allowing us to hold our elections in Jerusalem, and to establish our Palestinian state on part of our land – this would certainly open the door for the possibility of a relatively long-term truce that postpones the conflict and achieves a level of stability in the region. Is the world serious about pressuring the occupation to achieve this? We hope that the latest round has led to a shift in the awareness of international leaders to push for such a scenario.

We in Hamas, through our Charter* and through the National Reconciliation Document that we signed, along with the factions of the Palestinian people, have clearly stated that we are ready to accept the common denominators agreed upon by Palestinians. While these common denominators do not represent the political ideology of Hamas – our political ideology is clear and well-known: we stand for the removal of Israel through jihad and armed struggle; this is our belief. The occupation must be removed and swept away from all of our land. However, for the sake of Palestinian unity and the common Palestinian goals, and due to international will, we have said that we are ready to pursue this option. We have no problem with it if the major world powers and international organizations are prepared to compel the occupation to respect international law and international resolutions – so that we can establish our state on our land in the West Bank, Jerusalem and Gaza, with the dismantling of the settlements, the release of prisoners, the lifting of the blockade and the return of refugees. This makes the possibility of a long-term truce or ceasefire viable, relatively speaking. There is no doubt about this.

---

* Sinwar refers here to Hamas's 'Document of Principles and General Policies' that was issued in 2017, seen as the new charter of Hamas and where the movement accepted the premise of a Palestinian state within 1967 borders. See Khaled Hroub, 'A Newer Hamas? The Revised Charter', *Journal of Palestine Studies* 46, no. 4 (November 2017): 100–11, https://doi.org/10.1525/jps.2017.46.4.100.

FOURTH: THE INEVITABLE EXPLOSION: OCTOBER 7

In his threatening tone to Israel over Al-Aqsa being a red line, Sinwar warned of what could happen if Israel continues its squeezing policies on the Mosque and Palestinians in Jerusalem. The lines of the response that Sinwar anticipates could inform of what he had in mind while planning the October 7 attacks, specifically the anticipation of other fronts to immediately engage once the surprise strike comes out from Gaza. These are the details of what he imagined and wanted to happen if the red line of Al-Aqsa was crossed:

Al-Aqsa Mosque and Jerusalem are a red line. If you want more time to stay, then stay away from Al-Aqsa Mosque and Jerusalem. The decision to eliminate your state depends on implementing your plans in Al-Aqsa Mosque and Jerusalem. [We have] *an existing and known scenario, and the rehearsal has been made for it* [i.e. the Sword of Al-Aqsa confrontation]. *Gaza will launch its resistance with all its strength, and the West Bank will explode with all its power. Our people will attack all the settlements at once. Our heroes, even the security forces* [of the Palestinian Authority] *in the West Bank, will stand up for you at all the intersections and roads. They will attack you in all the settlements throughout the West Bank, and our people inside [in Israel] will rise up, a million demonstrators or more, who will take to the streets and close the roads, and I am absolutely certain that we have no less than ten thousand potential martyrs there* [ready to function] (emphasis added). ...

Hinting to his anticipation of regional forces like Hizbullah and Iran joining this imagined battle, Sinwar stated the following:

The masses of our people and our nation will rush across the borders, flowing like torrential floods to uproot your entity, and the resistance in the region, all the living forces, will rush to hit you with the utmost and most of their strength, God willing, and I am confident that the shape of the entire Middle East will become different from the Middle East in which we live.

Talking about the hard economic conditions in the Gaza Strip, Sinwar issued another chilling warning saying: 'And we, the leadership of the resistance, pledge that this year [2021], by the will of Allah, will not pass without a major breakthrough in the economic and humanitarian life of the Gaza Strip. This year will not pass, and the problems in Gaza, caused by the blockade, the war, and the destruction, will not remain as they are. Let the entire world hear: *we will burn everything – green and dry – if the problems of Gaza are not resolved now*' (emphasis added).

FINALLY

Sinwar's calculations about resistance flooding the borders once a strike from Gaza on Israel is conducted proved to be wishful thinking. He dedicated his attention to the details of the small picture and simplified the complexities of the bigger one, that included his allies in the axis of resistance. During his youth, in his high school and university years, Sinwar worked as a bricklayer in his free time to help his family and earn a living. Two people whose small homes were built by Sinwar, that I talked to, spoke highly of his patience, precision and meticulous work. He also built parts the long brick-walls surrounding the Islamic University in Gaza. As a bricklayer, and later builder of Hamas's resistance capabilities, he was dedicated to the details, the precise alignment and keeping things perfectly in line. It seems that he was overwhelming himself in refining the resistance in Gaza, while underestimating other imposing factors and limitations beyond his control. The jury is still out on his military and political decisions and may remain so for years to come.

But, aside from the vilifying Israeli and Western *hasbara*, Yahya Sinwar, for the Palestinian people and for many around the world, cuts a profile of a heroic figure that lived, fought and died legendarily. His was a rebellious and free soul as reported by Nabeeh 'Awada, a Lebanese communist who was imprisoned with Sinwar from 1991 to 1995, saying: "Sinwar used to play table tennis bare foot in Ashkelon prison," built on the land of the Palestinian village Asqalan, from which Sinwar's grandparents were expelled in 1948. Sinwar said he wanted his feet to touch the land of Palestine, shouting out: 'I'm not in prison, I'm on my land, I'm free here in my homeland!'* The pictures and videos released by the Israelis to brag victory over the man's dead body have backfired. These have gone viral on social media worldwide, turning him into a superhero who fought astonishingly until the last breath.

Khaled Hroub

---

* [' شهادات من السجن: السنوار كان نموذجا فريدا في القيادة'] Testimonies from Prison: Sinwar as a Unique Model in Leadership'], *Al-Jazeera*, 18 October 2024, https://bit.ly/3UsFVnV.

Recommended Reading

Abu El-Haj, Nadia. *Facts on the Ground: Archaeological Practice and Territorial Self-Fashioning in Israeli Society*. Chicago, IL: University of Chicago Press, 2001.

Aruri, Naseer H. *Dishonest Broker: The U.S. Role in Israel and Palestine*. Cambridge, MA: South End Press, 2003.

Aruri, Naseer (ed.). *Palestinian Refugees: The Right of Return*. London: Pluto Press, 2001.

'Azza, 'Abdullah Abu. *Ma'a al-haraka al-Islamiyya fil-aqtar al-'arabiyya [The Islamic Movements in the Arab Countries]*. Kuwait: Al-Qalam Publishing House, 1992.

Bishara, Marwan. *Palestine/Israel: Peace or Apartheid – Occupation, Terrorism and the Future*. London: Zed Books, 2001.

Baconi, Tareq. *Hamas Contained: A History of Palestinian Resistance*. Stanford, CA: Stanford University Press, 2022.

Chomsky, Noam, and Ilan Pappé. *Gaza in Crisis: Reflections on Israel's War against the Palestinians*. Chicago, IL: Haymarket Books, 2010.

Christison, Kathleen. *Perceptions of Palestine: Their Influence on U.S. Middle East Policy*. Berkeley, CA: University of California Press, 1999.

El-Awaisi, Abd Al-Fattah Muhammad. *The Muslim Brothers and the Palestine Question, 1928–1947*. London: Tauris Academic Studies, 1998.

Englert, Sai, Michal Schatz and Rosie Warren. *From the River to the Sea: Essays for a Free Palestine*. London: Verso, 2023.

Filiu, Jean-Pierre. *Gaza: A History*. New York: Oxford University Press, 2014.

Finkelstein, Norman G. *Gaza: An Inquest into its Martyrdom*. Berkeley, CA: University of California Press, 2018.

Gerges, Fawaz A. *America and Political Islam: Clash of Cultures or Clash of Interests?* Cambridge: Cambridge University Press, 1999.

Helmick, Raymond G. *Negotiating Outside the Law: Why Camp David Failed*. London: Pluto Press, 2004.

Hroub, Khaled. *Hamas: Political Thought and Practice*. Washington, DC: Institute of Palestine Studies, 2000.

Hroub, Khaled. 'A "New Hamas" through its New Documents'. *Journal of Palestine Studies* 35, no. 4 (Summer 2006): 6–28.

International Crisis Group. 'Islamic Social Welfare Activism in the Occupied Palestinian Territories: A Legitimate Target?' *Middle East Report*, no. 13, 2 April 2003. www.crisisgroup.org/middle-east-north-africa/eastern-mediterranean/israelpalestine/islamic-social-welfare-activism-occupied-palestinian-territories-legitimate-target.

International Crisis Group. 'Dealing with Hamas'. *Middle East Report*, no. 21, 26 January 2004. www.crisisgroup.org/middle-east-north-africa/eastern-mediterranean/israelpalestine/dealing-hamas.

International Crisis Group. 'Enter Hamas: The Challenges of Political Integration'. *Middle East Report*, no. 49, 18 January 2006. www.crisisgroup.org/middle-east-north-africa/eastern-mediterranean/israelpalestine/enter-hamas-challenges-political-integration.

International Crisis Group. 'After Mecca: Engaging Hamas'. *Middle East Report*, no. 62, 28 February 2007. www.crisisgroup.org/middle-east-north-africa/eastern-mediterranean/israelpalestine/after-mecca-engaging-hamas.

International Crisis Group. 'Inside Gaza: The Challenge of Clans and Families'. *Middle East Report*, no. 71, 20 December 2007. www.crisisgroup.org/middle-east-north-africa/eastern-mediterranean/israelpalestine/inside-gaza-challenge-clans-and-families.

Karmi, Ghada, and Eugene Cotran. *The Palestinian Exodus 1948–1998*. London: Ithaca Press, 1999.

Kear, Martin. *Hamas and Palestine: The Contested Road to Statehood*. London: Routledge, 2018.

Khalidi, Rashid. *Palestinian Identity: The Construction of Modern National Consciousness*. New York: Columbia University Press, 1997.

Khalidi, Rashid. *The Hundred Years' War on Palestine: A History of Settler Colonialism and Resistance, 1917–2017*. New York: Metropolitan Books, 2020.

Khan, Mushtaq Husain (ed.). *State Formation in Palestine: Viability and Governance during a Social Transformation*. London: Routledge Curzon, 2004.

Lybarger, Loren D. *Identity and Religion in Palestine: The Struggle between Islamism and Secularism in the Occupied Territories*. Princeton, NJ: Princeton University Press, 2007.

Makdisi, Ussama. *Age of Coexistence: The Ecumenical Frame and the Making of the Modern Arab World*. Berkeley, CA: University of California Press, 2019.

Malley, Robert, and Hussein Agah. 'Camp David: Tragedy of Errors'. *New York Review of Books*, 9 August 2001.

Masalha, Nur. *Palestine: A Four Thousand Year History*. London: Zed Books, 2018.

Massad, Joseph. *The Persistence of the Palestine Question: Essays on Zionism and the Palestinians*. London: Routledge, 2006.

Milton-Edwards, Beverley. *Islamic Politics in Palestine*. London: I.B. Tauris, 1996.

Milton-Edwards, Beverley, and Stephen Farrell. *Hamas: The Quest for Power*. Cambridge: Polity, 2024.

Nafi, Basheer M. *Arabism, Islamism and the Palestine Question 1908–1941*. Reading: Ithaca Press, 1998.

Pappe, Ilan. *The Ethnic Cleansing of Palestine*. Oxford: Oneworld Publications, 2006.

Piscatori, James P. (ed.). *Islam in the Political Process*. Cambridge: Cambridge University Press, 1983.

Rogan, Eugene L., and Avi Shlaim, *The War for Palestine: Rewriting the History of 1948*. Cambridge: Cambridge University Press, 2001.

Roy, Sara. *Hamas and Civil Society in Gaza: Engaging the Islamist Social Sector*. Princeton, NJ: Princeton University Press, 2013.

Roy, Sara. *Unsilencing Gaza: Reflections on Resistance*. London: Pluto Press, 2021.

Saad-Ghorayeb, Amal. *Hizbu'llah: Politics and Religion*. London: Pluto Press, 2002.

Said, Edward. S. *The Question of Palestine*. London: Vintage, 1992.

Sayigh, Yezid. *Armed Struggle and the Search for State: The Palestinian National Movement, 1949–1993*. Oxford: Oxford University Press, 1997.

Segal, Rafi, and Eyal Weizman. *A Civilian Occupation: The Politics of Israeli Architecture*. London: Verso, 2003.

Shlaim, Avi. *The Iron Wall: Israel and the Arab World*. New York: W.W. Norton, 2000.

Stern-Weiner, Jamie (ed.). *Gaza and Israel from Crisis to Cataclysm*. London: OR Books, 2024.

Tamimi, Azzam. *Hamas: A History from Within*. Northampton, MA: Olive Branch Press, 2007.

Index

The Pluto Press Newsletter

Hello friend of Pluto!

Want to stay on top of the best radical books
we publish?

Then sign up to be the first to hear about our
new books, as well as special events,
podcasts and videos.

You'll also get 50% off your first order with us
when you sign up.

Come and join us!

Go to bit.ly/PlutoNewsletter